# SELF
# MEDITATION FOR
# BEGINNERS

THE COLLECTION TO LEARN MINDFULNESS
AND RELAXATION MEDITATION. STOP
ANXIETY AND FALL ASLEEP WITH HYPNOSIS
FOR DEEP SLEEP. SELF HEALING GUIDE TO
DECLUTTER YOUR MIND

**Peace of Soul & Brain Foundation**

# TABLE OF CONTENTS

# SELF-HEALING POWER AND RELAXATION MEDITATION

BEGINNERS GUIDE TO MINDFULNESS THERAPY. STOP ANXIETY, LIVE STRESS FREE AND DECLUTTER YOUR MIND. BEDTIME STORIES: FALL ASLEEP AND

AWAKENING BETTER

**Peace of Soul & Brain Foundation**

# TABLE OF CONTENTS

# Introduction

**M**editation is about taming your mind. A lot of people struggle with trying to overcome anxiety, despair, agitation, and other habitual thought patterns that they may find difficult to break out of. Taming the mind through mindful meditation is how you give yourself control of your own well-being once more. Meditation will bring you a sense of fullness and completion. Believe it or not, it is the only way to truly achieve tranquility that is easily accessible to everyone on this planet. True, there may be other temporary forms of serenity, but nothing will come close to bringing you the long-term peace that you seek no matter what you may be going through in your life the way meditation will. And that is why we learn to meditate.

Meditation has been practiced traditionally for hundreds, if not thousands, of years. It is not something that just came about overnight as a new trend. Meditation is something that is inherent in all human beings, something that we all have in us to be able to do. Many are already reaping the benefits of what meditation has to offer, and now, it's time for you to start doing the same thing.

Learning to meditate is just like learning any other skill you put yourself through. When you learn to meditate, you exercise your mind muscles that you never or rarely worked on before. Meditation takes consistent practice for you to be more aware, mindful, and focused. There is no such thing as perfect meditation. Along your journey of mindful meditation, you will sometimes lose focus, your mind will wander, and you will also forget to follow your breath. Just remember that this is okay. Remember that it is a journey and not a destination.

This is why a lot of people find meditation to be a helpful practice. Those who avidly do this find that their mind is peaceful and free from worries and mental discomfort, making it easier for them to achieve happiness compared to those who do not practice meditation at all. If you have never tried it, you may scoff at the idea of how sitting quietly for a few minutes every day is going to make a difference in your life, but you would be surprised.

Think about it. What is it that successful people and motivational speakers often say they do as part of their daily routine? That's right; they spend a few hours meditating in the morning. Clearly, it's working for them, isn't it? They're able to go through life, even with the struggles that may come their way, with a positive attitude, and they don't let stress get the best of them. Now, you don't necessarily have to practice meditation in the morning the way they do; you can meditate at any time that works best for you. There is no hard and fast rule. You can even meditate more than once a day if you need to, and you find that it helps. You make your own rules according to what works best for you.

By spending a few minutes each day, training your mind and making meditation part of your routine, you will discover that your mind gradually is able to find peace a lot easier, and finding happiness is something that doesn't seem so elusive anymore, even if you have certain challenges that you may be going through in your life. Even in the most difficult circumstances, you will find that you are able to remain calm, steady, and still able to look at the bright side of life.

Learning to control our minds is one of the most difficult things we can do. It's easy to let our thoughts get the best of us, which is why it is so easy to be consumed by negativity, and external circumstances can affect us to such an extent. The thing about this is, we don't even realize just how severely we are affected by it all because we are not really thinking too much about it. Fluctuations in our moods seem like a normal, everyday occurrence, and we brush it off as being part of life, and we can't control it. But that's where you would be wrong.

The reason is that you can control it with meditation. Create that inner space and clarity in your mind that will enable you to always be in firm control of your thoughts, despite the circumstances you may be facing. Meditation is how you find that mental balance, so you are never at one extreme or the other (never too sad or never so happy). It is always about finding the right balance. You have always been told you need to live a balanced life and eat balanced meals, so why not have a balanced mind, too? Meditation is a way of bringing your mental clarity and change the way you look at the world around you.

# Chapter 1 Stress and Anxiety

From the outside, the distinctions between stress and anxiety can be difficult to detect. Both of these can result in sleepless nights, weariness, constant anxiety, lack of focus, and irritability. Even physical symptoms such as rapid heart rates, muscle pain, and headaches can affect people who are stressed or diagnosed with an anxiety disorder. For symptoms that may seem interchangeable, it can be hard to determine when to work on deep breathing and when to pursue medical assistance.

In short, stress is the response of your body to a stimulus and is usually a short-term experience. Stress may be either positive or negative. When stress comes into play and helps you get that deadline, it's positive. It's negative when stress leads to sleeplessness, poor concentration, and diminished ability to do things that you regularly do. Stress in any particular circumstance is a reaction to a threat.

Anxiety, on the other hand, is a chronic, stress-related mental health disorder. After the threat is mediated, anxiety doesn't fade away. Anxiety hangs over the long-distance and can cause considerable impairments in social, productivity, and other important functioning fields.

Most people experience occasional stress and anxiety. Stress is a demand imposed on your brain or body. People report being stressed when they are asked to make multiple competing demands. An event which makes you feel overwhelmed or nervous can trigger the feeling of stress. Anxiety is a sense of fear, worry, or discomfort. It can be a response to stress, or it can happen in people who cannot identify important stressors in their lives.

Anxiety and stress can help you overcome a problem or dangerous situation in the short-term. Symptoms of daily stress and anxiety include stressing about finding a job, nervousness before an extensive examination, or humiliation in certain social situations. If we have no fear, we may not be inspired to do what we need to do (e.g., preparing for this big test).

However, it can imply a more serious problem when stress and anxiety start messing with your daily life. It may be time to seek treatment if you avoid situations because of irrational fear, constant worrying, or severe anxiety about a traumatic experience weeks after it occurred.

## What Do Stress and Anxiety Feel Like?

Stress and anxiety can cause physical and psychological symptoms. People encounter various stresses and anxieties. Common physical signs are:

- Dizziness

- Diarrhea

- Muscle tension

- Change in appetite

- Trouble sleeping

- Rapid breathing

- Sweating

- Headache

- Fatigue

- Shaking

- Frequent urination

- Fast heartbeat

- Stomachache

People with long periods of stress and anxiety will experience negative health outcomes. They are more likely to experience diabetes, heart disease, hypertension, and even depression and panic disease.

## Eustress and Distress

Eustress translates to "good stress," a term that comes from a very significant insight amongst people. If you have a positive view of any scenario, you will never generate enough hormones to hurt you in the long run. Think of young people seeking strong sensations— such as those young people who go up in a helicopter and sprint directly from there on a ski hill without trying to think of the avalanches this could trigger.

In the field of stress science, researchers early on suggested that this situation should lead to a significant long-term stress reaction among these young people. When the researchers studied people in search of strong sensations, they found that these people created sufficient stress hormones to offer themselves a real "high," but not enough that they could hurt each other in the long-term.

Distress, on the contrary, refers to "bad stress." If you take me from a helicopter on a ski hill, I will be in total distress, even with my skis on, because I understand this entirely in an adverse way. I don't want to be there and do not want to participate in an activity that I think is too dangerous. Because I have a negative interpretation of the situation personally, I can produce sufficient stress hormones to cause long-term harm.

The scenario is similar in both situations (springing from a helicopter to a ski hill), but the person who interprets it positively will not be affected by the negative effects of stress, while the person with a negative interpretation is affected.

This example shows how the perception of a situation can significantly influence the development of good stress (eustress) or bad stress (distress).

Over the last few decades, we have devoted a lot of our focus to how stress is always negative, and we can do nothing. This is a false statement. In demonstrating that a stress response arises from an understanding of a situation as threatening (relative stress) or not, research has made it clear that we have immense power over our stress response. Nonetheless, it is important to explore how chronic stress takes root and can render us sick until we see how we can manage stress more effectively. If you know about the long, rolling road that can lead to chronic stress, I hope that the next time you come across it, you are able to avoid it.

# Chapter 2 Causes of Stress

**Work**

Work is such a popular source of stress that an entire scientific journal is dedicated to the study of it. For the past thirty years, Work and Stress has covered the impact of work and organizations on health. The American Psychological Association found that 65 percent of Americans named work as their top source of stress. It's not hard to understand why. We all want to do well at work because how we perform determines how much money we make, how we perceive ourselves, and how others perceive us.

Work is also where we spend most of our time. A 40-hour work week is often not reality, as work demands more and more of our hours. Many people find it hard to say no at work because they believe that if they don't say yes, their jobs may be in jeopardy. We often agree to new responsibilities as we wonder how we're going to fit one more task into our ever-lengthening day.

- **Work-Life Balance**

Even if you love what you do, the demands of the modern workplace can leave you feeling stressed and looking for balance because your life feels out of whack. What does work-life balance really mean? For each person, it means something different. I am now a remote worker who, as an academic, traveled as often as possible for the past 20 years during academic breaks and to far-flung conferences during the school year. And no matter how much I love my job; I can't imagine having only two weeks off. Some people love working from home or their local café or co-working space, whereas others feel disconnected and lonely and miss the interaction that office life brings.

## Finances

In a capitalist society where we constantly buy new and better items, it would seem that we're set up to be stressed about money. Money stress is often related to work stress because of salaries and benefits. In the United States, where our social welfare benefits are not very generous, it's on us to save enough to cover emergencies while still paying for our day-to-day expenses. Credit card debt is increasing as we spend more than we make and use debt to fill the gap. And with student loan debt in the trillions, too many of us will be paying back loans for a really long time. If you have children, planning for their college expenses can seem like a herculean task as tuition costs get higher and higher.

## Family and Friends

The relationships you have with family and friends can be both a blessing and a curse when it comes to stress. If you have loving, supportive relationships, then family is your refuge from stress and can be a key factor in reducing the impact of stress in your life. However, if your relationships are fraught with conflict, you may find yourself dreading going home at the end of a long, stressful day.

The amount of stress we experience from family life also depends on how demanding our roles are at any particular time in our lives. For example, if you're a new parent with a demanding infant, you may find that when your alarm goes off in the morning you feel as though you just can't keep going. Or maybe you're caring for a parent with dementia, or your romantic relationship may be going through a difficult time and you're not sure if you're going to last over the long haul.

## Toxic Relationships

Although friends and family can provide lots of support when we are going through trying times, sometimes it is these problematic relationships themselves that are the source of our stress. If you find that certain relationships make you feel drained and overwhelmed, sad, or frustrated every time you engage, then perhaps it's time to rethink the relationship. Being around people you love is supposed to make you feel good, loved, cared about, and supported, no matter what. Loving difficult people is hard; you don't have to stop loving them, but you don't have to perpetually feel bad because of them. Setting emotional boundaries for yourself will make you less stressed even as you mourn what you wish the relationship could be but clearly isn't. For more on setting boundaries, see Learn to Say No, here.

## Health

Stress and health are two issues that go hand in hand. People who experience a lot of stress may have related illnesses such as hypertension or cardiovascular disease. Stress also manifests itself in physical issues like hair loss, skin problems, asthma, and panic attacks.

## Social Media and Technology

The negative impact of social media is connected to our constant need to compare ourselves to other people. The problem is that on social media, friends, family, and influencers only show the best parts of their lives. Social media is also a distraction from work, and for some of us—including me—it is easy to get sucked down the rabbit hole when we have more important things to do.

Research has shown that we touch our phones thousands of times a day. Even if you are not connected to social media, your mobile devices keep you constantly connected to the world of work. You may check your e-mail at night and feel compelled to respond as soon as you can. Many people check and respond to their e-mail while on vacation because they're afraid that if they don't, their inboxes will be overflowing when they return to work. Technology often means that we are always reachable. This is why some companies have taken steps to shut down servers on weekends or after hours so that workers can disconnect, take a break, and be more productive when they are actually at work.

But it's not just work that keeps us on a leash. Even our cars come with the ability to connect to the Internet and to our phones, leaving us no place to hide and no time to ourselves.

Ask yourself why social media and technology are stressful for you and record your observations below.

## Major Life Changes

Major shifts in our lives cause stress because change is stressful, even if it is necessary or wanted. Major life changes such as the birth of a child, a marriage, moving to another city, or a change in employment can create a disruption in our lives that requires us to reinvent ourselves in some way. If you move to another city, you have to find a new salon, a new gym, and the shortest or fastest way to work. You need to find a new favorite restaurant and a new route to run or walk. If you have a new job, you have to learn the new office politics and get used to a new boss, new tasks, and new work relationships. Planning a marriage or preparing for a new member of the family can be very stressful, even though these events are a source of happiness. The same goes for sending a child off to college. You are happy for your child, but now you may have a little too much free time to manage.

## Loss

Whether it is the loss of a relationship or a loved one, these life changes require us to think for a long period of time about our identity or mortality. Yes, we know that we are all going to die, but losing someone who means something to us often makes us reconsider who we are and what we want out of life. Even if the loss is something that we wanted, like the end of a bad relationship, we still experience stress as we try to reorient our lives to accommodate a new role. Loss is particularly stressful because we may feel like we can't address the person who is gone.

## Environment and Surroundings

The environment where we live, and work can be a source of stress. Even for those of us who love living in cities, the density, concrete, pollution, and noise can put us on edge. This is why people often seek out green spaces, like rooftop gardens, to feel relaxed. Living in a neighborhood where you don't feel safe or living next to a noisy neighbor can also be a source of stress. Sometimes, where we live is a source of stress because we live in areas that are very socially competitive. No matter what your worries are, write them out so you can understand them better.

## Internal Stressors

In addition to the external causes of stress, some of the stressors in our lives are internal. These include our fears, such as the fear of flying, fear of public speaking, or fear about how we are viewed in social settings. Sometimes we experience stress because we don't feel as though we're in control, whether regarding the outcome of a medical test or the traffic jam on the way home from work. Beliefs about and expectations of we can cause stress, too. Maybe you believe you're on the outs with your family when you're not, or you may expect that you should have a perfect life, which isn't possible.

# Chapter 3 How Stress Develop and Transform to Anxiety

I t is fascinating to learn that our thoughts define what happens to us. From a psychological perspective, it means that we can control what happens to us by simply learning how to control our thoughts. This is a powerful technique indeed. Knowing that you have power over what happens to you is something that most people are unaware of. The reality is that you become what you think. If you look closely, whatever happens to you, good or bad, stems from your thoughts.

What you think about affects your mental health and wellbeing. Your thoughts lead to the emotional state that you might be experiencing. Often, this will affect your health. If your thoughts are preoccupied with sad events, then chances are that you will constantly feel sad. If you are constantly thinking about the fun activities that you engage in with your friends, then you attract the same energy to your life. From this, you will garner deeper insight into why your thoughts could be identified as the cause for your dwindling productivity at work, lack of sleep and your failing social relationships.

Your thoughts and feelings will work together to build an ideal future for yourself. Since you have the power to decide what you want, you ought to request a life that you've always dreamt of living. Your focus and energy should be in line with what you want to attract.

After understanding the fact that you are the creator of your world, you should begin thinking consciously towards creating a better life for yourself. In this case, this should encourage you to think positively since your thoughts define what you want in life. This requires that you channel your time and energy on thinking about the good things you want in life. It also means that you should deliberately manage your thoughts and emotions as they have an impact on what manifests.

## Anxiety: Stopping Negative Thoughts

Anxiety is caused by numerous factors. At times, it is caused by a combination of genetic factors and environmental factors. Fear within you can easily make you feel worried about things that haven't happened. In extreme cases, this leads to panic. Your mind can easily amplify the fears within you and make you believe that something bad will happen. In social settings, anxiety will leave you in a constant state of worry of saying the wrong thing in front of other people. Also, you might gain the assumption that other people will not like you. Such negative thoughts only prevent you from being yourself. It holds you back from living your life.

# Stress

You could end up developing a fear of lose your job. Indeed, this will stress you out a lot. In some cases, stress harms the quality of your sleep. This worsens your situation as anxiety tends to worsen when you don't have enough sleep.

Negative thinking will often lead to stress. When you constantly dwell on negative self-talk, this is what your subconscious mind will focus on. Instead of ruminating on how bad things follow you, it is vital to realize that such thoughts can hurt your emotional wellbeing.

# Stress and Negative Self-Talk

Self-talk is the inner voice that talks to you. Depending on how you use self-talk, it becomes a make-or-break situation. Positive self-talk will remind you of the great things that you can achieve. It will help you approach life with optimism. Negative self-talk, on the other hand, will attract negative energy. You will pay too much attention to the possibility of all the bad things that could happen to you. Negative self-talk will not help you overcome the stress that you might be going through. it worsens the situation as you will feel more stressed.

Overthinking can affect your life in many ways. Whether you are feeling anxious, stressed, or unmotivated, all these can be attributed to how you think. Your thoughts define who you are. Thinking positively can attract good things to you. The law of attraction will always apply to your thoughts and emotions. It is through these thoughts that you create the world that you want. Negative thinking breeds negativity in your life. It will affect your relationships, work-life, and your productivity in varying aspects. Instead of worrying about the future, you should use your energy to focus more on what you can do today for a better tomorrow. Frankly, your actions determine your future. Hence, thinking alone is just not enough. You need to act.

Overthinking is that inner voice that tries to bring you down. It criticizes you and destroys your confidence and self-esteem. You not only doubt yourself, but you also doubt those who are close to you. It pushes you to second guess everything. Thinking too much can be compared to a spreading fire. It burns down everything that it finds on its way. Therefore, you will suffer as a result of overthinking.

Overthinking is when your mind clings to the faults that you have made and takes you through them throughout the day. When you overthink, your life will be on constant pause. You will always feel as though you are waiting for the right moment to do something. The problem is that this moment never arrives. You're always anticipating that something could go wrong. You will be overly careful when doing anything. This is influenced by the fact that you are just worried things might not work out as expected.

# Chapter 4 The Importance of Not Underestimating Stress

We yearn for a happy, peaceful, fulfilled life, but if we do not make conscious efforts to mitigate and manage our stress levels on a daily basis, we can never really have that life. You need to be truly motivated to address your chronic stress positively and regularly. Let me walk you through the various ways through which stress affects and sabotages your life so that you understand the dire need to tend to this issue seriously.

## How Stress Affects Your Health, Wellbeing and Life?

Chronic stress takes a toll on your body, mind, sanity and every aspect of your life. It upsets, sabotages and disturbs your life in the following ways:

- Constantly staying in a state of stress disrupts your ability to stay focused and think clearly. When you are extremely disturbed, you ruminate on bad experiences and cannot pay attention to important tasks. This negatively affects your performance and productivity in tasks.

- Stress often makes you irritable and you lose your calm on even the most trivial issues. You find yourself yelling more often at your kids and loved ones and panicking at the slightest of disturbances.

- When you become a mere pressure cooker, people find it hard to be around you. they become distant from you and you miss out on valuable moments with loved ones.

- Feeling swamped and isolated from loved ones only upsets you more pushing you towards emotional disorders such as anxiety and depression.

- Moreover, when you perceive everything as stressful, you lose interest even in activities that once brought you happiness. Nothing brings you joy and meaning, and you start to sense a huge void in your life.

- Stress when it goes unchecked for long leads to physical problems such as constant headaches, shoulder pains, backaches, upset stomach, chest pain and insomnia. You feel more frustrated and find it difficult to live a comfortable life.

- In addition, stress is one of the most common root causes of high blood pressure, diabetes and heart problems. If you become prone to chronic stress, it is only a matter of time before you start struggling with these problems.

- Stress is also linked to six of the major causes of death: cancer, accidents, heart disease, lung ailments, suicide and live cirrhosis.

To sum it up, life only becomes more difficult and painful when stress becomes a constant in it.

Before moving on, here are a few preparatory measures and guidelines we would like you to understand.

## Preparatory Tips and Measures to Practice Stress Management

- Firstly, understand that stress management is not a one-time thing. You need to practice all the measures taught on a daily basis to yield a strong, compound effect. For instance, taking deep breaths when you panic on having to meet a deadline definitely calms you down. However, if you do not make a conscious effort to breathe deeply regularly, you are likely to panic again the next time. Remember to observe all the measures and strategies on a regular basis to gradually equip yourself with the ability to keep stress at bay at all times.

- Wrap your head around the fact that no matter how hard you try; some amount of stress will always affect you. It is inevitable so you need to stop trying to completely eradicate stress from your life and focus primarily on becoming strong enough to address it positively.

- Take your time and read one at a time. Go through it a couple of times, analyze the teachings and then practically apply them in your life. If you are asked to avoid seeing people who trigger your stress, you need to actually do that and observe the effects of this strategy. Remember, only practical and real-life application of strategies yields desired results; reading and accepting them alone would not do the trick.

- Keep a small pocketsize notebook with you at all times to record your stress management journey. When you start working on a certain strategy, note down how you feel about yourself and your life at that moment along with your stress levels. Once you have actually carried out a certain measure, observe your feelings and stress levels again, and write them down. If your stress levels have even dropped down a little, it shows the trick is working and you need to continue with it to gradually mitigate your stress better. Also, analyze how well or poorly, you carried out that strategy to become better aware of your strengths and weaknesses. If you are told to practice gratitude throughout the day, but you kept reminiscing bad memories instead of counting your blessings, that is a weakness you need to improve on. This journal helps you keep track of your performance, pinpoint your mistakes and strengths, and gives you an understanding of areas of improvement. If you follow it strictly, you will soon have your thoughts and stress levels under control.

These guidelines if observed regularly help you move closer to your goal; a stress-free, happy and meaningful life. Now that we have covered the basics, let us move on to the first step of stress management.

# Chapter 5 Difference Between Overthinking and Anxiety

The two terms are often used interchangeably, and since many of the symptoms tend to overlap, it's understandable to see why. While they share many similar traits, anxiety is a completely different matter altogether. From the symptoms we experience to the way we experience, one of the few common similarities overthinking and anxiety shares are the havoc they wreak on our psychological and emotional health. What are these subtle yet important distinctions between the two? Let's find out.

Anxiety is identified by the following characteristics:

- Originally, anxiety is a survival mechanism present in all of us. Its primary function is to alert us to the presence of danger, and it is not meant to be an emotion that lingers for long. Once the danger has passed, anxiety should dissipate, but that's not the case if you happen to be dealing with an anxiety disorder.

- Activates the body's fight or flight response.

- With an anxiety disorder, the body remains in an unnatural heightened state of alertness. Everything feels like a cause for alarm, and it triggers a constant flow of cortisol throughout the body.

- Diagnosed as a psychiatric or mental health disorder that is capable of derailing your daily life because of the persistent fear and worry that seems to follow you everywhere you go.

- It does not necessarily originate from a logical source, making it difficult to pinpoint what the underlying cause may be. It can be difficult to talk yourself out of an anxious episode.

- It has a stigma associated with it because it is classified as a mental health issue. It is not uncommon for those struggling with anxiety to be misunderstood, even by those who are closest to them.

- It can feel like a lonely and isolating burden to bear when you feel disconnected to the people closest to you. Many who struggle with anxiety are often embarrassed to admit what they're going through out of fear of being rejected.

- The anxious thoughts manifest differently from one person to the next.

- Anxiety tends to make you feel like you're running in a hamster wheel, going round and round in circles with no productive solution or end in sight.

- The emotions, fear, panic, and distress felt can make it feel impossible to function normally in your routine. Some people experience anxiety to such an extreme level they're too afraid to leave the house, let alone do anything else that requires venturing outside their comfortable or "safe" zone.

- Relentless and persistent worries that won't seem to go away, no matter how hard the person may try to reason with themselves. The fear felt can sometimes be so great that it leads to a panic attack episode.

- Insomnia and difficulty are trying to stay calm in a lot of situations.

- Irritable, frustrated, tired, and feeling like they are always on edge are some of the common emotions felt by those dealing with this disorder.

- The physical symptoms that are associated with this condition include shortness of breath, difficulty breathing, rapid heartbeat, sweaty palms, upset stomach, difficulty concentrating, and muscle aches and pains.

- A persistent sense of foreboding or dread, like something bad, is going to happen at any time.

- Some instances of severe anxiety may require medical intervention or treatment to help resolve the situation.

Overthinking, on the other hand, is associated with the following traits:

- Originally meant to be used as a method to resolve. When experienced in excess, overthinking disrupts our ability to think rationally and logically.

- Part of the usual thought process cycle for many people.

- Situations, events, or thoughts can cause immense stress and a lot of unnecessary worries. However, the concerns tend to be a lot more realistic than those of anxiety.

- A source or trigger is almost always immediately identifiable. Since the worrying thought stems from something specific, you may be able to talk yourself out of it and calm your thoughts.

- Overthinking is mostly a mental experience, unlike anxiety, where the symptoms are severe enough to manifest physically. With overthinking, we tend to be caught up in our thoughts more so than anything else.

- Less likely to produce a strong cardiovascular response the way anxiety does.

- In some cases, overthinking could trigger problem-solving and acts as a strong enough motivator that gets you actively thinking about the solutions, so you don't have to deal with the problem any longer.

- The emotional distress felt is a lot milder than what you would experience with anxiety. Aside from impeding your ability to focus, overthinking is less likely to cause any real problems to your ability to function in your daily routine.

- Overthinking is a condition that is a lot more manageable than its anxious counterpart. Since overthinking has the potential to lead to problem-solving, every solution you come up with means your worry diminishes your worries a little bit more.

- The worries experience here can either be temporary, or they can linger longer than they should. Generally, once a problem has been resolved, the mind should be put at ease and move on to something else to focus on.

- Less likely to impact our professional and personal lives the way anxiety would. Overthinking does not have the same stigma associated with it the way anxiety does.

- Worrying and the tendency to overthink is still considered a normal psychological state, unlike anxiety. However, overthinking excessively is not healthy either.

- It does not require medication to treat the condition.

Almost similar yet subtly different. Anxiety and overthinking are neither healthy nor helpful. The anxious brain is not an easy entity to deal with. It's hypervigilant and always on alert for anything that might be perceived as dangerous or a threat. The fight or flight response is the body's primal mechanism for protecting itself against danger. It is what the earliest humans used to help them survive and thrive when the living conditions were a lot more dangerous than what they are today. This response is also referred to as acute stress response, and it shares the same reactions or feelings, such as shaking anxiety and fear that occurs when our body is preparing for a possible emergency. The term fight or flight first started going around sometime in the 1920s as the first part of involuntary general adaptation syndrome.

Our fight-or-flight response is a reaction to stress, and this is a reaction that most likely evolved out of the survival needs from our early ancestors who lived in dangerous times. For example, prehistoric cavemen were in constant danger of animals. One minute they might be lighting a fire, and the next minute, there's a stampede coming their way, and they need to evacuate as soon as possible. The human body's natural survival design then kicks in and we have a full surge of energy and strength to quickly respond to the threat by removing ourselves from danger and increasing our chances of survival. Numerous physiological changes have been identified by researchers that happen when the flight-or-fight response takes place. It is believed that these changes are triggered by the sympathetic nervous system that is released through stress hormones into our bodies. When this happens, it causes a quick and instant physical reaction in preparation of the muscular activity that is required to fight or flee the danger. However, the body is not meant to remain in this state of alertness for long. All that cortisol pumping through your body will eventually take its toll on your mental, physical and emotional health.

When anxiety is thrown into the mix, our brains are churning out an endless stream of worried thoughts that never seem to end. Day and night, and even when we're trying to go to sleep at night, these thoughts won't leave us alone. We never seem to have a moment's rest, and we can't remember what it was like to feel relaxed anymore. Since these thoughts seem to be relentless and go on for a prolonged period, we eventually run the risk of believing what the mind is trying to tell us. That's dangerous territory to venture into. After all, if your thoughts have the power to shape your reality, then everything you allow yourself to believe is going to manifest one way or another. The good news is, neither of these conditions needs to be part of our permanent existence for long.

# Chapter 6 What Causes Mental Clutter?

What comes into your mind when you hear of mental clutter? Do you visualize a physical clutter that you know of? Mental clutter simply means mental overload, mental stress or mental fatigue. This is anything that gives you anxiety, depression, frustration, sense of overwhelm, and anger. This clutter comes in the form of:

- Regrets for past failures and regret for not doing some things that you should have done

- Too many bills to pay and increasing debts as well as unfinished projects

- Worries and insecurities

- Inner critic

- Feeling bad for failing to achieve something

These thoughts hinder us from focusing and working to improve ourselves. They divert our thoughts to the past instead of focusing on now and tomorrow. Mental clutter occupies our mental space, messes with our minds, eliminates our mental clarity and it is bad for our mental health.

# What Causes Mental Clutter

## 1. Worry

When we encounter challenges in our daily activities, our brains naturally go to a state of worry. Although it is a natural reaction, we can always control it because it will not solve any of our problems. Instead, worrying will worsen the situation. Worrying will take away your peace of mind and it will stress you. Worrying is a waste of energy.

The best thing you can do is to stop worrying. Find something to do that will divert your thoughts to something better like going for a walk, dancing, cooking or anything that interests you. You can also write down those things that are robbing you of your peace of mind and write how you are going to solve them.

## 2. Regret

Gee whiz! "I wish I worked hard in school my life could be better!" Such remarks are common when having a conversation with friends or family members. We all have those things we wish we had done or not done in our lives! Sometimes our minds can focus on those things, but we should not allow it. Focusing your minds on regrets will rob you of your happiness and cause you mental fatigue and stress. You cannot change the past so put your energy into creating a better vision for your life.

## 3. Fear

Fear is an enemy of progress! You should not allow fear to hinder you from taking chances and chasing after your dreams and enjoying life.

Do you dream of owning a business, but you are afraid that it might not take off if you start? Start it anyway and silence the fear that you have.

## 4. Guilt and shame

We should take responsibility for our wrongdoings and learn some lessons from it. Never allow yourself to be a prisoner of guilt and shame because it will cause you to have resentment self-hate, and even kill your self-esteem. The best way to get rid of guilt and shame is to acknowledge your mistake, forgive yourself and move on. This will empower you, motivate you to become a better person, make you value yourself. You should never repeat the same mistake.

## 5. The inner critic

How do you perceive yourself? Do you frequently have negative self-talk dominating your mind? Negative self-talk will limit our mental growth and lower our self-confidence. Remember your brain will believe what you tell it. If you constantly tell yourself that you cannot do it, your brain will act according to that belief.

You need to learn to refuse negative self-talk and replace it with positive talk. If the inner critic is telling you that you cannot do it then do it and you will silence that inner critic that is hindering your progress in life. Talk to yourself positively every day and you will see changes and your self-confidence and esteem will improve making you feel good about yourself.

# The Negative Effects of Mental Clutter

## 1. Clutter is not good for your health

Research has shown that mental clutter can harm your health and physical wellbeing. This is because of the following reasons:

- It increases your stress levels

When you have an endless list of unfinished projects, unpaid bills, and debts, it can lead to stress. Mental clutter will stress the brain and it will release a stress hormone cortisol. This can lead to some undesirable health conditions like chronic stress, high blood pressure, slow digestion, poor sleeping habits, and depression that can cause mental illness.

Stress will exhaust your mental energy leaving you feeling tired and overwhelmed. It will also make you lose focus and concentration on important things and it promotes negative self-talk.

- It interferes with your eating habits

Mental clutter can make you lose appetite or crave for more unhealthy food because of the rise of stress levels. Research has shown that people with mental clutter eat twice as many cookies, sweets, and snacks than those people who do not suffer from mental clutter. That means when you have a mental clutter you will not prioritize a healthy diet, but you will crave junk food, which is unhealthy, and it can make you fat.

## 2. It steals your productivity

Mental clutter promotes stress and anxiety that will suck your energy making you feel lazy, unproductive, and useless. Clutter will distract your focus because so many things are fighting for your attention and this can affect your productivity. Having an endless "to-do" list can be hard to handle and it can make you feel like you are losing your mind. This feeling of never completing projects will ground your mind and it will create negative self-talk that can hinder your progress.

When your mind is full of clutter, you may find that you do not remember where you put certain files then you spend so much time looking for those work files. These can delay your work, you may fail to meet deadlines, and this may make you feel like giving up.

## 3. Less efficient thinking

Mental clutter will prevent you from processing important information. It can also lead to temporary memory loss. Mental clutter will take away your focus leaving you confused with endless "to-do" tasks. Such overwhelming feelings will render you helpless and you may find that even doing a small task is difficult. It can also affect your parenting styles negatively because you will project your anger and frustration on the children and that is not good for their mental growth.

## 4. It interferes with your relationships

Mental clutter will consume your energy and you will not have the energy to give your loved ones. You can't give full attention to the people you love when your mind is full of clutter because mental clutter is distracting since there is so much stuff fighting for your attention in your mind. The inability to give the people you love your attention and energy will make them suffer.

Clutter will give you stress, and mental fatigue and you will feel overwhelmed from the pile-up of things that needs your attention as a result, you will project some frustration onto your loved ones. Although you will be doing this unknowingly it will affect your relationships negatively because you will be moody and resentful most of the time. You might end up treating them harshly and they may develop a negative attitude towards you.

Mental clutter may isolate you from other people. Since you will be feeling stressed out and mentally tired, you may not want to interact with other people because their presence will irritate you. If you have children, your mental clutter will not allow you to have a good time with them and this will affect them psychologically because they will feel like you do not value them. Such children may suffer from unhappiness, anxiety, and they may have difficulties in socializing with their peers.

## 5. It will rob you of your peace of mind

Your mind can never relax if you are suffering from mental clutter. It will always be wandering! This will leave you with stress, frustration, discontent, and these feelings can be overwhelming to your mind. Find something that can help you decongest your mind and relax. You can listen to soothing music, meditate or take a walk in the park, anything that will relieve your mental clutter.

## 6. It can lead to procrastination

Since mental clutter will drain your energy, you will end up postponing some tasks because of mental fatigue and stress. The best way to stop procrastination is by clearing your mind of unnecessary thoughts so that it can focus on doing important things that can make you a better person.

## 7. It will keep you in the past

When your mind is full of clutter, you will not be able to receive new ideas because there is not any room left for them. Your life will only be revolving around the clutter in your mind that are normally worries from past events and uncertainty of the future. Whining about your past situations will derail you from achieving a better tomorrow. So, let go of your past and have a clear plan of how you can achieve your aspirations and goals in life.

## 8. It affects your emotions

There is no way you can be happy with mental clutter. It will bring you feelings of anger, sadness, discontent and it will be hard for you to have positive feelings like being happy, confident or proud. The mental clutter will spike your stress hormones giving you dull feelings every day!

## 9. Encourages bad money management

Mental clutter can cause you to have surprise bills because you may have forgotten to pay them. The clutter in your mind may make you forget to pay bills on time, and this can cause you to pay some penalty fee. It can also cause you to have bad credits. You may also find yourself buying stuff that you already have but you cannot remember. Mental clutter can also make you forget to keep count of how much money you use per week or month and this will make you a poor financial manager.

## 10. It will derail your career and prevent you from getting promoted

When you lose focus and concentration in your work, you become less productive and this is not healthy for your career. Most managers demand performance in the workplace, and you cannot keep up with that if you have mental clutter. If you want to be successful in your career, you need to clear your mind and focus on doing your best in everything you do.

# Chapter 7 Decluttering Your Mind

You must declutter your mind; it is essential to your mental health, productivity, and ability to concentrate. If you have a cluttered mind, you may struggle to sleep at night. You won't be able to focus on work. It will be difficult to enjoy your life when you are weighed down with countless thoughts and filled with worries. There are a few ways that you can work on decluttering your mind.

One way to declutter your mind is to declutter your physical space. You may be mentally overwhelmed because of the physical environment that you are in. If your workspace is unorganized and filled with junk, your mind will reflect that; you won't be able to focus on your work. For this reason, it's necessary to go through your space and get rid of anything that you don't need. This will allow you to focus on what's important. Your home, workspace, and car will all influence your mental health. Put yourself in an environment that helps you to focus instead of distracting you from focusing.

Another way to declutter your mind is learning how to not multi-task. It is instinctual to multi-task, as it seems like a way of getting more done. However, you are splitting your focus among several tasks instead of giving your total focus to one. This will result in work that is of a lower quality, and you will feel overwhelmed as a result. Start making it a habit to completely finish one task before moving onto another. You will notice a dramatic change for doing so, as you will accomplish more and feel better about your work.

You can also declutter the number of decisions that you must make. You may also prepare ahead of time so that you feel better when it actually happens. For instance, you may plan your outfits for the entire week on Sunday night. You may meal-prep so that you don't have to worry about food when it's mealtime. Make a schedule for routine tasks you must complete, such as doing laundry every Thursday morning or vacuuming every Wednesday night. Reducing your decisions and coming up with a schedule can really help you to stop overthinking and have a schedule that you already know works for you. You may make a schedule for yourself so that you know exactly what to do.

| Sunday | Monday | Tuesday | Wednesday | Thursday | Friday | Saturday |
|--------|--------|---------|-----------|----------|--------|----------|
| Pick clothes | Bathroom | Dishes | Vacuum | Laundry | Trash | Meal-prep |

Minimalism

Minimalism isn't simply getting rid of things or decluttering your belongings. It is seeing what truly matters to you and sticking with that. Marie Kondo's method is to only keep items that "spark joy." This means that you only keep the items in your life that truly make you happy. It can really help you to go through each item that you own and decide what matters to you. You may have some things that you keep out of guilt or for "someday in the future." However, these items will only disappoint and frustrate you each time you see them. It is important to eliminate any items that bring you negativity or remind you of failure. Surround yourself with items that bring you joy and make you a better person. Your surroundings should be a reflection of you and what you love. You may choose to go through the items in your house, at work, in your car, and any other places that you may have. Do not bring any other items into your life that bring you down in any way; only own what you truly need to make you happy. This can help you to have a much clearer mind.

Learning to Focus

Take some time to reflect on where you stand with your focus. Are you happy with your ability to focus? Do you wish that your focus could be improved? Figure out what your goal is. Do you find yourself getting distracted easily, unable to continue work after taking a break, or simply can't finish tasks with ease? Determine what it is that prevents you from focusing.

You may try to challenge yourself. Give yourself a task and a time limit and do your best. Become aware of how often you become distracted and how easily you can regain your focus. Write down anything that distracts you; you may not even realize how distracted you become! Afterward, ensure that you rid yourself of any distractions. Turn off your notifications. Make sure that it's quiet and peaceful. Whatever distracts you, make sure it's eliminated. You may also come up with a schedule for your breaks. Figure out what works best for you. Perhaps you like to work for fifty minutes and take a ten-minute break. Perhaps you prefer to work longer and have a longer break. It will depend on your personal preference. Regardless, it's important to remain completely focused while you are working and to also take breaks regularly. This will increase your productivity and allow you to be less stressed. Determine what sets you off. What is it that makes you lose your focus? Why do you overthink? Reflecting can really help you to determine the causes of your actions.

Overall, it's important to take care of your mental health so that you can focus better. By taking some time to yourself and doing small things that you love, you can really help yourself to feel better. When you are happy, you will feel much more motivated and find it much easier to focus.

Prioritizing

Perhaps you are able to focus, but you simply aren't focusing on what you should. It can be quite easy to get caught up in tasks that are unimportant or aren't urgent. You may think that you're being productive, but you're really procrastinating. This is why prioritizing is so important. You must be able to recognize where you should be placing your focus. Otherwise, it's like you're on a treadmill. You're still getting something done, but you aren't actually going anywhere. You must learn to prioritize your tasks properly so that you focus first on what's important. After that, you may move on to other tasks.

One way to prioritize is by making to-do lists every day. It is helpful to make them the night before so that you can plan ahead of time. At the moment, you may not feel as motivated to accomplish every task. It helps to have one to three major tasks for the day. These are your top tasks. Even if they are the only things you accomplish for the day, you would be happy with yourself. These are your top priority, and it is what you should focus on accomplishing first. This will allow you to focus on what you must.

You should also write down any additional goals that you have for the day. Write every possible thing that is on your mind. Make a list of all of the potential tasks, even if they aren't necessary for the day. By doing a "brain dump," you are freeing yourself of clutter in your mind. This will really help you to focus on the present instead of the past or future. Additionally, you will feel better knowing that you won't forget anything that you would like to do. It will all be written down, so you can feel more at peace.

Decluttering your mind will help you to remove all of your unnecessary thoughts. You will learn how to focus on what matters so that you may direct your energy towards that. Similarly, practicing minimalism will help you to understand what you value in life. You will realize what you should put your focus on, and what you find important. You can learn to focus by means of a few methods. Physical and mental health will play a huge role in your ability to focus. Finally, prioritizing will help you to learn what you should focus your attention on. You will feel more at ease when you can focus on what you need to.

# Chapter 8 Declutter Your Physical Environment

Sometimes, we forget that living in an environment that is messy, cluttered, filthy and disorganized, can take its toll. There is no one out there who will tell you they like feeling overwhelmed. The word alone invokes feelings of unpleasantness, isolation, and failure. Almost like you feel disappointed with yourself for being unable to cope. That's the word you're going to be using a lot, though, if you live in the kind of environment that is described above. Walking into your garage, you can't find anything that you're looking for and it's a struggle to maneuver past the boxes and piles of stuff that are scattered all over the place. You open your drawers and there's a pile of items scattered in there you don't even use anymore. Doing a quick inventory of your home might surprise you with several items you don't recall buying. That's the thing about stuff. It tends to pile up and if you're like so many others out there, it's hard to let go.

Feeling "overwhelmed" by the clutter that surrounds our lives has become a common dirty little secret. Most of us go through it, but nobody likes to talk about it because talking about it means you've got to admit you have a clutter problem. A lot of us have this obsessive need to fill everything we have. We fill our houses, our cars, our offices, our workstations, our mobile phones, tablets, laptops, storage units, cupboards, shelves, and we fill both our minds and our hearts with unnecessary clutter. It's more than we can manage, and it's no wonder we feel as overwhelmed as we do. Why do we continuously keep taking more? Because we believe "more" will lead to happiness. We believe if we buy the latest mobile phone, we're going to be happy. If we buy the newest car on the market, we're going to be happy. A new watch, a new pair of jeans, shoes, items for the home. Advertisements and commercials often portray a feeling of happiness when we purchase their product or engage in their services. Does retail therapy really make us happy? On some level, it does, but it's not the kind of happiness that lasts for long.

We keep buying and collecting believing with each new purchase that it's going to finally make us happy. In reality, all it does is perpetuate the overwhelming feeling we already have. The words "clutter", "decluttering" and "minimalism" has exploded in today's society because this is a very real problem. We know by now that clutter is not limited to the physical belongings that clog up our space, it could be digital, mental, spiritual, and emotional. The physical clutter is the one our minds automatically go to when we hear the term "clutter". To tackle the other aspects of a cluttered life, you need to work on the physical and the rest will gradually fall into place. When your life is simpler, your brain automatically becomes less cluttered. Coming home to a space that is neat, organized, and with plenty of room to move around is a breath of fresh air after the noisy outside world you left behind when you walked in the front door.

## Your House Is a Container

We certainly treat it that way. Yes, we need to accept that our homes are a container. It's where we keep everything that we own. What we need to learn how to do now is to stop the overabundance. Messiness, even the minor ones, eventually takes its toll. It may not seem like a small pile of stuff here and there scattered haphazardly around your home is going to cause any real damage, but every type of clutter demands your attention. It might not be conscious or mindful attention, but your brain is still processing these stimuli whether you're paying attention or not.

Your home is a container, and it happens to be one container you spend a lot of time in when you're not at work. If this environment is constantly going to overwhelm your brain, you'll find it increasingly difficult to focus, make decisions, and the mental fatigue is going to leave you feeling exhausted and drained of energy all the time. In the pursuit of keeping up with this constant, on-the-go and hectic lifestyle, we have forgotten that there are other aspects of our life that need looking after. Our health, relationships, personal growth, and mental health have taken a backseat as we race for what else we can buy, who has what new item and finding reasons to constantly make new and unnecessary purchases we don't need. We have become far too consumeristic and materialistic, and it is time to change all of that.

A home should be a space you look forward to coming back to each day. A space that makes you happy, lifts your mood and elevates your spirits. It should be your sanctuary, not a place that fills you with even more stress. To create such an environment, you need to accomplish two goals:

- Simplicity for Greater Clarity - Get rid of anything that is unnecessary, that's the rule of thumb for simplicity. If you don't need it, then toss it (or donate it). One study done by Princeton University reveals that cleaning up the environment within your immediate field of vision can help prevent your brain from overloading. Without the brain fog, it becomes a lot easier to think clearly.

- Break Away from Boredom - As much as we need routine, after a while it can become boring. When it does, you lose motivation and any desire to get things done. The American Psychological Association believes that the reason you feel bored could be because what you're doing now lacks purpose. Meaning there are steps in your daily routine or environment that don't make you feel happy or fulfilled. Research done on this subject indicates that a change in your environment, even if it is a slight shift, might be what you need to change your outlook and get a different perspective on life. If your work desk is cluttered and makes you feel uninspired, clearing it out and leaving nothing more than your laptop and a notepad on it can leave you feeling rejuvenated. Your brain is processing this as something new, and that sparks excitement. It's been a while since it saw a desk this empty and simplistic, and that change wakes the brain up, renewing your sense of purpose while it's at it.

## Valuing Space Over Stuff

Space is an asset that is underrated. We put so much value on our material belongings that we forget the space we have is limited. There's only so much your home, car, desk, garage, closet, and drawers can handle before it's packed to the brim. Yet, we can't seem to bring ourselves to stop buying. Space is no longer considered "space" when there's no room to move around anymore. Have you ever felt that there was no room to breathe? Claustrophobic? Trapped? Confined, perhaps? That's your brain trying to signal to you that there is too much going on. Now, compare those feelings to the way you feel after you've done a little spring cleaning. Do you breathe a sigh of relief? Immediately feel lighter. Better? If we learn how to place value on the precious space we have, then perhaps we wouldn't be so quick to fill it up again as soon as we've made some room.

The benefits of valuing your space and decluttering go beyond trying to make your home look like something out of a Pinterest board. It's the mental, physical, emotional and even financial benefits that you gain which makes this process worthwhile. Understandably, the thought of getting rid of most of what you have accumulated over the years can be daunting. Some people have a very strong emotional attachment to certain possessions that they own, even if they may not have used or touched those items in years. The question of "What if I need this?" is always going to linger at the back of your mind. But ask yourself this: Is the mess worth your stress?

We all have different battles we're fighting with clutter. Some are more physical, while others could be more emotional or mental. But once you start valuing your space, you're going to see the following changes unfold:

- You Feel a Greater Sense of Relief - Clearing away the clutter in your life is going to feel like a big weight has been lifted off your shoulders. Suddenly, you have room to breathe again once more. We often don't realize just how much we are affected by the clutter and accumulation of possessions around us until we get rid of it and feel much better when we've tossed out a few items.

- You're Clearer About What You Don't Want - As you methodically work through your items, you'll start to realize which are the ones you value the most. Gaining clarity of what you don't want simultaneously creates clarity about the things you do want. Decluttering seems like a simple enough exercise in clarity, but the ability to separate what you want from the things you don't want will carry over into other areas of your life too.

- You Feel Motivated Again - There's an added benefit to being able to clearly identify what you want and what you don't. Your motivation is reawakened, thanks to the newfound, clearer purpose in your life. Without the unnecessary distractions taking away your focus, you are once again able to see your purpose, remember what your goals are and what you want to accomplish.

- You're A Lot More Efficient - You are able to concentrate better, your priorities more in focus, you find yourself feeling lighter, happier, and able to work a lot more efficiently and make more productive use of your time because you have fewer things around you that distract you.

- Less Stress Means Better Mental Health - Greater focus and clarity reminds you of what you have been neglecting all along. That you matter more than any material possessions you could possibly buy. The moment you start focusing on yourself again, your mental and physical health starts to shine because you're working on becoming a better you. If you continued to live with stress, none of this would be possible.

# Chapter 9 Overthinking and Its Causes

What exactly is overthinking? Experts overview overthinking syndrome as spending much of your time thinking of anything and something which causes stress, fear, restlessness, concern, dread, unease, and many others. This mental condition is not just about too much thinking of something, but also about spending more thoughts, which affects the capability of the person to work and finish the daily tasks.

If you worry about your friends, your job, your family, your boyfriend, and girlfriend, your life and anything else; You believe that you do not have overthinking condition; No matter what you are thinking about, perhaps concerns you for a moment, then a short span of time, you continue with other parts of your life. Yes, you return wondering every so often. However, you do not continuously wonder, and you do not find it getting in the way with the rest of your life. With this kind of mental condition, however, the troubled is all that you can think of. Even if you may not be troubled on the same thing regularly and repeatedly, you always worried about something.

No two individuals will suffer from this kind of mental issue in the same way. But people who do suffer overthinking will find that their daily living and lifestyle is at stake. This is due to their lack of capability of efficiently and successfully controlling negative thoughts as well as emotion. Thus, they find it hard to hang out and socialize. They also find it hard to enjoy their sidelines and hobbies. They are not helpful and not creative at work. All these happen since their mind spends an inconsistent amount of energy and time on particular lines of thoughts. There is a feeling that they do not have complete power over their emotions or minds that can be extremely destructive to mental wellbeing.

Making friends, meeting up with someone as well as keeping friends is hard with this mental condition as you resist interacting with them. You will experience difficulty in talking to the people that surrounds you. This happens because you are too much trouble with the things you do or say. You are also too much concerned about what will happen or how you will do it. If you, your friends or any member of the family experience, this mental disorder might struggle to make general conversation with others. It will also be hard to interrelate in a typical setting. You might find it so hard to go out to the department store or to your appointment, which affects your whole life in general.

Do you worry too much, even on simple things? Are you an extreme worrier? Maybe you automatically think that when you wonder/worry enough, you are able to avoid bad things from taking place. However, the reality is that worrying, and wondering are able to affect your system in so many ways which might astound you. If you think too much on everything or if you have excessive worrying, it can result in feelings of high stress and even lead to a serious health condition.

# Causes of Overthinking

There is always a reason or a cause behind everything that happens. This includes the thoughts you have. Very rarely do thoughts randomly spring to mind for no apparent reason. When you catch yourself overthinking, there is always going to be a reason behind it. Something that sparked that train of thought. It is now up to you to identify what those triggers are. Now, this may be something you're reluctant or hesitant to do at first, but it needs to be done, nonetheless. It is important to identify your causes. Only when you know the root cause of any problem can you then begin to fix it. You're not alone. Excessive thoughts are something a lot of people struggle with each day. Let's look at some of the common excessive thinking triggers:

**Trigger #1: Social Media**

Social media usage has skyrocketed within the last decade. We spend more time on platforms like Facebook, Twitter, Instagram, and Snapchat more than we do on any other online space. What do you do when you find yourself idle or with some free time on your hands? Whether we like to admit it or not, social media is changing why and how we do certain things. It is even changing the way we think and has become one of the many triggers for the tendency to overthink. Why? Because when we're on social media, we start comparing.

We compare the life we have to the ones we see on social media. We compare our lives to that of our family and friends who seem to be having it all. Someone just got engaged. Someone's celebrating an anniversary. Someone else is about to jet off on a holiday you've been dying to go on. Someone just got promoted. When you look at all these, it becomes almost impossible not to compare. You look at all the smiling faces and enthusiastic announcements and start to think: Why not me? Why do they seem to have it all? Why can't I get that lucky? Why does my life have to be this way? It's no wonder social media usage has been linked to higher levels of depression on loneliness. An entire generation is growing up with lower self-esteem levels than the past generation. As if that wasn't worrying enough, they're growing up with higher levels of anxiety and a penchant for excessive thinking. They don't want to be obsessed with their thoughts, but they can't seem to help it.

## Trigger #2: Relationship Anxiety

There could be several reasons why relationships might become a trigger for your excessive thoughts and anxiety. It could be a bad dating experience you had in the past that left you scarred to this day. Perhaps you struggle with insecurity and low self-esteem. Maybe you're afraid to open yourself up to your partner and expose the vulnerable side of yourself out of fear of getting hurt. Even the fear of getting hurt could send your thoughts and emotions hurtling out of control. Here's the interesting bit: People who struggle with relationship anxiety would STILL rather be in a relationship than be alone. Yet, when they become intimately involved with someone, the anxiety rears its ugly head and sabotages the relationship, thanks to all the overthinking and doubt, insecurities, and fears that are present. Without any way of controlling your thoughts or emotions, they can quickly get out of control, and it won't be long before you end up pushing your partner away.

## Trigger #3: Living Up to Expectations

The fear of not living up to other people's expectations is a fear that haunts many anxiety-ridden overthinkers. When you spend too much time caring about what other people might do, say or think about you, you're not spending enough time caring about your happiness. Trying to live up to someone else's expectations prevents you from being fully present in your life. Why? Because the things you do are not done for you. You're not making decisions based on what's going to move you forward in life. You're not making decisions based on what's best for you. You're not investing time in tasks that are going to contribute to your future success.

## Trigger #4: Worrying About Life in General

You worry about work, money, your family, the future, being stuck with an illness, school, your job, and the list could go on. Worrying about life, in general, is a big cause of overthinking, and it's no surprise either since there seems to be so much to worry about in the first place. We're worried all the time despite trying to paste a smile on our faces and present a calm, composed facade to the rest of the world. Overthinking in this category can feel pretty unbearable at times.

Your anxious excessive thoughts are often about specific or particular things, and most of the time, these excessive thoughts roam free in your mind when self-awareness is not present. Without self-awareness, it becomes difficult to see just how little control you have over the contents of your mind if you continue to allow overthinking to be the dominant force. The biggest trigger of anxious and excessive thoughts in this category is the fear of what we cannot control and the fear of what the future holds. Every facet of your life is going to bring with it some form of worry or another, and if you gave in to each of these thoughts, it could spell emotional disaster. Given the sheer number of things that could go wrong, indulging your overthinking mind is going to skyrocket your anxiety faster than you can keep up.

The human brain hates uncertainty. It doesn't take kindly to unknown variables and any element that is out of its control. That's why worrying about life, in general, is a major cause of overthinking. This is why anxiety sufferers and overthinkers find the prospect of the future so alarming. The fear of the unknown happens to be all the fuel their brain needs to start working overtime, churning out one negative thought after another.

# Chapter 10 What are the Symptoms of Overthinking?

B elow are symptoms that you are an overthinker:

When you talk fast

A person may appear to be nervous when they talk fast without pausing. However, this could be a sign that the person is an overthinker. A lot is usually happening inside an overthinker's mind. A person's mind may wander deep in thoughts, causing them to have a lot to say even though other people may not follow precisely what that person is talking about.

When you find yourself comparing people?

Sometimes overthinkers shift to a perfectionist mindset, and they start comparing other people and things to imagined standards of perfection. Such measures could come from Social Media and Media in general, where people make out everything to be perfect.

You Overanalyze Everything

If you notice that you overanalyze everything around you, then you are certainly an overthinker. This means that you may try to find a deeper meaning in all the experiences that you go through. When meeting new people, instead of engaging in productive communication, you may focus instead on how other people perceive you. Someone could be giving you a particular look and you may make several assumptions just based on that look. Overthinking consumes you. You end up wasting a lot of energy trying to figure out and make sense of the world around you. What you don't realize is that not everything has intrinsic meaning.

You Think Too Much but Don't Act

An overthinker will be affected by something called analysis paralysis. This is a scenario where you think too much about something but don't do anything about it in the end. In this case, you spend a lot of time weighing the options you have at your disposal. At first, you make up your mind on what the best alternative might be. Later, you compare your decision to other possible decisions that you could take. This means that you can't stop thinking about the possibilities and whether or not you made the right decision.

You Can't Let Go

Often, we make erroneous decisions that could lead us to fail. When this happens, it can be daunting to let go more so when you reflect on the sacrifices you have made to get to the point you are at. You might feel that it is painful to let go after you have invested a lot of money on a certain business.

You Always Want to Know Why

Without a doubt, the notion of asking why can be helpful to solve problems. This is because this probing attitude gets you the answers that you might be looking for. Nonetheless, it can also be damaging when you can't help but always wonder why. Overthinkers maintain such investigative attitude throughout their lives.

You Analyze People

The way you see other people can also say a lot about you. In most cases, you get lost thinking too much about how other people behave. You may tend to judge everybody that you come across. This one walks in a funny way. That person is not dressed well. You wonder what someone sitting at the park is smiling about. When these thoughts fill your head, you will only drain yourself. Spending too much time focusing on other people will only deter you from using your mind productively. Instead of visualizing your goals and your future, you waste your energy mulling over little things that add no value to you.

Regular Insomnia

Do you find it hard to sleep sometimes? You may get worked up over the idea that your brain cannot shut down and stop thinking. Sadly, this can paralyze you since your brain doesn't get the rest that it deserves. Gradually, you will notice a decrease in your productivity. You are unlikely to feel good about yourself since there is little that you achieve. Worrying too much about not being able to sleep can make you uneasy and you may find yourself in a state of captivity.

## You Always Live in Fear

Are you afraid of what the future has in store for you? If you answer yes to this question, then chances are that you're caged in your mind. Living in fear could drive you to resort to drugs and alcohol as your best remedy. You will gain the perception that by taking drugs, it will help you drown your sorrows and help you forget.

## You're Always Fatigued

Do you always wake up in the morning feeling tired? This could be a result of stress or depression. Instead of living a productive life, you find yourself waking up late, tired, and unmotivated. This happens because you don't give your mind an opportunity to rest.

## You Don't Live in the Present

Do you find it difficult to enjoy life? Why do you think you find it daunting to sit back, relax, and be happy with your friends? The mere fact that you can't stay in the present implies that you won't focus on what is happening in the present. Overthinking blinds you from noticing anything good that is currently happening around you. You will often think about the worst that can happen. The issue is that you are trapped in your mind and there is nothing outside your thoughts that you can constructively think about.

You crave for affection, yet don't always get it

Often, overthinking is just a ploy to get attention. While this isn't always the case, it might be worth asking yourself if it is just the comfort that you seek.

You pay attention to others' assessments as well

Considering the opinions of others is crucial in understanding your feelings and what you can do about those issues which worry you.

An overthinker attempts to locate importance in all things

Indeed, everything is urgent, everything is a life and death struggle, and everything is headed toward a tragic end.

Experience the ill effects of sleep deprivation

It is common for overthinkers to lose sleep regularly. While it's normal when you have something important to worry about, the chronic overthinker will experience sleep deprivation issues as a result of their pathological worrying.

Overthinkers recollect every word and detail from a discussion

If you find yourself keeping a play by play account of your conversations, then there is a very good chance you fall under the category of overthinkers.

Overthinkers have trouble relating to others

These folks will find it hard to build lasting relationships especially if they are bent in seeing the worst of every situation.

When your mood constantly changes

Overthinking causes hormonal imbalance in people, which is manifested by frequently occurring mood swings. Also, a person may experience anxiety, obsessive-compulsive disorder, addictions, and other mental health issues.

When you notice weight variations

Overthinking causes stress, which leads to weight variations. It causes loss of appetite and loss of weight. Weight loss can happen over a few days, weeks, or even a few months. That is how the body responds to overthinking habits that increase metabolism. The body uses 'fuel' from the body's fat reserves when metabolism increases. In that way, a person experiences weight loss.

When you are anxious and restless

Too much thinking leads to anxiety and restlessness, which, if not treated, become worse over time. When a person constantly thinks about finding a job, or feeling nervous before doing a big exam, or being embarrassed in particular social situations, her mind becomes restless, and even causes the person to develop fear.

When you lack patience

A person will often feel impatient when they become too much engrossed in their thoughts. They may also become angry, irritated, and intolerant.

The body reacts to overthinking by releasing adrenaline or cortisol, which helps the body to respond to a stressful situation. For overthinkers, a stressful situation could be as small as someone else interrupting their thoughts. The overthinker will react in a way that could irritate another person.

# Chapter 11 Decluttering Your Thoughts, Your Life Obligations, Your Relationships and Your Surroundings

## Decluttering Your Thoughts

We all worry from time to time. You worry about yourself and others on a daily basis. This is normal, to an extent. You may worry about the potential of failure, about your safety, or other possible factors. It is instinctual, as animals must worry about their hunger until they feed themselves. However, there is a certain point where worrying is unhealthy. If you find yourself constantly worrying to the extent where it takes over your life, you need to take action. You must be able to enjoy your life. While you will certainly worry occasionally, it should not prevent you from completing your daily tasks. When worrying becomes severe, it needs attention.

You must learn to stop worrying. There is always the chance of a negative event occurring, but you must be able to find positivity and hope instead of dwelling on the potential for something going wrong. You must be able to live in the moment and focus on enjoying yourself instead of worrying about what you did incorrectly in the past and what could go wrong in the future. Here are some ways on how to declutter your thoughts:

## Stop Worrying

It sounds simple enough: just stop worrying. Although this seems easier said than done, it is possible to train your brain to worry less and be able to enjoy yourself more. Worrying can be lessened, and you may greatly minimize it and even prevent it from occurring. However, this will take a lot of practice and patience with your progress. If you tend to worry naturally, this will be an ingrained habit that will take time to replace with better habits. You must be able to change your mind so that you may reduce the amount of worrying that you do.

## Live in the Moment

Learning to live in the moment can really help you to stop worrying. Often, worrying is a result of the past or future. We don't typically worry as much about what we are doing in the present. You must be willing to accept the past and live without regrets. Every mistake is a learning opportunity, and every issue will only make you stronger. The future is unpredictable; the best you can do is to work your hardest towards making it a future you want. However, that's pretty difficult when you spend your time worrying!

## Stop the "What-Ifs"

Everyone experiences "what-if" thoughts from time to time. This is normal and can help with the decision-making process. However, they can harm your daily life when they start to interfere with your routine. If you struggle to go about your everyday routine because you are too focused on the potential for negativity, you need to make changes to yourself regarding your worrying. When you can't control your thoughts, it's problematic.

To control these thoughts, you can try a few methods. One way is to write down these thoughts when they occur. By doing so, you are becoming more informed of how you think, and you may realize that these thoughts lack logic behind them. It will help you to realize what you are thinking, and you may understand why you think that way as a result. You should also take action on these thoughts. If there is a way to solve the problem that you are worried about, do it. If there isn't, find a way to let go of that thought. Talk to someone, write it down, or think it through. You may also take a moment to understand what the thought is, how it makes you feel, and what your reaction to it is. This will help you to have a better emotional response to it and behave properly to solve the issue. You must also become more comfortable with change and uncertainty. Recognize that some things will simply remain unknown until they occur and worrying will not alter the outcome.

Become More Aware of Yourself

Self-awareness can really help you. It can make it much easier for you to understand your emotions and feel more in control of your mind. You will realize why you act and think the way that you do. You can understand what your strengths and weaknesses are. It will also help you realize what motivates you. You will become more aware of your purpose and goals in life.

To become more self-aware, you will have to make a conscious effort to do so at first. Take some time each day to really reflect on how you are feeling. Understand your current emotions, the causes of them, and the effect they have on you. You may also reflect on your day as a whole. Did you accomplish what you set out to do? If not, what held you back from doing so? Use this time to constructively criticize yourself. Do not simply criticize yourself, compare yourself to others, or think about how you failed. Instead, realize what worked for you and what did not. Doing so will benefit you, as you can learn from that and apply it to the next day. You will not be perfect at first, but if you can make improvements each day, you will be much better off. Only compare yourself to who you were yesterday. You should always be learning, improving, and changing for the better. This is a natural way to progress in life, and it's important to do so to be the best person that you possibly can be. Remember to think about both what can be improved and what you did well, as it is important to remind yourself of your successes and remember that you are capable of success.

You may ask others to help you in several ways. One way is to talk out your emotions with another that you trust. This can help you to verbally express your thoughts. You may also ask others for feedback, as they will be able to give you an opinion outside of yourself. However, this must be healthy. You should trust the other person's word and ensure that you take everything they say as a way to improve, not as an attack on the person that you are.

It's important to stop your habit of worrying, and there are a few ways that you can work on it. You must, however, keep in mind that it will take work to stop yourself from worrying. It's also important to discover how to live in the moment so that you can enjoy life and feel greater happiness. Stopping the "what-ifs" that you think can really help you. Most of these are unnecessary, and you will feel better for not thinking these thoughts. Finally, you must become more aware of yourself to worry less.

## Decluttering Your Relationships

The first step to breaking out of any toxic relationship is to identify the signs around you, acknowledge and then accept them as a truth that is negative to your health and needs to be amended. Everyone's relationships are different, but here is a closer look at some of the most common signs connection to toxic relationships:

- Emotional manipulation is one sign that is prominent in any kind of toxic relationship or connection

- The definition of this symptom varies because it can include a wide range of actions and behaviors that vary from case to case

- At its core though, emotional manipulation refers to the intentional alteration of behaviors or way of speaking in order to avoid or manage the emotions of someone else

- In the case of the toxic person, this can refer to an intentional intensification of tense emotions and responses when their friend or partner is talking in order to get them to leave the room or feel powerless in their current situation

- In the case of the victim, they know that when their friend or partner is in this mood that their tense emotions will only intensify if they try to talk to them so instead they intentionally find something to do in a different room to avoid talking to their friend or partner until they are in a better headspace

- Isolating oneself from other close connections with family or friends to spend more time with their toxic friend or partner

- In many cases, this isolation is directly linked to and even the result of their friends and family seeing the way their loved one has changed in this relationship or connection and confronted them about it

- This confrontation is seen as an act of aggression by the individual and they get defensive, siding with their toxic friend or partner and hindering their relationship with their supportive loved one

- Being dismissed as overly emotional or overreacting to things whenever you voice your feelings or opinions (particularly if they are counter to the toxic friend or partner)

- In some cases, the individual is not dismissed but rather teased and ridiculed making them feel even worse about speaking their mind

- They can be accused of imaging problems that do not exist if there is an issue the toxic friend or partner does not want to deal with

- Some toxic partners might try to make the individual feel selfish or guilty if their thoughts, opinions or desires are centered around anything they need or want

- A variety of controlling behaviors have been associated with toxic relationships and connections

- Calling a person names and speaking with a sarcastic tone in situations where it is inappropriate or hurtful

- Endless and harmful criticism that is meant to damage their self-esteem and confidence so that they are easier to control and manipulate

- Using intimidation and fear tactics when the person becomes too bold or exploratory for their liking

- Blaming the person from things they had no control over or were not even connected to and throwing out unnecessary accusations in an attempt to make their partner feel guilty about something that may not even have happened

Whatever the specifics are with toxic people, they are unhealthy influences on men and women of any age or profession. The more toxic people that are around and the longer or more connected their relationship with the individual becomes, the more power and negative influence they will have on the person. These types of relationships are often neglectful and even dangerous, and they can be some of the most difficult to break free from.

## Decluttering Your Surroundings

1. Determine the department of the house you want to start decluttering.

This is the first and foremost step you need to undertake. You can't declutter all the areas of the house in a day. Even you do, that means you, leaving work, school or that vital task that you were supposed to handle for the day. It can be so overwhelming if you think you can declutter your home in a day, especially if it's your first time. It can also be time consuming, so you need to decide where you are going to start decluttering from. Start with the easiest one so that you won't get tired easily. Then, ascend to harder areas. When you have chosen an area to declutter, it's time to move to the next step on this list.

2. Give yourself 5-10 minutes decluttering period.

Decluttering is a gradual process. A process that you ought not to rush. You can dedicate 5 or 10 minutes of your time every day to declutter your home. As you proceed, increase the time and add more tasks on your list as you go on. For example, the first day can be 5 minutes. The second can be 10, the third can be 15, and so on. Don't start decluttering with 10 minutes on your first day and spend 5 minutes the next day. It simply won't work. Before you realize, you are finding it hard to dedicate even a minute to declutter your home. Start with the lowest possible time and ascend accordingly.

3.  Get a trash bag ready

You would want to get rid of those items that are causing your home to be cluttered. Get a trash bag, throw them inside. Old items that you feel you don't want to get rid of, give them to charity. If you're going to store any item, get large boxes. Move them to the appropriate places and create space in your home. You will be amazed to see the number of trash bags that you have taken away.

4.  Create a to-do list of items you want to throw in the trash

Surely, there will be a good number of items in trash bags that you would want to get rid of. Get a paper, write out all the items that you want to get rid of. Each item that you take to the trash cross them on your list. Also, it's important you create a to-do list of all your tasks, so that you cross each one you have accomplished. As you get rid of each item, the clutters get reduced. Creating these lists will help you keep track of tasks that you have completed and the ones that you haven't. It's easier to declutter if you have a picture of where and how to get started.

5.  Declutter one item every day.

Each day that you decide to declutter your home, try to at least get an unwanted item out of your home. Imagine doing this for a month? That's 30 items. Do this for a year, and you must have for rid of 365 items. How about you increase it to 2 items every day? In no time, you will be able to declutter your house and get those items thrown into the trash. Your home will stay completely clean and devoid of dirt.

6.  Take a picture

This isn't necessary, but it's quite helpful. You can decide to take a picture of a cluttered area, like your kitchen and then, take another picture of your kitchen. This time, a decluttered one. Observe those photos, and you will see how proud you have become that you have begun the step in decluttering your home.

7.  Use the four-box system

Establishing a system will make it easier to declutter your home than having none. The four-box system is an example of such systems that will help you become more efficient in tidying up your home. Get four boxes and label them as follows with descriptions.

- Give away: These are boxes that should be filled with things that you don't need or use but are still okay. In other words, these are items that you can either sell online or donate to some charity organizations.

- Keep: These boxes should contain items that you plan on keeping. They are items that you can't do without. That is the items that you use frequently. Examples of these items are your clothes, sound system, chairs, etc. They mostly have a fixed place where they are kept.

- Return: In this box, things that are misplaced in your house should be kept in this box. For example, your soap shouldn't be in the sitting room. Your cutlery shouldn't be in the bathroom, and so on. These items should be kept in their appropriate places and not the other way round.

- Trash: Items or possessions that are worthless should be kept in this box.

Each room that you enter identify items that should be placed in their respective boxes. Any item at all, irrespective of its size, should enter their appropriate boxes. It may take you some time, but it's worth it. You will discover items and will now what to do with them.

8. Don't be afraid to ask for assistance

Asking for help from a friend or relative is a cool way to get suggestions on how to declutter your home. Your friend or relative can go through all the items in your home and suggest which one is to be thrown, given out, or which one is to be kept. You might want to defend your reasons for keeping such an item, which is totally cool. If your friend or relative see the same reasons as you do, then your decision is valid. If otherwise, then it's wise to get rid of such item.

The best thing about this is that your friend or relative doesn't need to be a professional to help you get rid of any clutter. Just that having someone by your side all through the decluttering process will make it easier and faster for you to get rid of certain items that you have doubts getting rid of.

# Chapter 12 Mental Declutter Habits

**M**ental clutter can greatly lower your productivity because you will lose focus and concentration. Assess your life, identify the source of your mental clutter, and try to fix it. Remember the design of the brain does not allow it to divide its attention in too many directions. That is the reason why it needs to be orderly and peaceful so that it can filter information into the right place and act.

To get your mind in a good state, you need to clear it of any clutter. You should organize your thoughts, worries, and tasks so that your mind can have somewhere for focusing and acting accordingly. The following are some of the tips that can help you to get rid of mental clutter.

## 1. Declutter Your Physical Environment.

When you sit in an environment that is full of clutter, it will cause your mental clutter. This is because the clutter will keep on telling your mind that it needs to work extra hard to clear the clutter. These excessive stimuli will likely suck your mental energy. If you clear the clutter from your physical environment, you will also be clearing your mind from the mental clutter.

Get rid of the non-essential items and put everything else in its rightful place. The best way to clear your mental clutter is by clearing your environment or workspace every day so that clutter does not pile up. Tidying up your workspace will promote your mental clarity.

## 2. Write a "to-do" list

You do not have to overwork your brain by storing so much information in it. Having a "to-do" list where you write all that you have to do will free up your mind. The list should have priorities of tasks and you should check them daily and work on them depending on their priorities on the list. The list can have appointments, projects, bills to pay and so on. You can always tick against a task when you complete it.

## 3. Keep a journal

A journal is almost similar to a "to-do" list but here you document those things that disturb your peace of mind and give you anxieties and worries. You can write down your worries, plans for achieving certain goals, and even problems in your relationship that are draining your peace of mind.

## 4. Commit to remain in the present

You need to let go of your past. Holding on to regrets from past mistakes or missed opportunities, or people who have hurt you, will clutter your mind and rob you of your mental peace. Getting rid of unnecessary thoughts and fears will reduce stress and improve your confidence. These negative memories do not help you at all so try to delete them in your mind so that you can have a better focus on the things that are more important in your life.

## 5.  Avoid multitasking

Organize your work well and tackle them on a priority basis. This will prevent you from straining and you will reduce stress and overwhelm. Multitasking will eventually limit your concentration span and stress you. If you find your home or office is in a mess, start by clearing the clutter before handling any other business. Clear your mind of any other thoughts and focus on clearing the clutter.

## 6.  Limit the amount of information you consume

The amount of information that we consume can have an impact on our mental health. Too much information from the media, newspapers and the internet can clog our brain causing stress and anxiety. Spending so many hours reading some information on social media, blogs or any other platform can clutter our minds with unnecessary stuff causing mental fatigue and mental stress.

You should limit the amount of time on social media and select only important information to read. You should never allow yourself to consume negative content and cancel any blog subscription that does not help improve your life. Ensure that the information you read is authentic and from a credible source, then store only relevant information while you discard the rest.

## 7.  Set priorities

What are your goals in life? You should identify which things are most important in your life and which ones are not. Setting priorities can help you in taking control of your life and it can help you in identifying and reaching your goals in life. Having an endless "to-do" list can clutter your mind. You should know that you could not do everything in one go. So, decongest your mind by having a top priorities list.

You can start by writing down a list of what you want to do and achieve based on priorities. The next thing is to plan on how you will do the tasks and how you will achieve your goals. After writing down how you are going to execute your plan, you can now allocate each task the time you will take to finish it. Keep checking and updating your priorities to ensure that they remain relevant because they can change over time.

## 8. Make decisions on time

Postponing decision making will clutter your mind with pending decisions. So, act right away and avoid procrastination. However, remember to evaluate your decisions first before implementing them. Therefore, if you delay decisions, you are simply cluttering your mind. Check your emails, letters, bills, requests and respond to them accordingly so that they do not pile up giving you mental clutter.

## 9. Practice meditation

Meditation is a great way of relaxing your mind and clearing it of any stressful thoughts. You need to make it a daily practice to help you eliminate any unnecessary thoughts and to calm your mind.

## 10. Take some time to unwind

Take a break from your busy schedules and stressful situations. Take a walk in the park, go swimming, go to social events, and go for hikes or anything that will calm you and make you happy. Give your mind rest and let it recharge so that you can improve your focus and mental clarity.

## 11. Share your thoughts

Sometimes talking to someone eases the emotional burden and clutter in our minds. You can share your thoughts with a trusted friend or a family member. This can help you to see things differently and make sound decisions.

## 12. Practice breathing exercises

Taking a deep breath and exhaling slowly can work magic by calming your mind and relaxing your nerves. Deep breathing can also clear your mind giving you a calm mood. It is also helpful in reducing stress and promoting concentration.

## 13. Eat healthily and get enough sleep

A good diet and good sleep are essential to your mental health. Getting enough sleep will help your mind to rest and recharge. This is also the best remedy for reducing stress and fighting depression and anxiety.

# Chapter 13 What Should You Know About Hypnosis?

Hypnosis is a different, stronger form of meditation. It is something that needs more guidance as you progress. With this practice, we will provide you with commands that help reshape your brain. Let your mind wander and keep it open so we can provide you with the right kind of tools to tweak the way you think ever so slightly.

You need to be completely relaxed in order to be properly hypnotized. We are going to start this hypnosis first by making sure that you are regulating your breathing and that you are free from any tension. Once you have found that relaxed state of mind, it will be easier for our guided hypnosis to tap into the deepest parts of your brain. Make sure that you are willing to let your thoughts go and don't stay too attached to any negative emotions that pass through your mind in this process.

These thoughts and commandments will make it easier for you to keep a positive outlook each and every day. Towards the end, if you stick with it, you will be astonished at the vast improvement to your overall mental health.

# Hypnosis for Life-Changing Positive Thinking

In this hypnosis, what you're going to do first is to make sure you are in a very comfortable seated position where your legs and your arms are loose. You don't want to keep anything bent to the point where you might cut off circulation. Position yourself in a way that blood can flow easily through your body.

These are going to help you better create a positive mindset rather than trying to do this all on your own. We are going to be giving you what you need to understand. These are your daily thoughts, and things that you are going to constantly need to remind yourself. We will use these thoughts to rewire your brain.

Begin by noticing your breath. Notice it come in and out, in and out. It is a very natural process that is making you feel so much better from the moment you begin.

The air needs to cycle through your body because it is what's helping you get stronger and grow into a healthier person. It keeps your blood regulated, which is very important for feeling good. When your mind feels good, your body is going to feel good, and that will show. Keep your eyes open for just a moment. Right now, look up as high as you possibly can. Do not move your head. Only look using your eyes. Look up so high that you can see your eyelids. On three, you're going to snap forward and look straight ahead of you. Then we're going to close your eyes and countdown, so first begin by looking up. Look up as high as you can. You should only see your eyelids and nothing else. Do not move your head. On the count of three, you're going to snap and then look straight ahead.

One, two, three.

Now, place your head gently back onto a pillow or something else where you can rest it comfortably for the next several minutes.

Begin by breathing in, once again. Breathe in as we count down from five. Breathe out as we count up from five. Counting down is going to get you prepared and counting up is going to help build that energy so that this hypnosis is a lot easier. Breathe in for five, four, three, two, and one. Breathe out for one, two, three, four, and five. And again. Breathe in for five, four, three, two, and one. Breathe out for one, two, three, four, and five.

You should now be incredibly relaxed and focused. It is time to make a promise to yourself. This hypnosis is going to be like a contract that you are signing with yourself, to think more positively. By the end, you should have a new, healthier mindset that will take away the mental blocks and make it easier for you to get the things that you want from life. No longer will you have to live with mental anguish, constant anxiety, or depression that only makes it harder for you to find happiness.

You are doing something good here. You are doing something healthy.

Staying positive is never a bad thing. Being positive is good. It is going to help you achieve the things that you want the most.

The first promise that you are going to make to yourself is to always look for the positives. You are going to do whatever you can to make sure that you see the bright side. Your mind is going to have to learn how to be able to pick up on a different perspective.

No matter what happens in life, you will now be an expert at finding the good. Even in situations that are difficult with no silver lining, you will know exactly what you need to do in order to find the positive side. You will be able to recognize the good from the bad.

This does not mean that you will lose your grasp on the reality of the situation. There are plenty of bad situations that you have to deal with. Each one with varying degrees of severity. Knowing how to find the positives doesn't mean that you are ignoring it.

You are now somebody who is focused on making sure that the positives are more apparent. We don't want to overlook the positive, just like how we might overlook the negative. You are going to be able to pick up on both sides of the coin. You will realize the black and the white while understanding that the gray still exists.

No matter how small this distinction might be or how fine the line is, you will understand the truth.

Let's do another breathing exercise now to make sure that this sticks in your mind. Repeat this, as a promise to yourself.

Say now, "I will always look for positivity."

To establish this further, let's breathe in again. Breathe in now for five, four, three, two, one, and breath out for one, two, three, four, and five.

Repeat, "I will always look for positivity."

Breathe in now for five, four, three, two, one, and breathe out for one, two, three, four, and five.

Now let's move on to the next commandment. You are always going to accept the things that are out of your control.

A positive life does not mean one where we will never have to deal with negative issues again. We are always going to run into things that are beyond our control. Now, at this moment, completely relaxed, happy, open, and free, you are also accepting of all things.

You are going to know exactly what to do in a situation where you don't have all of the power.

It is not always going to be that easy, but when you are dedicated and passionate, you can make sure to keep a positive mindset.

When you are presented with a challenging situation, you will be able to identify if you have any control over it or not. You will be able to understand whether there is something that you can change, or if things are just the way they are for a reason.

You are always going to look for a way to find positivity, but when you cannot, you will focus instead on making sure that you at least have a good mindset. When you are continuously focused on the negative and not looking for ways to make it a positive experience, that is only going to hold you back.

You have to realize that it is going to be a struggle, and there will still be challenges. You are promising to yourself that you are going to accept the things that are out of your control. You are okay with this because you know that in the end, it is going to make you a stronger person.

You know you can't control other people. You are aware that there will always be a certain level of uncertainty, even in the most planned out situations. You understand that even when we have a specific outcome in mind, things still won't end up looking exactly the same as we might have predicted. You accept the fact that you will not always be able to change these situations. You are very aware of things that you control and the things that you cannot. You are going to use a positive mindset to help you work through the issues that you have.

This is a promise that you're going to make to yourself.

Continue to focus on your breathing. Notice the way that the air is coming in and the way that it is leaving your body. This is to help keep you relaxed and let these thoughts come into your mind as if you were creating them on your own.

Breathe in now for five, four, three, two, one, and breath out for one, two, three, four, and five. You promise to accept the things that are out of your control.

Repeat this phrase: "I will accept the things that are out of my control."

Breathe in now for five, four, three, two, one, and breathe out for one, two, three, four, and five.

Repeat one more time. "I accept the things that are out of my control."

The next commandment is that you are always going to look for ways to include more positive activities into your life. There are many things that we can do, aside from having a healthy mindset to increase overall positivity. This includes things like eating healthy, exercising, getting the proper amount of sleep, and hanging out with people that we love. Also doing artistic activities, mindfulness activities, puzzles, and other fun solitary games will increase your ability to focus.

You are always going to look for things that make you feel good. It doesn't have to be one of these activities. These are just some common things that people enjoy helping make themselves feel good. You are promising yourself now that you will find something that makes you happy.

Pick out an activity that you can do when you are extremely stressed. Find something that will always put you in a better mood. You are going to be looking for something to increase your overall good feelings. You will be able to better decipher the difference between something that makes you feel good and something that you just simply feel obligated to do.

You don't have to subject yourself to tasks that you don't actually enjoy. There will always be certain things that we have to do, like chores or going to work, but you will know how to keep a positive mindset throughout these situations. You are always going to be looking for ways that you can include more positive activities in life. You are dedicated to yourself, to make sure that you are spending time alone and growing your skills that you enjoy more than anything else.

Breathe in now for five, four, three, two, one, and breath out for one, two, three, four, and five.

Repeat after this phrase, "I am going to look for ways to include positive activities in my life."

You are dedicated to making this promise to yourself because you want to live a happier and healthier lifestyle. You no longer want to live in misery, where you don't feel like you have an identity, or where you can find joy from simple things that you used to do.

Repeat the phrase for is one more time. "I am always going to look for ways to include more positive activities into my life."

Breathe in now for five, four, three, two, one, and breath out for one, two, three, four, and five.

Moving on to the fourth commandment. You will allow yourself some discomfort from time to time. Don't try to avoid these uncomfortable moments, whether it is stress from work or a relationship issue, you have accepted that life will always have its flaws.

There will always be moments that you wish that you didn't have to go through. This might include significant change or loss. These are natural things in life that should not be ignored. We cannot pretend as though we are free from ever having to experience a bad situation. There will always be challenges that you have to learn how to overcome.

The best way to overcome these things is through the use of your positive mindset. You are going to be able to work through these challenges because you are thinking positively. You are going to be able to pull yourself from even the most challenging situations because you understand what it takes to live happier and healthier. You are aware of all the ways that a positive mindset is going to help you work through some of these most challenging issues.

You are going to keep the endpoint in focus and not just the bright side. You now know that you are stronger and better because of these issues, especially in the aftermath. You are promising to yourself that you won't avoid these situations. You are not somebody who pretends everything is fine. You are going to confront the issues head on.

You will come face to face with your biggest fears and your greatest struggles. You will know exactly what it takes to get through the most challenging situations. You are going to be incredibly understanding that there will always be moments in life that we wish didn't happen. You are going to know exactly how to get through these. You are going to do everything within your power to make sure that you are living a healthier life in the long run.

Breathe in now for five, four, three, two, one, and breath out for one, two, three, four, and five. Repeat this statement. "I am going to allow myself to feel discomfort in order to learn."

This does not mean that you will be intentionally torturing yourself. This also does not mean that you are living in constant misery. It simply means that you aren't going to run from fear. You will not run from the hard situations.

The fifth and final commandment is always knowing how to identify a positive. Being able to see the good and pull it out is a skill that you'll need to develop. At first, you're going to be stuck on the negative, and that keeps you thinking everything is always bad.

Rather than continuing on with that mindset, you promise yourself that you are going to be like an investigator in life. You will always be able to pick up on all the clues that lead to something being more positive. It will be a lot easier for you to know exactly what is good and bad in your life.

Breathe in now for five, four, three, two, one, and breath out for one, two, three, four, and five.

You are going to continually remind yourself that you have everything that it takes to live a happier and healthier life. You will always know how to find the positive even the most challenging negative situations. Repeat after this.

"I promise to always know how to identify the positive in everything that comes my way."

Breathe in now for five, four, three, two, one, and breath out for one, two, three, four, and five. Repeat, "I am always going to know how to identify the positive and everything that comes my way."

You are going to make sure that you are doing everything possible to live a happy and healthy life. You are somebody who is ready to come face to face with the challenging things that you struggle with. You know exactly what it takes to live a happy life. You won't be waiting around for somebody else to tell you what to do anymore. You take action and live the life that you choose.

You are always going to be looking for ways that you can find positivity and even the darkest of times. You are resourceful, and this means using everything that comes your way and recovering value from it, you are exceptionally skilled, talented, and knows what they have to do to get the things that they want. You are somebody who is always going to be looking for ways that you can increase your experiences.

You take value in even the smallest most minuscule moments, and you know exactly what to do in order to make sure that you are living a happier and healthier life. You are not afraid of anything that is going to come your way. You are prepared and ready for all that you will have to face. You are in control of your life.

You are focused on your breathing once again. You feel so grateful for all the air that is coming in and leaving your body. You know everything to find the positive, even in the most negative situations, you are prepared, relaxed. You are calm, you are collected, and you are cool. You are perfectly happy. You are positive, and you are prepared. You are resourceful, and you are virtuous. You will always be looking for the good and all that you see.

As we countdown for 20, continue to focus on this.

Once we reach one, you will be snapped out of hypnosis. You will be able to continue with your life, always living by these commandments that we have wired into your psyche.

# Chapter 14 Managing Stress and Anxiety with Relaxation Techniques

**M**any people within society are facing severe issues about anxiety. Some people end up losing their lives while a good number leads to a frustrating experience for the rest of their lives. Emotionally, they are failing on how to control themselves. Usually, anxiety forms part and parcel of our emotions. Sometimes, it is healthy and falling on the positive side of your health. In this case, you may call it a good feeling. However, anxiety can build up in a person to some toxic level. You end up harboring anxiety at a disproportionate level, forcing you to make a short call at the hospital. That is a situation of a medical disorder. Your mental health starts incurring diagnoses that result in severe fear, worry, excessive nervousness, and even apprehension.

Disorders have high impacts on the behavior of someone. Your mind gets altered, and all these lead to physical symptoms, which are very severe and sometimes harsh. You start experiencing some strange emotions. Therefore, you can either have mild anxiety or severe anxiety. In the case of severe anxiety, you will emotionally suffer, and this will affect your day to day activities. However, mild anxiety has got vagueness issues plus unsettling kind of disturbances. Therefore, due to what has been so far, we can now define anxiety. Anxiety refers to an emotion embraced with wild thoughts, tension, feelings, and even physical changes such as high impulse rates. You can control and manage your anxiety in many ways, such as meeting your demands. Doing the correct thing and filling those gaps that caused you this kind of stress will help you a lot. However, you can also control the level of your anxiety through a proper step by step meditation. We are going to take a look at the meditation techniques you can employ or implement to counter your anxiety.

The first meditation technique in this category is breathing. When you are emotionally anxious, your impulse increases, leading to faster breathing. You may feel droplets of sweat at your armpits and face. You will feel lightheaded and sometimes wholly dizzy. At this moment, getting your breath at a stable level becomes a little bit difficult. There are several meditation techniques you can do to overcome the anxiety and bring your breathing under management. These include the following:

You can start by sitting in a comfortable place and completely quiet. Place your hand on the stomach and the other hand on your chest. Breathe in and out, slowly making sure your stomach moving faster than the chest.

Next, use your nose to have regular and slow breathing in and slowly breathe out using your mouth. Try as much as possible to watch your hands, sensing them more often. Your hand at the chest should not move; however, you should slightly move the other side across the stomach.

Now your anxiety is a little bit becoming weak. You can go ahead with this process as many times as you wish till you feel a little bit relaxed. At this moment, your anxiety will lessen up.

Secondly, visualize. In this case, you can work on your visualization state of mind. It will help you realize a happy place in your mind. Visualization paints a flowering picture in your mental mind. It comes a feeling of relaxation, and this will eventually calm and cool both of your body and brain. You are anxious, look for a comfortable place, and remain completely quiet and silent. Start having thoughts of your best site for relaxing. While you are doing this, try to think of a place that gives you peace, happiness, and more so, a calming state of mind. However, this place can be either in the real world or instead of a hypothetical situation. You should put more effort here to get the optimum level of relaxation. More so, this place should also be more comfortable to think about and use it as a future referral to all of your anxiety conditions.

Now go ahead with your visualization. Take your time to think of those small details and things you would find in that place if at all you were there. Think of the feeling of the site, how it would smell and sound. In sound, I mean all kinds of music within the happy atmosphere, and this would be caused by the following factors such as birds, swaying of trees, and so on. Think of the rivers flowing with a soothing sound and a cooling effect of wind breeze. Start envisioning yourself while thoroughly enjoying and making fun in that place. Now that you have this picture in your mind, you can start by closing your eyes and making some regular but slow breathes using your nose and breathing out through your mouth. Maintain both the breathing and visualization process until your anxiety starts to lessen. Since your anxious emotion will lift, do not forget to revisit this place during anxiety conditions.

You can also do exercises that relax your muscles, whether within the short run or long run. Anxiety causes tension, strain, exhaustion, and weakness of your muscles. In most cases, it is not that much; however, sometimes, this cannot allow you to concentrate on other issues. Muscle stress act as a hindrance to your anxiety management. It has that nagging and annoying trend of creating difficulty in your way to control your anxiety. Therefore, the only way to achieve your anxiety elimination is to first destroy or eradicate any element of stress within your muscles. There are several meditation exercises that you can get on your way to start the process, as you can see below. Since you want to delete muscle tension during anxiety moments, you can do the following:

☐ Look for the right comfortable place and in total silence. Make sure you have closed your eyes and concentrate on your breathing. Breathe in and out for sometimes. Make sure it is slow breathing, which you do with your nose and breathe out using your mouth.

☐ Still breathing, make a tight fist using your hand and tightly squeeze your fist.

☐ While still squeezing your fist, hold it for few seconds and detect all the strain and tension you are feeling now, especially in your hand.

☐ Go ahead by opening your fist, note how you feel in this situation. At this juncture, you may notice some element of tension deserting you, and this reflects on your hand, resulting in a more relaxed and lighter situation.

Another meditation technique you can also employ to counter anxiety is counting. Many people always avoid it for various reasons that are funnily unknown to me even though several books of psychology talk much about it. Many psychologists, taking psychological therapy as a living or as a hobby, also are busy doing it to their clients. Counting is a simple and easy way to ease up your anxious mind. When you get yourself in that mix of anxiety, get yourself the right place; make sure it is a little bit quiet and silent. It should be comfortable too since that will create a relaxing feeling without many disturbances. After meeting up with these conditions, you can go ahead with your counting process. Start counting from one to ten, and you can go with this even up to 20 times. Counting is not limited; therefore, you can move to higher figures until you feel you are recuperating well. That is, your anxiety is lifting and subsidizing tremendously. Sometimes, you might get a quicker and faster relief; however, other times, this may prove to take a little bit longer. In this case, you should only be patient and stay calm as you focus on your emotional healing process. It is better to note that healing is a process that requires patience and time.

Staying present is also another meditation technique that will help you counter your level of anxiety. You must look for ways to create your mindfulness at all times. That's, you should practice as hard as possible to be present in your state of mind, and no one should judge you under any circumstances. Staying in this situation will help you eradicate several groups of anxiety that might be building up. Therefore, you can at least bring back your state of mind by doing the following exercises:

☐ Look for a quiet place and make sure it is very comfortable where you can eventually sit while closing your eyes.

☐ You can as well make a note on how you feel, especially about your body, and this should be extended to your breathing too.

☐ After this, make a slight change in your awareness of your surroundings. Take every note of anything that's happening, especially in the external world. What you smell or even here will eventually bring back your physical balance in terms of your mindfulness. Again, there is that feeling of an environment that will invade your presence. This will also give you that chance of having your present state back, thus countering your anxiety.

☐ You can also change your awareness by shifting it from your environment to your body. Repeat it until your anxious mind become free, and the level of anxiety diminishes ultimately.

You can also counter anxiety by interrupting it. That is, interrupting your thinking here. It is always hard to have an honest thought when you have a high level of stress. Again, even less level, such as mild anxiety, instills in you that unsettling feeling that prevents you from thinking very well. Anxious thinking is hazardous since you might end up thinking of something that's not true. You end up making severe accusations followed by some critical steps in life that you might regret later on as time passes. Also, you may get yourself doing things that would only worsen your already worse situation. The only way to avoid this is by breaking the anxious thoughts that are lingering on your now stressed up mind. The following guidelines will eventually help you to come up with a clear thing far off from the anxious mind.

☐ You can start asking yourself about your usual worries and if at all these worries are complicated and offer a problem to you. If your answer is yes, then you are off to the process of starting up your meditation as quick as possible.

☐ After this, you can now start your anxiety interruptions using the following steps.

☐ You can try singing any song whether you know it or not as long as you have mastered some parts of it. Again, you can speak aloud your anxieties or try shouting or talking them to yourself.

☐ After this, think of an excellent task for your next focus instead of your anxiety. Therefore, this focus could be on your spouse, children, a person you cherish, your happy place, or even some tasks that you have saved to undertake them later on during the day, such as having a meeting somewhere.

Another way to interrupt your anxiety is by investing much of your time in listening to music or even having some excellent collections of different books touching on various life chapters.

Last but not least, on this, try as hard as possible to handle yourself with much dignity and notice your feeling after every meditation practice you undertake. Note the way your anxiety diminishes.

Another meditation technique you can also use is the self-stress management. Anxiety comes as a result of the stress of not getting something or not achieving something. When you learn to eliminate stress, then you will be in a position to fight off your anxiety. Again, understanding how you can manage stress help you to strike off the possible triggers of your anxious mind. You can, therefore, manage this through proper organization of your upcoming deadlines and various pressures. Do this by compiling them correctly in a manner that you can eventually achieve them. Make sure that those daunting tasks are achievable and more manageable. Still on this, you can take some time off for your benefit. Locate for yourself some free time so that you can make even a nature stroll to release some hidden anxiety.

You can also offer yourself some relaxing techniques. These relaxing techniques provide you that kind of meditation feeling to counter your anxiety. There are several ways in which you can have a relaxing posture in your mind, and these include breathing exercises, resting, and even staying in the dark. Yoga, long baths, and even mild slow sex are part and parcel of these relaxing techniques that are part of meditation. Breathing exercises such as breathing in through your nose and taking and taking the air out through your mouth have been seen as good ways to release the toxic level of anxiety. Long baths, especially within the bathtub, can release some tensions within your strained body. You will feel a little relaxed in the end. As a result, this will lead to the eradication of anxiety. We have slow sex and romance, too, which also contributes to the reduction of anxiety level. If well maintained and managed, the issues of anxious thoughts and worries will never be an issue. Yoga helps you not only to reduce anxiety but also a reduction in weight. Due to this, you will lead a life free from health-related complications. There are several ways to carry out your yoga activities and always struggle to get the best. If you cannot find one, then you can consult your doctor or trainer. You can also rest in the dark for longer times as expected. Darkness is a quiet, silent place with little or no disturbance at all. In this place, you can even perform other meditation techniques such as breathing, counting, and so on. You can also listen to the sounds made by several animals within the atmosphere and expose your whole body to the prevailing fresh air. All these will leave you in a situation where you are not anxious and, if any, then very minimal or little.

Other forms of meditation techniques include performing some exercises to replace your negative thinking with positivity. On most occasions, anxiety comes about as a result of having some negative thoughts within your mind. You start off thinking of things that are not there, or instead of having a clear state of consciousness, you end up having a dirty mind. To start on this, you can make a good list of every bad or negative thought that lingers on your consciousness mind every day. Make a corresponding list but positive things you can eventually use to counteract the negative ones. You should make sure that these lists are manageable. There and then, establish a mental image with a notion of conquering all your fear. For example, you have worries about not completing your job today, and this has been bothering you for quite sometimes.

On the other hand, without completing your job today, you will have to forfeit the wages. The feeling of not getting paid at the end of the day gives you many worries that at the end of the day, you become highly anxious. The best positive thing to note down is how you can still have money. It seems in your worries, and money was the anxiety trigger. If you can as well get other sources of money as long as they are legit, then you will be able to avoid anxiety in this manner. This might be a short-run solution to the predicament, and next time you may think of having a long-term solution. As much as you look for an immediate solution about your worries that later on leads to anxiety, try as much as possible to get the long-term solution. A long-term solution, in this case, is to come up with a drafted plan containing a step by step guideline on how to complete that task within that located time. There are other meditation techniques such as getting involved in volunteering work within your society. Society is full of life-threatening and complications that affect their day to day activities. People are suffering from a particular illness due to negligence. Others are undergoing traumas caused by fire, death of the loved ones, and much more. Some, on the other hand, need physical and emotional encouragement to keep going. So, you can eventually chip in within this society and help them solve these life disputes that seem to devour them in the next moment of their lives. Touching someone's heart has the power to accelerate their lives once more. You can also get into their contribution lists and donate a few of the items you no longer need though still in good condition. Therefore, you will realize that your anxious mind and all the worries that came with it have reduced or even eliminated.

# Chapter 15 What is Relaxation?

The art of relaxation is a state of mind. In other, you need to set your thoughts in such a way that leisure is essential. Even when you are eating, you can`t just keep consuming all the time.

You need to relax and take some break that will help your mind settle and think of other things.

The minds also need to shift from one aspect to the other. In other words, if you keep doing something for long, there are chances that you will get bored and hate it. In the same way, you can`t eat for more than an hour and expect that all is well. Even your jaws, let alone your teeth need to relax and prepare for another meal.

Also, if the snack is so sweet, there are chances that you can`t take all the time and eat everything at a go. You need to relax and allow the process of digestions to swallow, let alone.

Several studies have been carried out to determine the effects of failing to relax while eating. It is worth noting that if you eat without allowing your gut to shallow well, there are chances that you will be choked.

There are other cases where one fails to register in the brain that one is full since they are not relaxing. In other words, if your minds do not have time to relax, there are some complications that one may develop.

For instance, people who develop the disorder of binge eating do not improve the condition in a single day.

However, it occurs gradually such that the minds fail to register that one is full. The desire to keep eating develops, and one thinks of eating rather than deducing anything else. They are the kind of people who will prefer eating at night, during the day and at any time. The art of eating in such a manner is not right as the mind does not relax.

Experience shows that the ritual of gratitude combines very well with the ritual of viewing ("spend" the day ritual), and from their combination, a single powerful ritual can be formed. In addition, both of these rituals are in harmony with specific assistive techniques, such as a warm bath. Among the more active components are walking, as well as all forms of active relaxation, such as muscle relaxation, according to the Jacobson method.

How to relax when something really bothers you? "Nothing will work out for me," "I am like a squeezed lemon" or "I have my nerves to the limit" - these are some of the expressions that accompany us during severe stress and anxiety. Sometimes we tend to get by with pills or even with visits to the doctor so that he will prescribe a "wonderful injection" from all problems. I will try to give you some recommendations on how you can make yourself a "wonderful injection" without having to take pills or going to the doctor. Learn to relax when you are overwhelmed by anxiety and stress! First, discover the Jacobson's Progressive muscle relaxation method.

In any case, first, we need to learn a little about what anxiety or sleep anxiety is in order to understand why there is no need to take medication to overcome it. When anxiety overcomes us, we feel a sense of fear, and even come to the conclusion that one day we can die from one of the attacks of severe anxiety: there is nowhere else to go. In this case, fear is a natural emotional response to an imminent threat, real or imagined, while anxiety is a preliminary reaction to a future threat (which may or may not occur).

Both of these concepts are productive in a sense because they warn us of the existence of danger and help us prepare for trouble. As they say, forewarned means armed. The problem arises at the moment when we are too long in a "state of alert" in high-intensity mode. This can lead to the so-called "anxiety attack," the symptoms of which cause a sharp deterioration in well-being, and as a result, we are forced to consult a doctor. However, we must understand that anxiety is nothing more than a combination of symptoms. This is not a disease, and this condition can be controlled.

Let's get back to anxiety. In order to understand what it is, imagine that a lion is chasing you, and you try to run as fast as you can. But actually, there is no lion! "Lion" exists only in our head. That is, the cause of these symptoms of malaise was the idea of something non-existent, fictitious (for example, fear of death or the obsession to die, fear of leaving home, or fear not to survive a heart attack).

In the case of the lion, we see that the solution lies in the palm of your hand: "you just have to stop," because the lion does not really exist, and there is no real danger. This would be the only way to reduce our anxiety, stop sweating, and soothe a heart jumping out of our chest. These are the same symptoms that provoke a real fit of anxiety or even panic.

The practice of conscious meditation, some fascinating activity or hobby, etc. This is something that constantly keeps your mind busy with something. So, we move away from this idea of danger (or from any other obsession), which can be a good strategy and help us reduce the symptoms of anxiety.

I will tell you about a very effective method for learning how to relax when anxiety overcomes you: the method of progressive muscle relaxation by an American scientist and Doctor Edmund Jacobson.

## Jacobson's Progressive Relaxation

What is Jacobson's progressive relaxation? This is a physiological method focused on the state of rest. It promotes deep relaxation without much effort, which allows you to set arbitrary control over the level of bodily tension. It allows you to recognize the close relationship between the level of bodily tension and mental stress, and to understand that the reduction of one of them involves the relief of the other.

It helps to achieve a state of dominance and relaxation in a gradual but continuous form (progressive relaxation), each time more intense and effective. The method teaches us to relax the muscles with the help of willpower, and through this, we achieve a deep state of inner peace, which comes when excessive bodily tension leaves us.

The areas in which stress builds up are numerous, and sometimes they cannot be seen with the naked eye, so it is important to learn how to relax all muscle groups in the body.

## What Does the Method of Progressive Muscle Relaxation of Jacobson Give Us?

Using this method, you can reduce periods of general anxiety, learn how to relax muscle tension, improve sleep quality, as well as increase self-control, and achieve a high level of relaxation. The method of progressive muscle relaxation of Jacobson consists of three main stages:

1. Tension-Relaxation

We are talking about the consistent tension and relaxation of various muscle groups throughout the body. This is done in order to learn to recognize the difference between the state of muscle tension and muscle relaxation. Thanks to this, a state of complete muscle relaxation is achieved, which is gradually transmitted throughout the body. Muscle groups should be in a state of tension for several seconds (7-8) and slowly relaxed for 5-10 minutes.

2. Observation

All participating muscle groups are mentally tested to make sure they are relaxed to the maximum.

3. Relaxation of Consciousness

At this stage, you need to think about something pleasant and positive or completely free your mind from thoughts (if you know how to do it). You need to learn how to relax your mind while your whole body continues to relax. Your meditation training comes to play here.

These three phases usually last from 10 to 15 minutes each. The method should not be applied in a hurry. This method can be repeated several times a day.

## About the Jacobson Method or Progressive Muscular Relaxation

We all strain and relax to move and live. Any action is a rather complex combination of muscle contractions and relaxation. Any thought can cause a similar combination of contractions and relaxation, even if we do not take active actions, and even if it seems to us that we are not moving.

A sudden sound will make us freeze and squint our eyes towards the sound source, even if we do not turn our heads in this direction. An unpleasant conversation will cause tension in the facial muscles, and even the muscles of the upper shoulder girdle, despite the fact that we carefully monitor the expression of our face and our posture. Pleasant signals from outside also affect us: we relax, facial features soften, we catch our breath.

If our life is full of events and thoughts related to stress, muscle tension will prevail and become our habitual state to such an extent that we ourselves will not notice it. However, such an overvoltage will not be completely invisible. Sooner or later, we will find it by pain in the neck, shoulders, sore muscles, headaches associated with tension, steady gloomy facial expression, and other delights of the effects of prolonged anxiety associated with stress.

The method of progressive muscle relaxation of Jacobson is among the best ways to handle your own body to reduce the effects of stress.

The long-term psychological effects of the regular practice of progressive muscle relaxation include:

- Reducing general anxiety.

- Reduced anxiety expectations associated with phobias.

- Reducing the frequency and duration of panic attacks.

- Expanding your own capabilities in frightening situations when applying the method of desensitization (graduated exposure).

- Improving concentration.

- Increased mood control.

The practice itself is that you perform a certain sequence of simple exercises. You mentally give yourself certain commands that you yourself execute. Exercise should take place daily, preferably twice a day, at a time convenient for you and in a quiet place where you can take a comfortable position and remove or loosen clothing and accessories that are restricting you. The room should have a comfortable temperature. The supine position is optimal, but not required. Estimated lesson time is 20 minutes. Do not strain muscle groups in places where you are experiencing pain without first consulting the Energy Cleaning (EC) meditation. Try to exercise without excessive perseverance, but with enviable regularity.

# Chapter 16 Relaxation Techniques for Anxiety

R elaxation is an incredibly effective way of dealing with anxiety, and it applies to all groups of people. It allows the body to activate its natural response to combat stressors. Relaxation comes in many forms and depends on what works best for you. Some of the relaxation techniques that have been proven to beat back anxiety are:

- Body scan technique

- Abdominal breathing for quick relaxation

- Progressive muscle relaxation

- Mind body relaxation to decrease stress and anxiety

- Relaxing self-massage

- Focus on breathing

- Deep breathing

- Roll breathing

- Box breathing

- Progressive relaxation

- Autogenic training

- Relaxing poses

There is a common belief among many people that relaxation involves sitting idle and or doing something you enjoy, like watching a movie or sleeping. No, relaxation is a task that needs concentration and energy input. Its sole purpose is to reduce the effects of stress and anxiety. If your definition of relaxation doesn't meet this goal, then it is far from relaxation. Relaxation achieves this by putting your body to a state of deep rest and restores normalcy such as slowing the heart rate, reducing blood pressure, improve blood circulation, and, most importantly, checking stress and anxiety. Activities that involve relaxation are those that touch on the most affected organs like the heart, blood vessels, and those in the breathing system. Try things like muscular exercises, meditation, yoga, and deep breathing. Most of these exercises are a form of self-treatment, so you don't need a professional to do them. However, they are quite demanding and require a lot of discipline. If you are the type that needs to be pushed, you might consider looking for a professional therapist to help you do the exercises. The word 'professional' is key because not anybody can make you do things that make you uncomfortable, especially if you're an adult. You need someone that will be hard and a little harsh on you. Also, people have diverse systems that respond differently to changes. If one or two of these exercises don't work for you, look for one that you are comfortable doing and is compatible with your system. You don't have to kill yourself trying to make a particular technique work even you can see that it is not working. Furthermore, all these techniques have been proven to lead to the same results, which is slowing down stress and anxiety. Just don't be too lazy to give a particular technique trial and error period before giving up on it entirely. Remember, things take time; you need to give your body a chance to get used to these changes. You will get used to those exercises in no time, and they will become a habit.

There is a thin line between relaxation exercises and meditation exercises. The main difference being that relaxation exercises engage various parts of the physical body while meditation engages the brain. The similarity between them is that they both put the entire body and mind in a state of rest to relieve affected parts and organs from stress and anxiety. Both exercises are carried out in systematic steps to the end. Skipping one step will likely jeopardize the whole process. If you are not sure about these steps and the order in which they are done, it is advisable that you seek the help of a therapist who will take you through each step.

## Body Scan

As you meditate, it can be helpful to do a body scan. This involves bringing attention to each part of your body. Allow your feelings to come to the surface and release them. You can complete this exercise lying down or sitting in a recliner. Focus on your breathing first. Then notice your toes. Breathe through your body and expel tension out through your toes. Focus on sensations, tension, and feelings in each part of your body and then breathe them out through that part of your body.

Conducting a body scan helps you identify areas in which you are holding tension and learn to release it. Do this as often as you feel necessary or when tension arises.

## Abdominal Breathing

Slow breathing from your abdomen can help alleviate symptoms of panic by slowing your respiratory rate, reducing the constriction of your chest wall muscles, and decreasing symptoms of hyperventilation.

When you feel dizzy or disoriented during a panic attack, it is because you are breathing rapidly from your chest. After three or four minutes of slow abdominal breathing, you should notice your symptoms are reduced. In addition to breathing this way in the moment of panic, you should also practice five minutes each day to train yourself to breathe more deeply on a regular basis.

To practice deep breathing, find a comfortable position. Close your eyes. Notice your breath. Is it shallow from your chest? Are you breathing slowly or quickly?

Now inhale deeply and slowly through your nose and expand your stomach as you breathe. Put your hands on your stomach so that you can see them rise and fall. Gradually, exhale through your mouth, letting out all of the air. If you feel worse during deep breathing, take a break for about 30 minutes and then try again.

If you practice abdominal breathing regularly, it should become natural for you. You will be able to initiate it during a panic attack to cue your body to relax.

## Progressive Muscle Relaxation

This is a two-step process of muscular contraction and relaxation involving various groups of muscles in the body. This exercise is important because it demonstrates how your body physically responds to stress and anxiety. Remember, this is a mental disorder that is not easy to detect, but if we incorporate physical aspects in detection, it will be much easier to know when we are experiencing anxiety. The exercise can be combined with deep breathing to yield maximum results. For you to carry out this exercise, you must be in your best form health-wise; no muscle spasms, no back pains, or recent injuries that might put unnecessary strain on the muscles. In case you have or suspect to have any of these problems, consult your doctor before starting the exercise. Here is the procedure.

## Mind-Body Relaxation to Decrease Stress and Anxiety

The purpose of this mind-body relaxation meditation is to get rid of fear and anxiety. This guided meditation session will take you deep inside your mind. You will be able to get rid of your fears and anxieties. You will get a chance to face them and defeat them.

This guided meditation is very helpful in relieving stress and anxiety. It helps you in sleeping better and provide complete physical, mental, and emotional relief. You can practice it anytime you like.

## Relaxing Self Massage

The objective of this meditation session is to physically release the tension from the body through self-massage and mentally release the tension through meditation. It is going to be a completely relaxing session. You can sit in any comfortable position you want. If you wish you can sit on a chair or even in the cross-legged posture.

## Focused breathing

Breathing is one of the body's involuntary actions, meaning you do not really need to command your body to breath, it just happens. However, you can turn your breathing into a form of meditation just by taking notice of every breath that you take.

In focused breathing meditation, you take long, slow, deep breaths; breaths so deep that you fill your abdomen with air as well. To practice this form of meditation, you disengage your mind from all thoughts, and focus all your attention on your breathing. This is especially helpful for when you start noticing that your thoughts are starting to go out of your control.

However, this technique might not be appropriate for those who have respiratory ailments, like asthma and some heart ailments.

# Deep Breathing

Throughout any day, there are bound to be things that cause your stress levels to rise slightly. There are also going to be thoughts that pop into your head and cause you to feel anxious. Our mind can be our own worst enemy, but the good news is we can take control. There are many ways that we can help ease our fears, and deep breathing is one of them!

These techniques are extremely easy to do and can be done anywhere, even at your desk or on the bus to work! If you find it hard to concentrate, you can also purchase a guided relaxation tape, or download a stress-relieving app, as these will guide you through breathing exercises until you get the hang of doing them yourself.

This is a method you can use for any type of stress or anxiety that is bothering you, and it's a great way to get rid of an issue that is upsetting you at any stage during the day.

Another essential breathing technique is ensuring that we are taking deep, full breaths. When we are even the slightest bit stressed, we start breathing shallowly. These shallow, short breaths do not give us enough oxygen and can even lead to full-blown panic attacks. To stop poor breathing, place your hand an inch or two above your stomach. Now, slowly breathe in through your nose until your stomach touches your hand. Go with our usual 5 counts inhales and hold for a few seconds before slowly exhaling out through your mouth.

When our breathing is shallow, we only fill up the top portion of our lungs with air. Placing your hand above your stomach ensures that you are breathing deeply enough where your entire lungs are filled!

Deep breathing is the foundation of many calming strategies. It can be done on its own or with other methods like meditation, tai chi yoga, etc. Deep breathing is easy because we need to breathe to remain alive, but strongly and efficiently for mental relaxation and stress reduction. Deep breathing focuses on breathing the stomach thoroughly and clean singly. It is easy to learn that you can do it anywhere, and it regulates your stress levels. Sit down with your back straight, inhale through the nose as the belly grows. Inhale as much clean air as possible into the lungs. It makes it possible to get more oxygen into the blood. Exhale the mouth as the belly drops to force as much air as possible out and close the abdominal tract. If you find it difficult to do this sitting, first try to lie down. You could put your hands on your chest and stomach to see if it's wrong.

## Roll Breathing

Roll breathing causes you to grow full utilization of your lungs and to concentrate on your relaxing. You can do it in any position. Yet, while you are learning, it is ideal to lie on your back with your knees bowed.

Practice move breathing day by day for a little while until you can do it anyplace. You can utilize it as a moment unwinding apparatus whenever you need one. Some individuals get tipsy the initial couple of times they attempt move relaxing. In the event that you start to inhale excessively quick or feel woozy, slow your relaxing. Get up gradually.

## Box Breathing

One of the simplest and best breath work procedures is box breathing. No, this doesn't include sitting in one of those goliath boxes you get when you move to another house, yet rather alludes to the example itself. Known to be highly effective in promoting peaceful sleep, Box breathing includes giving equivalent time to a nasal breathe in, first breath hold, nasal breathe out, and second breath hold. The rhythm and cadence of box breathing makes it relax. It urges us to concentrate on tallying the corner of each of the four "sides."

Since the inbreath and outbreath are equivalent, this method adjusts to your sensory system and help you simply settle and bring your body and mind back to the focus. Box breathing is ideal for relaxing, especially when one of its advantages include promoting sleep.

Box breathing is an extraordinary procedure for us to deal with everyday stressors as well. The system works in a wide range of stressful circumstances. Hence, it is recommended for everyone. Except children younger than 7-8 years of age, this procedure can be advantageous to anybody, particularly the individuals who need to think or reducing stress.

It is recommended to attempt to rehearse box breathing technique for 10 to 20 minutes on a daily basis, ideally simultaneously of day. On the off chance that that target appears to be unattainable, you may attempt it for a couple of minutes at whatever point you feel and stop it when you become uncomfortable. On the off chance that you practice this technique at list for 5 minutes daily you will see a huge effect in your everyday life.

## Autogenic Relaxation

This means something that comes from inside you. Using this relaxation technique requires the use of your visual imagery, as well as your bodily awareness. With this technique, you repeat affirmations and words that help you to reduce muscle tension, as well as make you relax. You can imagine a peaceful setting, and then focus your mind and relax your breathing. Meditation is one such technique that uses autogenic relaxation.

# Relaxing Poses

Numerous individuals state that some poses causes them rest better. These are relaxing poses that can help you to fall asleep as they help to cultivate a quiet mind if you practice it for a period of time.

By focusing on deep breathing, and by fully relaxing and releasing your body you will evoke a meditative state. These postures are very easy and can work for anyone and you can do this sequence right in your own bed.

### Neck Stretches

Your neck holds a lot of tension and stress and this is a great stretch to help to let go of some of that tension. Unlike neck rolls, which are not really very safe for your neck, this stretch is chiropractor approved!

### Fan Pose

Fan Pose is a relaxing forward bend that opens up your inner thighs and stretches the lower back. It helps quiet the organs and get any stagnant energy in the legs moving again. Use this pose to direct your focus inward after a long, busy, stressful day.

# Chapter 17 Understanding Guided Meditation

This is all about using your senses, such as the sense of smell, sounds, taste, textures, and sights as much as possible. You form mental images of places or situations you find relaxing in your mind, and a teacher may guide you.

Guided relaxation uses several techniques that may be used separately or in combination with each other. It may last as long as ten minutes and helps reduce impulses that trigger automatic behaviors. Guided relaxation uses abdominal breathing, visualization, progressive muscle relaxation, and mindfulness.

You will learn to breathe deeply as you imagine a serene environment using guided imagery. This sort of visualization activates the imaginative and sensory faculties of your brain. Relaxation meditation may also focus on relaxing the muscles so that you may feel the difference between tense and relaxed muscles when you are responding to stimuli. Mindfulness techniques are relaxing because the mind does not cling on one particular thought. It wanders and hops from thought, emotion, sensation, etc. Mindfulness meditation is about being present in the now.

Guided meditation is whereby you listen to the soothing voice of a meditation teacher in a meditation session to help you fall asleep. Meditation instructors give you a guide throughout the entire meditation session. An instructor may ask you to inhale deeply and exhale and relax your toes or legs. However, you should also note that this is not necessary you do with a guide by a specialist, but one can perform it alone.

Let's say you are using the help of the instructor. He/she may ask you to imagine a series of relaxing images. For example, some may invite you to imagine yourself at a beautiful sandy beach and envision yourself happily seated along the water's edge as the wavelets tickle your feet.

The clouds, the mountains, and the oceans are the most commonly chosen scenes of imaginations. However, you can choose to focus on anything you want as long as it is calming. There are no rules about what one should imagine and focus on. Some people enjoy visualizing their office- brushing everything off his/her office desk and going to sleep. One only needs to pick a place he/she feels safe, and using imaginations, invite all the senses to explore it. It is simply because the brain doesn't often know the difference between what is real and what is not. For example, when you watch a horrifying movie, your adrenaline may go up, or when you start to salivate when you imagine yourself eating something.

Apart from helping with insomnia, meditation can help one to let go of negative thought patterns and emotions, giving one insight on how to deal with grief or trauma and thus encouraging healing. Therefore, meditation has a wide array of other benefits when diligently practiced.

Meditation can also help to develop compassion towards other people. Yeah, a pretty nice and wholesome way to get to sleep! Goodnight!

Gratitude meditation is a kind of meditation, whereby instead of one focusing on the breath, it requires you to concentrate on the things you are grateful for. It is one of the easiest and effective ways to fall asleep, as one never lacks anything to be grateful for. The things you are grateful for could be something small as having a nice coffee, or something big like your partner or your job. All you need here is to challenge yourself to think of the things you are grateful for in life. I am sure such things are uncountable, now you can use them to gain some sleep if you are having trouble falling asleep at night.

Deprivation of sleep can have a devastating impact on one's health and general productivity. Therefore, it is essential to put a lot of considerations in the quality of our sleep. And since sleeping has been proven to contribute to the healing process of our body, it is high time we get some good night sleep. The good news is that you don't have to take medications for you to have a night of quality sleep. All you have to do is to put into practice one of the above meditation techniques for deep sleep and enjoy yourself a pretty good sleep.

People think that their life is complete. No. Fear pops up. Have a huge event coming. Most of the cases of anxiety are unexpected. Meditation is the cheapest way to deal with stress. It is more effective than drugs. Its effects are long-lasting. When compared to drugs, it is more affordable and more effective. This therapy is very successful in treating depression and anxiety. These effects are long-term. The method is also less costly. Just after a few months into the program, some of the patients were already well. So, meditation works better than antidepressants to reduce anxiety. The world is full of chaos. Chaos can exert some stress in you. However, with a peaceful mind, we can deal with the disorder. Therefore, this is where peace in the brain is required.

The subconscious mind is generally put off balance by two major issues, the first being fear and the latter being worry or the re-living of fear in conscious moments with conscious thoughts. In order, therefore, to cleanse the soul of all forms of negative reenactments, we have chosen to push forward with what is called guided meditation on positive consciousness.

Paths of consciousness are all intertwined. As you grow older, you will begin to realize that each of these paths underpins your actions by filtering the energy with which you choose to process your life's force. As such, the best way to rebuild your bridge to relaxation is to work on a positive filter through with you can view your own self and transform your consciousness while also healing and moving forward.

# Chapter 18 Importance of Guided Meditation

You are most likely here right now because you have heard amazing, life-changing aspects meditation can bring to your life. Whether you are looking to improve your mental health, performance, physical health, or better your relationship with yourself or others; meditation could be the perfect practice for you.

Unfortunately, there are many individuals who suffer from mental health issues. Whether you are dealing with anxiety, depression, or something along those lines; meditation can help place you in a better mindset when practiced on a regular basis.

1.  Decrease Depression

In a study done in Belgium, four-hundred students were placed in an in-class mindfulness program to see if it could reduce their stress, anxiety, and depression. It was found that six months later, the students who practiced were less likely to develop depression-like symptoms. It was found that mindfulness meditation could potentially be just as effective as an antidepressant drug!

In another study, women who were going through a high-risk pregnancy were asked to participate in a mindfulness yoga exercise for ten weeks. After the time passed, it was found there was a significant reduction in the symptoms often caused by depression. On top of the benefit of less depression, the mothers also showed signs of having a more intense bond with their child while it was still in the womb.

Reduce Anxiety and Depression

In general, meditation may be best known for the mental health benefits of reducing the symptoms associated with anxiety and depression. It was found that through meditation, individuals who practiced meditation such as Vipassana or "Open Monitoring Meditation," were able to reduce the grey-matter density in their brains. This grey-matter is related to stress and anxiety. When individuals practice meditation, it helps create an environment where they can live moment to moment rather than getting stuck in one situation.

While practicing meditation, the positive mindset may be able to help regulate anxiety and mood disorders that are associated with panic disorders. There was one article published in the American Journal of Psychiatry based around twenty-two different patients who had panic or anxiety disorders. After three months of relaxation and meditation, twenty of the twenty-two were able to reduce the effects of their panic and anxiety.

When you are able to relax, you would be amazed at how much better your brain will be able to function. By letting go of stress, you leave room for positive thoughts in your head and will be able to make better decisions for yourself. It's a win-win situation when you can improve your mood and your performance simply from meditation.

Better Decision Making

A study done at UCLA found that for individuals who practiced meditation for a long time, had a larger amount of gyrification in the brain. This is the "folding" along the cortex, which is directly related to processing information faster. Compared to individuals who do not practice meditation, it was found that meditators were able to form memories easier, make quicker decisions, and could process information at a higher rate overall.

Improve Focus and Attention

Another study performed at the University of California suggested that through meditation, subjects are able to increase their focus on tasks, especially ones that are boring and repetitive. It was found that even after only twenty minutes of meditation practice, individuals are able to increase their cognitive skills ten times better compared to those who do not practice mindfulness.

Along the same lines, it's believed that meditation may be able to help manage those who have ADHD, or attention deficit hyperactivity disorder. There was a study performed on fifty adults who had ADHD. The group was placed through mindfulness-based cognitive therapy to see how it would affect their ADHD. In the end, it was found that these individuals were able to act with awareness while reducing both their impulsivity and hyperactivity. Overall, they were able to improve their inattention.

Relieve Pain

It has been said that it's possible that meditation could potentially relieve pain better when compared to morphine. This may be possible due to the fact that pain is subjective. There was a study done on thirteen Zen masters compared to thirteen non-practitioners. These individuals were exposed to painful heat whilst having their brain activity watched. The Zen masters reported less pain, and the neurological output reported less pain as well. This goes to show that pain truly is a mental aspect.

Along the same lines, mindfulness training could also help patients who have been diagnosed with Fibromyalgia. In one study, there were eleven patients who went through eight weeks of training for mindfulness. At the end of the study, the overall health of these individuals improved and reported more good days than bad.

Avoid Multitasking Too Often

While multitasking can seem like a good skill to have at some points, it's also an excellent way to become overwhelmed and stressed out. Unfortunately, multitasking can be very dangerous to your productivity. When you ask your brain to switch gears between activities, this often can produce distractions from your work being done. A study was performed on students at the University of Arizona and the University of Washington. These people were placed through eight weeks of mindfulness meditation. During this time, the students had to perform a stressful test demonstrating multitasking before and after the training.

It was shown that those who practiced meditation were able to increase their memory and lower their stress while multitasking.

While mental improvements are fantastic benefits of meditation, physical benefits can help motivate individuals to begin meditation as well. Unfortunately, the standard of health is to turn to medication. If you are an individual who hates popping pills for every issue you have; meditation may be just what you need to help improve your health.

Reduce Risk of Stroke and Heart Disease

It has been found that heart disease is one of the top killers in the world compared to other illnesses. Through meditation, it's possible you could lower your risk of both heart disease and stroke. There was a study done in 2012 for a group of two hundred high-risk people. These individuals were asked to take a class on health, exercise, or take a class on meditation. Over the next five years, it was found that the individuals who chose meditation were able to reduce their risk of death, stroke, and heart attacks by almost half!

Reduce High Blood Pressure

In a clinical study based around meditation, it was also found that certain Zen meditations such as Zazen, has the ability to lower both stress and high blood pressures. It's believed that relaxation response techniques could lower blood pressure levels after three short months of practicing. Through meditation, individuals had less need for medication for their blood pressure! This could potentially be due to the fact that when we relax, it helps open your blood vessels through the formation of nitric oxide.

Live a Longer Life

When you get rid of stress in your life, you may be amazed at how much more energetic and healthier you feel. While the research hasn't been drawn to a conclusion yet, there are some studies that suggest meditation could have an effect on the telomere length in our cells. Telomeres are in charge of how our cells age. When there is less cognitive stress, it helps maintain telomere and other hormonal factors.

There are some people who are looking for a little bit more peace in your life. In the world we live in today, times can be very trying. There are constant deadlines, bills to pay, people to deal with; but now is the time to look at stressors in your life under a different life. Through meditation, you can become a more caring and empathetic individual to create a more peaceful life for yourself.

Improve Positive Relationships and Empathy

When we undergo stressful situations with obnoxious people, it can be very trying to remain empathetic. There is a Buddhist tradition of practicing loving-kindness meditation that may be able to help foster a sense of care toward all living things. Through meditation, you'll be able to boost the way you read facial expressions and gain the ability to empathize with others. When you have a loving attitude toward yourself and others, this helps develop a positive relationship with them and a sense of self-acceptance.

Decrease Feelings of Loneliness

There are many people who are not okay with being alone. Often times, we try to fill our time with activities so that we are never alone with ourselves. The truth is, it can be healthy to spend some time with yourself so that you can self-reflect on your life choices. In a study published in Brain, Behavior, and Immunity, it was proven that after thirty minutes of meditation per day, it was able to reduce individuals' sense of loneliness while reducing the risks of premature death, depression, and perhaps even Alzheimer's.

Along with feeling less lonely, meditation also opens up new doors to feeling a positive connection to yourself. When you love yourself, and you are happy with your own company, you may spend a lot less time on negative thoughts and feelings of self-doubt; both of which can lead to self-caused stress.

# Chapter 19 Types of Guided Meditation

O ur will power is continuously put through its paces, making it harder to control ourselves in an increasingly chaotic world. Luckily, we are not born with fixed willpower; like anything else, willpower can be cultivated and increased. After all, studies have shown that willpower breeds success. Training the brain with meditation helps fortify your strength (self-control) in dealing with the physical circumstances.

When you practice meditation once a day, every day makes it easier to control your focus, energy, and tenacity when trying new things that require dedication and effort. Guided meditations are designed to help boost our willpower to reduce the negativity in our lives, like stress and bad habits, and focus on love, positive energy, and behaviors. Meditation not only increases willpower, but it also reduces stress and increases our ability to learn.

Concentration Meditation

This practice takes about 15 minutes, and it focuses on concentrating your mind on one thing. On different days, the focus of your mind will be different. You can choose to do the exercise in five, ten, or fifteen minutes.

Sit still with your eyes closed for the proposed length of time and resist the urge to indulge your impulses. When you think you are still is when your body itches- try not to scratch. Do not move, allow the noise and the world around you to continue their flow but do not engage. When time lapses, finish the meditation and acknowledge the stillness you managed to achieve. With time, your mind will learn to remain still and focus on one thing at a time.

Breathing Meditation

This exercise focuses on the feeling of breathing. Close your eyes and inhale. Note "inhale" in your mind, and "exhale" when you breathe out. When your mind wanders off, allow it to label all the other sensations of the body, such as "back itchy," or "sound of dogs barking," etc. You can also ask yourself how it feels to breathe. Is your body relaxing? Can you feel the tension leaving your body? Then pull your mind back to breathing. Allow this rhythmic movement of the mind and thoughts from the breathing pattern, to the sensations.

Breathing meditation will help you become more aware of your environment and assist with impulse control in response to your surroundings. It also activates the brain's prefrontal cortex, quieting the stress and cravings.

Desensitization Using Meditation

This practice is used to control fear, anxiety, stress, anger, and other forms of psychological trauma. It is useful as a healing/ coping tool. This meditation exercise begins with relaxing your body, use relaxation meditation techniques to bring your body and mind to calm. Then, invite your mind into an environment that causes anxiety for you. The situation may cause you anger, distress, uneasy, etc. If the emotions become overwhelming, and it starts to feel less like meditation and more of trauma, return your mind to the feeling of relaxation.

This technique does not always work, especially for fragile people. If you are beginning to heal, it is best to start with other forms of meditation before you try out this practice. However, the exercise helps you handle stressful situations better with what is called "graduated exposure."

Compassion Meditation

Self-compassion is of tremendous importance when making a difficult life change in your life, such as healing from trauma. Self-love will help you overcome challenges that may seem impossible. It involves the repetition of specific phrases that shift the attention from judgment, dislike, and ridicule, to caring, love, and understanding.

In this meditation practice, the instructor will ask you to come up with thoughts and memories when you felt love for yourself, care, happiness, and contentment. You will also be asked to imagine sending thoughts of love, peace, and affection to the people dearest to you. Assume that with every breath you inhale love from them, and exhale love and affection back to them.

Yoga Nidra

This practice takes approximately 30-minutes. It promotes body relaxation while maintaining alertness of the mind. Yoga Nidra is also referred to as dynamic sleep, where the balance between wakefulness and sleep is nurtured.

This form of guided meditation will take you through the active thinking stage, then the relaxing, thoughtless, second stage, the instructor takes you deeper into a third, slowed state of thought. In this state, thinking has been considerably slowed, and it is possible to learn copious amounts of information at this stage (super-learning). Finally, the body and mind enter the last phase, known as the delta stage, where restorative functions happen. Your organs regenerate and heal, and the body releases all the pent-up stress. Do not try to skip the steps as every phase has its purpose, and the therapeutic process will not be reached if parts of the exercise are omitted.

You can practice these techniques one at a time, and do not feel pressured to master them all. If one does not work for you, it is okay, move on to the other. Meditation is not a quick-fix solution; therefore, dedicated practice is necessary for the desired outcome.

The next time you feel downcast or undisciplined, retreat to your meditation and remember that willpower is a muscle, and you have it within yourself. Resisting the power of your thoughts is difficult, but once mastered, you can as quickly learn to overcome other habits and temptations. The more control you gain over your internal turmoil, the better placed you will be to deal with your immediate surroundings. Constant practice will yield gradual improvement as meditation is the most straightforward and effective way to improve willpower.

# Chapter 20 What is Meditation?

**M**editation is a skill that is acquired through dedicated training of the mind and practice. Meditation is compared to fitness and exercise in relation to body training and overall fitness. The training is inclusive of claims to train the attention or to achieve a calmness or a compassionate mood. The dictionary defines meditation as the deep thinking of something or focusing one's mind for some time on one specific thing without losing focus. Meditation is also defined as the artistic nature of giving attention to one thing, or the engaging in mental exercise to reach a heightened level of spiritual awareness and understanding.

According to psychology, meditation is highly characteristic of its role in attention with an attempt of getting beyond the reflective discursive thinking beyond the logic mind achieving a deeper, more devout and more relaxed state. Another psychologist sees meditation as having a set of self-regulation practices which help to focus on the training attention and awareness to have the mental process under greater voluntary control. It brings forth general mental well-being like calmness, clarity, and concentration. On the other hand, meditation is also viewed as a practice that self regulates the body and mind, hence affecting mental events. Other psychologists define meditation as a stylized mental technique that is practiced in repetition with the main aim of attaining a subjective experience which in mind describing it will be having a very restful, silent, blissful and highly heightened alertness state of mind.

Meditation is, hence, believed to be the acquisition of peace and quietness against everyday stressing life and the opening of doors to the deepest and divine parts of our lives. Meditation helps to train in awareness, thus getting a healthy sense of perspective by learning how to observe your thoughts and feelings without being judgmental on them but instead with time, get to understand them.

Having mentioned that meditation is a skill that means meditation has to be learned, it is reasonable to look at meditation like muscle exercise, which one has not done before. Therefore, for the muscle exercise to work and be comfortable with the body system, one will need to do a lot of practice. To get to a level of comfort, understanding, and doing the right thing, one must have a teacher or a trainer who will guide and help one to do the exercise in knowledge. The ability to learn from a knowledgeable person is key in getting it right, and within a specific time as concerns. There are several people who over the years have learned the art and the skill of meditation and are willing to pass the knowledge to those people who are interested. As such, it is necessary to take advantage of such people and learn more about meditation.

Meditation is a practice that is not always as easy as it may seem. Those who have done it for long will say how when meditating there are times when they will lose focus, and the mind will wander, and consequently cause them to forget to follow the breath.

They say the way the mind loses focus and begins to wander is just part of the memorable experience they are creating. The important part of meditation is consistency and willingness. Meditation, in other words, is termed as one of those things where the journey is what is more important than the destination. Meditation puts more value on the journey, the practice, the commitment, and the dedication employed to achieve a peaceful state of mind.

During meditation, it might take time before your mind gets comfortable to the whole exercise. Chances that setbacks will be present are very high, but the good news is that those setbacks are part of the meditation process. It needs a lot of practice, and just by the fact that you are creating time for the training and learning, is very important in the journey of meditation. One primary invariant ingredient in meditation is the crucial need of the meditator to try and sustain their attention, be it through the concentration or the mindfulness of the whole process. With the retention of concentration achieving the skillful nature, o meditation can be attained.

More often than not, we are controlled and dominated by our thoughts or feelings. Under normal circumstances, we tend to believe we are precisely what those thoughts and feelings say we are. For example, when we have ideas that this is a sad situation, we somehow reflect the sadness on our faces and in the long run we feel anxious and stressed. The same applies to the feeling of joy and happiness. We focus on something as being good then the feeling of satisfaction is reflected on our faces as laughter or a smile. Meditation picks us up by letting us be, giving us a positive experience without any interference of our state of being. Meditation is then concluded to be the natural state of nature, and that is why more than often it is thought that we can read an individual's thoughts by looking at their faces which is a clear reflection of what is their minds or what they are experiencing at that exact moment.

Meditation is made up of different techniques which we shall expand on each later in the teachings. The meditative methods, techniques, or devices are then the means through which we create an intimate personal ambiance which is the facilitation force that disconnects the body and the mind and allows one to be. Of great importance is to set aside time from practicing the meditation techniques and find which method would work well in an everyday life practice context without affecting your work schedule, leisure and your interaction with people at different levels.

# Chapter 21 How Does Meditation Work?

To a bystander, a person in the meditative state may look like an idle person sitting in a cross-legged posture with eyes closed. There is no complexity. One doesn't even need to be in this position to meditate. You can meditate while sitting on a chair, while walking or even while lying on the ground.

The body may look inactive while in the meditative state, but the mind is very active. You can unfold some of the most complex mysteries of mind in the meditative state.

On the physical level, meditation strongly influences the activity of the brain. It helps in clearing the mind and also brings objective focus.

Every important thought that comes to your brain leads to a certain type of chemical reaction. The positive thoughts have a calming effect. Happy thoughts lead to the secretion of chemicals that suppress anger and anxiety. When you have a lot of negative, stressful, and fearful thoughts, the production of stress hormones increases in your body. This will not only cause emotional trouble but will also weaken your immune system.

A person trying to lose weight will find it really difficult to burn fat while in a stressful emotional state. The reason being the increased production of the stress hormone. This hormone keeps the body in a constant fat storage mode.

Meditation is a wonderful way to relax your mind as well as the nervous system. It increases activity in the specific regions in the brain associated with decreasing anxiety and depression. Your body also develops a better tolerance for pain. Memory, self-awareness, and the ability of goal setting also improves with the help of meditation.

Our brain in its active state produces beta waves that are fast and choppy. The thoughts in this state can be jumbled up. There are too many thoughts at the same time with very little control over them. However, while in the meditative state, the brain starts producing slow alpha waves. These waves cause relaxation. The stress level starts to go down. The rambling of thought also goes down. You will start feeling greater control over your mind in this state. These waves are associated with feelings of love, positivity, and happiness. The level of alpha waves keeps increasing as one starts to practice meditation for longer.

Meditation can bring physical change in the shape and size of your brain. Studies conducted on long-time practitioners have demonstrated that meditation leads to an increase in the gray matter in certain areas of the brain.

Two important areas are:

Insular Cortex: This area is associated with an awareness of breathing and heartbeat. The longer you meditate the better will be your breathing and heart. This would mean that your body would be in a better position to carry oxygen and carbon dioxide. You would have better immunity against diseases.

Premotor Cortex: This area regulates attention, emotions, and thoughts. Your learning power and memory would also improve if the gray matter in this area gets denser. You would have better control over your emotions and thoughts.

The Amygdala in your brain deals with stress, fear, and anxiety. Studies have clearly demonstrated that meditation can help in decreasing the gray matter in this area. It can greatly help in reducing stress, fear, high blood pressure, and immunity-related disorders.

With practice, your brain can also start producing gamma waves. These waves can help in bringing deep concentration and an unwavering focus.

Apart from the physiological stuff, meditation also helps you in developing better ability to deal with your thoughts and emotions.

Our mind remains mostly confused between wants and needs. The problems begin when it starts treating both interchangeably. Our expectations from people, jobs, relationships, personal wealth, and other such things are always high and when they aren't met, we start having negative thoughts.

Meditation helps you in viewing your thoughts objectively. You will be able to understand the true value of things and also judge the futility of wants. This can make life much simpler. Most of the things that deem essential are not even required in life, but we waste our lives pursuing them. We simply follow them endlessly because we see others around us doing the same. We acquire the herd mentality and get involved in the mind-numbing rat race. Meditation helps you in objectively analyzing our thoughts, needs, and wants to choose the best course of action.

You'd find yourself much more calm, relaxed, and peaceful after meditation sessions. Decision making would become easier and your mind wouldn't be constantly battling decision fatigue. Your perspective about things would improve along with your ability to look at things objectively.

# Chapter 22 Why Practice Meditation?

### 1. It Turns You into A Better Decision-maker

One of the main problems of making a habit out of DMN is that you think that you only have limited choices to make decisions. Rather than considering if something can be good (or bad), you just act on whatever things might come by default. The more you subject yourself to this habit of yours, the more ingrained in your mind it becomes, until such time comes when you do it without even thinking about your best interests.

### 2. It Provides You with A Place Where You Can Be Free from Conditioning

How many times have you watched the evening news and there always seem to be at least one news item that grinds your gears? It is quite unfortunate that most people go through life reactively. Mindfulness provides you with awareness and a space in your head that allows you to choose how to respond, rather than having a knee-jerk reaction to things. You get a chance to choose your reaction rather than letting your mind default to the kinds of reactions that society has ingrained into you.

### 3.  It Allows You to Increase Your Emotional Intelligence

Medical studies have shown that people who practice mindfulness have better control over their emotions compared to other people. In fact, the US Military conducted their own research on mindfulness and how it could help sufferers of PTSD. Their research yielded that mindfulness can actually help minimize stress, and even ease the effects of chronic stress.

Mindfulness training not only makes you more mature emotionally, you also gain more empathy, compassion, and you also become more altruistic. After even just eight weeks, you will feel more empathy with others, and you are also more able to take compassionate action.

### 4.  It Helps Your Body Thrive

Mindfulness can also increase the amount of physical activity that your body can endure. Most people distract themselves from their workouts, but it is actually better when you practice mindfulness while you are working out. For instance, if you are in a hurry to finish your weight training workout, you will only focus on doing the requisite number of repetitions, and not pay attention to your form. And when you are not careful about your lifting form, you are more prone to getting seriously injured. With mindfulness, not only are you careful about your weightlifting form, you will also feel more accomplished with every set that you complete.

### 5. It Helps You Become More Creative

Creativity arises from the DMN. In these periods of unfocused rest, you have the chance to have a different perspective, you can make new associations between ideas and strike upon them. For instance, if you are a sculptor, you do not immediately know what to carve out of a huge chunk of stone. You need to sit in front of that huge slab of stone and visualize what you can make out of it. The only way to see the final sculpture clearly is to eliminate all distractions around you.

With mindfulness, you can say goodbye to all of your distractions, and say hello to an almost infinite source of inspiration.

### 6. It Helps Strengthen Existing Neural Connections and Build New Ones

Mindfulness can actually reshape the human brain, it meant in terms of creating new neural connections. Practicing mindfulness as often as you can cause your brain to build new neural pathways, and ultimately new neural networks, thus making it function more efficiently. This helps your brain by improving concentration and awareness.

### 7. What Do You Need to Do to be More Mindful?

Practice mindfulness ad nauseam. There is no shortcut or magic pill that will help you become instantly more mindful. Instant results are not promised, although you will receive tips that will make the process much easier, but it will still take you some time before you can become fully mindful. Being mindful means that you are training your mind to be aware of what it is thinking, rather than becoming what it is actually thinking.

This is where meditation can help you. There are many ways to meditate, the traditional method of sitting in a quiet place and observing your thoughts without being judgmental is the easiest way and is also the best place to start for beginners. It might sound simple, but the problem is that most people are not living in the present, they are constantly worrying about things that are yet to happen or happened already. Your thoughts are constantly running around uncontrolled in your brain. With mindfulness, you can put a bit of space around your thoughts so you can easily let go of comparisons, judgments, and control of them.

# Chapter 23 Best Meditation Techniques

Meditation in itself is a simple and great way to bring better clarity in mind and attain greater peace. All meditation techniques take you towards these goals. Various meditation techniques followed these days have been designed to achieve this objective. The only difference is in the way they help you in doing them.

It would be unfair to say that one technique is better than the other as the objective of all the techniques is the same. They all have the potential to deliver the results. You must choose a technique that suits you the most. The technique in which you are most comfortable would be the best. One that works for others might not work for you. Therefore, it is important that you choose a technique in which you are most comfortable and find your rhythm.

Some of the most popular meditation techniques are:

Breathing and Relaxation Meditation

This is the easiest form of meditation best for beginners. In this meditation, you will have to focus on your breathing and that would help you in relaxing the body. This meditation helps greatly in releasing tension from various parts of the body and also helps in relieving stress and anxiety. You can do it at your home without any guide or supervision. This meditation can also be done whenever you are feeling anxious, stressed, or angry.

1. Mindfulness

It is one of the most popular forms of meditation being practiced in the west these days. It doesn't bound you with particular settings or restrictions of time and place. You can do it anywhere anytime. The most important aspect of this meditation is to be mindful of all the thoughts entering your mind. You don't need to restrain your thoughts or train your mind to think in a particular way. You simply need to observe the kind of thoughts you are having. This meditation helps you in thinking objectively. You also get a chance to look at your thoughts in a non-judgmental way and understand their root cause. It is one of the best ways to suppress anger and stress.

2.   Loving-Kindness Meditation

It is a form of Buddhist meditation and is also known as Metta meditation. It is a wonderful meditation for people who always feel agitated and have sudden anger outbursts. If negative thoughts and depression and making your life difficult then this meditation can help you a lot. In this meditation, you direct love, kindness, and gratitude toward yourself and the people around you. This meditation helps you in addressing your anger and you develop the ability to manage your sudden anger outbursts more effectively.

3.   Body Scan Meditation

This is a great way to meditate if you want to relax your body completely. It gives you a chance to feel each and every part of your body and observe the sensations closely. It will relax you completely and instill a feeling of wellness. You can do this meditation in standing, sitting, or lying positions. It is easy to do and can be followed for around half hours daily for best results.

4.   Mantra Meditation

It is a great way to shun all thoughts and focus your mind on a particular sound. Mantra meditation is a very popular practice and is very effective in bringing calmness. You will be able to shun thoughts and focus your mind on one sound, place, or object. Every mantra has unique vibrations that focus your mind on one thing. This meditation is very effective if you want to meditate for longer periods and maintaining an unwavering focus is very easy through mantra meditation.

## 5. Chakra Meditation

This meditation practice originated in India. It works on the principle that our body is divided into various energy circles with each circle having its unique role. Indian mythology says that when these energy chakras are out of sync, there are physical as well as mental problems. Through this meditation, all these energy chakras are activated, and a balance is sought. Every chakra has its own color and can be activated through specific sound vibrations. You can follow guided meditations for chakra awakening for faster results.

## 6. Third Eye Meditation

The third eye is the sixth chakra in our body also known as 'Ajna' chakra. This chakra dominates our intellect and also controls our sixth sense as well as our psychic abilities. Third Eye meditation helps in awakening this chakra and honing the psychic abilities. If getting greater spiritual consciousness is your goal, then also this is a great form of meditation for you.

## 7. Gazing Meditation

This meditation is used for bringing greater focus on things. This is an externally focused meditation and requires you to focus on physical objects like a candle, painting, dots, and other such things. You will have to gaze at the objects and hold their mental images in your eyes. This practice can help in relaxing the mind completely. The mind gets absorbed in the process to such an extent that all other thoughts causing agitation or anger pass away. You can do this meditation anytime.

8. Zazen or Zen

It is a Buddhist meditation practice. It helps in relaxing your body, mind, and soul. It isn't a religious practice but a spiritual one. You can follow it irrespective of your religion. It is done while sitting in a cross-legged posture with the eyes closed.

The first part of this meditation is to sit straight in a fixed position. You keep your body straight yet relaxed. This helps in taking away all the stress.

The second part of the meditation is controlled breathing. You will have to keep your breathing focused. This relaxes your mind completely. It drives away all the racing thoughts.

The third part is to bring your thoughts in line with your body. As you meditate, you start getting better control over your thoughts and emotions.

9. Guided Meditation

Guided meditations are the best if you want to meditate regularly but don't have the time to go to a guru or a teacher. With the help of the instructions and imagery given through guided meditation, you will be able to meditate in a much better way. It is a very easy and convenient way to meditate in the comfort of your home or office. You can use guided meditation for all types of meditations mentioned above.

# Chapter 24 Guided Mindful Meditation for Anxiety

## Reducing Anxiety Around Wins and Regrets

Time: 5 to 15 minutes

In this exercise, you'll focus specifically on what we call wins and regrets. We all have things that we are working on, positive habits we want to strengthen and negative ones we wish to eliminate. Our awareness of, efforts towards, and results with these things can all be anxiety-provoking, especially if we are not succeeding. This exercise is designed to assist you in this area and reduce your anxiety.

**Steps**

1. Find a comfortable place where you won't be disturbed but won't fall asleep. Sit comfortably but remain alert. Focus on your breathing, becoming mindful and letting your mind settle. Remain in that state for a minute or two.

2. Think about the goals you have set for yourself, and those you are working on; both things that you want to achieve, as well as things to eliminate. Take 1 to 2 minutes to do this.

3. Now, review your day with these two areas in mind, noting where you won and where you have regrets.

161

4.  Think about the successes, while remaining mindful and relaxed, and let yourself enjoy the positive, good feelings that go with that. Enjoy that for 1 to 2 minutes.

5.  Next, recall the regrets that came out of the day, and notice what those feel like. See if you can inquire into what happened, and where things went wrong or fell short. Notice how you think about it, breathing into and through the unpleasant emotions or sensations. Note if any amends or reparations might be in order, or if you need to alter your strategy and be more mindful around certain things. Do mindfulness meditation on all of this for 2 to 3 minutes.

6.  Remember that tomorrow is another day, and you will have a chance to improve. Try and let all anxiety and stress go.

7.  Sit for a few minutes, in regular mindfulness meditation, letting go of all those things that you were working on. Return to your breath, just focusing on the respiration, and allow yourself to calm and settle as you wind down for the evening.

## Reduce Negative Thinking to Reduce Anxiety

Time: 10 to 15 minutes

The way we think, positively or negatively, has a massive impact on our emotions, and by changing our negative thinking, we can allay our anxieties.

We are mentally talking to ourselves, whether we are conscious of it or not, almost all of the time. Unfortunately, we are often saying some very negative and scary things, with the result being an enormous amount of anxiety. It's time to change that.

**Steps**

1. Find a quiet, comfortable place to sit, with back straight and relaxed. Find your breath at the nostrils and follow it for a couple of minutes as you settle.

2. Think of something that causes you a lot of anxiety. Go over the story around this thing, and as you do, begin to notice the thoughts that go along with it.

3. Pay particular attention to the negative thoughts, and how you feel when you have these thoughts. Take several minutes to do this.

4. Choose one or two of the main negative thoughts and examine them. Look and see if these cynical, anxiety-provoking thoughts are really accurate and supported by data. Do this for 1 to 2 minutes.

5. Notice what you found; most of our negative and anxiety-provoking thoughts have no immediate basis in reality. There is no one holding a gun to your head or about to run you over, and you are not dying this very moment. This is an important discovery to make. Take 1 to 2 minutes to examine this.

6. Feel the feelings that are behind all of these serious, scary thoughts. There are things that we are afraid of and that we have not dealt with emotionally. Now is the time to do that. Take 3 to 5 minutes and breathe into the fear that is behind the scary thoughts. Feel a bit of the emotion, find the physical sensation that goes with it, and direct the breath into and through it.

7. Some underlying fears should begin to subside, though grave underlying concerns may need to be worked with in this way many times.

8. After some of the underlying fear has been lessened, go back, review the negative thoughts, and change them to something that is at least neutral, if not positive. Take a couple minutes to do this.

9. 9Return to the simple mindfulness meditation for at least a couple of minutes while you settle, make a few notes, and return to your day.

10. 10You can benefit from doing this exercise more than once for recurring issues or whenever negative self-talk arises. Do this as often as you need or like.

## Plan Ahead to Reduce Anxiety

Time: 5 to 20 minutes

If you think about it, you may realize that a lot of your anxiety is tied up in thoughts about the future; things you dread either happening or not happening, and it may also be related to painful events from the past. Since so much worry is directed at the future and negative things happening, one beneficial way to deal with anxiety is to plan for the future you want. You can do this meditation as a future planning exercise or when you're having anxious thoughts.

## Steps

1. Find a comfortable place where you won't be disturbed, settle in, and begin to follow your breath. Bring something to write with.

2. Think about and review the sorts of fears and worries that you have about your future. Notice if it's about your health, wealth, relationships, work, or something else.

3. Try to identify the main one or two things causing you the most worry about your future.

4. Notice the main worry thoughts and feel the fear regarding what you dread for the future. Allow yourself to breathe into and through the fearful emotion and any related sensations. Stay with this for a while and see if it begins to relax and shift.

5. From this more settled and clearer place, think about how you would like your future to be. Think about what things you want to have happen instead of what you fear.

6. Lay out a plan as to how you can create the outcome that you want, instead of reacting to and avoiding the result that you fear. Later you may want to write this down.

7. What is an action step you can take right now towards realizing the future that you want? Visualize taking that step.

8. Recognize that you are either actively envisioning and creating the future that you want or fearing and worrying about that which you don't want. The choice is yours.

9. Sit for a moment, return to the easy breath, settle, come out of the meditation, and return to your daily life.

10. Build these review and action steps into your daily life, at least for a while.

# Chapter 25 Guided Meditation for Sleep

## Mindful Bedtime Meditation

Time: 5 minutes

Anxious people often have difficulty going to bed early. This difficulty can be due to the internal energy buzz, or a worrying mind that is turning and spinning, but regardless, they have considerable difficulty choosing a reasonable bedtime and adhering to it. Going to bed earlier and getting more and better sleep can significantly reduce anxiety, as well as improve overall health, focus, and our ability to follow through and be productive.

### Steps

1. Find a comfortable place to relax and settle, while you lightly enter into mindfulness meditation.

2. Think about what the ideal bedtime for you might be, taking into consideration your age, health, nutrition, workload, and any other relevant factors. The first time you do this, you may need to be more formal and extensive as you figure this out. Be sure to include such things as what the ideal time for you is to wake and get up the next day, especially considering your schedule.

Take 1 to 3 minutes to do this. In the future, you can likely do this in 30 seconds to 1 minute.

3.  Now, think about what usually gets in the way of your adhering to this bedtime—maybe such things as binge-watching a series on Netflix, getting involved in activities on the Internet, exercising too late, eating too late and feeling uncomfortable, or a myriad of other things. Think about what your usual nemesis is. Take 2 to 3 minutes to do this. In the future, it may require less than 1 minute.

4.  Return to the mindfulness meditation, watching and following the breath, as you note any significant reactions to what you found. Think about actually planning to go to bed on time and sticking to it. Imagine and feel that for a minute or two.

5.  Plan out the rest of your evening to follow the script that you laid out, and take 1 to 2 minutes to do that, as you continue with your mindfulness meditation, then finish your evening.

6.  Hopefully, you will follow the script, and get yourself to bed earlier, reducing your stress and increasing your ease and focus.

7.  If something else happens, make a note of it and factor it into the next time that you do this exercise. You may want to keep records of this, such as writing sleep times in your calendar or using an app to keep track.

# Chill Out: A Sleepy Meditation

Time: 5 to 20 minutes

This is one of my favorite meditations for late evening or if I need a short nap during the day.

In our usual meditation, we sit reasonably upright, eyes often open, and focus on remaining quite alert. This meditation exercise is best done in or near bed, often slouching, and with eyes usually closed. You want to calm down and settle your mind, avoid revving back up, and encourage yourself to move into sleep. If it's during the day, you could choose a comfortable chair, slump down in it, and let your eyes close.

## Steps

1. Find a quiet and comfortable place where you can really relax and let go. Make sure you have no place to be for at least 20 to 30 minutes. If it is daytime, you may want to set an alarm.

2. Sit very comfortably, likely slouched, and let your eyes close. Focus on your breath and let yourself really settle and relax. Take 2 to 5 minutes to do this.

3. Don't try to keep your eyes open, and don't try to sit up straight. Get as comfortable as you can and let yourself relax and let go as much as you can.

4. If thoughts or other things try to arise, just barely notice them and let them go, and keep returning to moving towards dozing and/or sleeping. Take as long as you need.

5. At some point, you will likely begin to doze off. This is a good thing and should not be avoided or resisted. Just keep letting yourself go, taking as long as you need.

6. If it's daytime, when you awaken or your alarm goes off, take a moment to slowly rouse yourself, breathe mindfully for about a minute, and then return to your day.

7. If it's nighttime, you can adjust your pillow and slide down into your comfortable bed, letting yourself continue off to sleep.

## Insomnia: Tips and a Restful Meditation

Time: 10 minutes to an hour or more

Insomnia is a condition that most people experience at some time in their life. Occasional difficulty going to sleep, such as before a big event or medical procedure, is not uncommon and not much cause for concern. It's the regular, ongoing difficulty falling asleep that is problematic and concerning. It can result in depression or anxiety, weight gain, cognitive clouding, immune system suppression, and decreased motivation. Some people have insomnia related to sleep apnea, a condition that can have serious medical implications. Check with your doctor to rule out any medical basis for your insomnia.

I strongly suggest avoiding caffeine or other stimulants, especially after 2 p.m., as this can affect your ability to sleep later.

A regular bedtime that's not too late is best. Also recommended are measures like slowing down in the evening, avoiding stimulation, putting away the electronics, not exercising vigorously or overeating in the evening, and keeping the room dark and not too warm. Failing to follow these measures can lead to a heightened arousal state of the nervous system and make sleep very difficult. If you are prone to insomnia, I suggest doing this meditation before you try to go to sleep.

## Steps

1. If you have tried the approaches listed in the introduction and still can't sleep, your insomnia is likely driven by anxiety. You can verify this by noticing the incessant worrying thoughts. Take a minute or two to become aware of this.

2. Lie on your side and get comfortable. I prefer lying on my right side with the left nostril up, as breathing through the left nostril is less stimulating. While lying on your side, do the basic mindfulness meditation, with an even in and out and a slightly longer exhalation. Do this for 5 to 10 minutes.

3. Find what body area stands out the most and imagine directing your respiration into and through it. Continue for as long as you need to and come back into it as needed. Ideally, your mind will slow down, things will shift, and you will ease off to sleep.

4. If you are unable to actually fall asleep, at least you will be getting rest, though not deep sleep. Continue with this as long as you need to.

5. Some sleep specialists recommend getting up to read or watch TV, but something light and not action-packed, instead of lying

in bed and worrying about not being able to sleep. Keep the lights low. Writing your thoughts can also be helpful—whether it's a to-do list or a problem to solve—writing it down can transfer ownership from your head to the paper, clearing your mind. Often you can then go back to bed and sleep.

6. If the insomnia is frequent and severe, I strongly suggest that you consult with your medical doctor.

## Get Back to Sleep

Time: 2 to 15 minutes

Waking up in the night is another unpleasant sleep issue. If your waking up is due to needing to use the bathroom, and you quickly fall back asleep, then it's really no problem. It's when you wake up and have a hard time falling back asleep that it's a real issue. Usually, when this happens, we've awakened with a start, and there is a strong emotion, upsetting thoughts, or a combination of the two. This situation is what we will focus on for this meditation.

### Steps

1. When you wake up unexpectedly the middle of the night or early morning, turn on your side and begin the basic mindfulness meditation. Focus your attention on the breath and do this for 2 to 3 minutes. This simple approach may result in you going back to sleep.

2.  If the wakeful state persists, become aware of the primary emotion and sensation associated with it. Focus your attention on that as you breathe into and through it. You can do this for as long as you need to, though it will often shift within 5 to 10 minutes, and you will ease back into sleep. Repeat this as necessary.

3.  If it still persists, add some of the cognitive approach and question whether your fearful thoughts are accurate. Continue directing the breath into and through the experience.

4.  If all else fails, you may wish to get up for a while to stretch lightly, walk around a bit, journal, read a book, or even watch something light on TV until you can settle enough to go back to sleep.

# Chapter 26 Guided Meditation for Good and Happy Wake Up

## Guide Meditation for Super Motivation

At times we need to find the cause of motivation for us to keep doing some things. Take, for instance, an individual who works for long hours. They have to find things that motivate them to get up each morning.

If you are asked what your reason for living is, what would you have to say? What is that one thing that makes you want to try harder without giving up? There is some power that results from motivation. It allows us to want to do better in the activities that we undertake.

It makes us have meaning in what we go. One of the best ways to stay motivated is to have goals that you want to accomplish. In this case, the goal is to lose weight.

As an individual, you have to ensure that you are focused on that goal for it to be effective. If you wish to cut off some extra weight, get something that inspires you. For instance, you can be inspired to weigh a certain amount. In that process, you can be evaluating how much you way daily and how far away you are from getting to your goal.

Hypnosis is a great way to help those in need of weight loss. There are various reasons a person may be overweight. Some may range from behavioral issues or underlying conditions that will require to be addressed to lose weight successfully. In this chapter, we will take you through a guide for a weight loss program through hypnosis as well as how to lose weight through meditation. After losing weight, a person needs to maintain it. We shall further discuss how hypnosis can help one maintain their new weight and avoid becoming overweight again.

A person needs a lot of help and motivation to succeed. With the help of hypnotherapy, one can easily stay the course and watch the pounds melt away. Following the guide above and with a credible hypnotherapist or mastering self-hypnosis will help you in achieving your goals.

For any get-healthy plan to work, it begins with shaping an association with nourishment. When they must be aware of how they eat, why they eat, and the health benefit of what they eat. The motivation behind trance for weight reduction is to empower an individual to be aware of their eating examples and nourishments to have a fruitful adventure in weight reduction.

At times fear motivates us into doing certain things. For instance, you might fear to get obese or acquiring some lifestyle diseases. Such fear ensures that you stay focused on losing weight. You ensure that you strictly follow your diet plan or that you exercise regularly. Instead of fear motivating you negatively, it motivates you in a positive way. Another case example is the fear we have before taking tests or exams.

The fear of potentially failing can make you burn the midnight oil to ensure that you do not fail in the tasks that you have engaged in.

You find yourself trying to do your best in the various tasks that you are undertaking. Eventually, you may pass in your test, with fear as the motivating factor of success. All you need to do is ensure that you convert that energy into something useful and helpful in your life. At times the fear of failure in life makes us work hard towards making a better living. This makes you wake up very early each day, determined to make that day better than the previous day. It ensures that you give your best in life for you to live well.

We, at times, find our motivation from other people. At times you find that you may not be able to inspire yourself enough, but you feel inspired by other people. When you are unable to walk alone, you can always seek help from individuals that are more inspired than you are.

They ensure that you are always working hard towards achieving your goals and that you do not deviate from other things.

This type of motivation is positive and useful in your life. It ensures that you give your best in the activities that you undertake. Walking alone can, at times, be challenging.

Anytime you feel like giving up, and there is no one to remind you why you started the journey in the first place. You are prone to making wrong decisions that you will end up regretting.

One needs to have individuals that encourage them in the journey they take. As you start your weight loss journey through meditation, you can look for an individual with the same goal. You get to keep encouraging each other to accomplish certain things, and it becomes easier to achieve the set goals.

## Guide Meditation for Boost Positivity

You need to shed off any unimportant attachment.

Unimportant attachments are things that no longer have any effect on your life.

These are things that will only let you down, thus derailing your life goals of achieving a mind-set full of happiness. Your future success depends heavily on this, and for you to get at that position, you will need to detach yourself from anything that might let you down. You must note that anything might also mean any person.

We have people in our lives that always try very hard to put us down. These types of people are afraid of your success in life.

They will try their best to pull you down, no matter how hard you try to embrace only positivity in your life. It is time to get yourself going and void them like the plague. Remember, you must live and not only live but choose a pleasant experience.

It will only be possible if you manage to refuse anything or anyone that is holding you back. Since I have said this, it is now my wish that you may practice this affirmation and use it as your routine daily. Practice makes perfect, and you will only realize that when you train.

You are enough just as you are. You must release that demonic notion of having comparisons between you and others. For you to stay specific, you must have some success standards. After developing all these, set your own goals and ambitions. Your vision should relate to your mission in life. After all these, you can now judge yourself using the basis of your success.

Those rules and regulations you created in your success standards should enable you to judge yourself accordingly. Just know you are just enough the way you were born. You are a complete soul, and no part of you is lacking. So never try to make a comparison with others.

You should note that affirmation helps in the realization of worthiness. Within a short period, you will be able to control your body image. Also, it will be of a great deal as it helps you in achieving some of the personal goals in life and having a sound body is one of them.

You must be in a position to fulfill your purpose. The world should know your existence, and you must be ready to show your achievement. Showing your accomplished goals will need some positive deeds that lead to a successful life. On most occasions, people who trend are our trendsetters.

They trend because of having done something positive or negative. They are then known all over the world. However, in this motivational affirmation, you need to focus on positive things.

You need to be a trendsetter in showing the whole world what you are capable of offering. If you have been employed somewhere to sweep, you must clean until the country president cuts short his journey to congratulate you. Achieving your best is always one decisive way to be successful and lead a happy life free from stress and distress. Remember, this affirmation reminds you that no one has that power to stop you from doing or rather fulfilling your purpose in life. Sharing this thought every morning when you wake up will eventually get you somewhere. You must now stay focus and have this habit of telling yourself that no one can prevent you from achieving.

You must be results-oriented. In your daily life, you need to stay focus in life. Your primary focus should be on your results. It is through this that you will be able to realize your productivity.

To achieve this, you must be able to create some space for success. Get more success in your life. Avoid any derailing excuses that will only demean your reputation, thus lowering your success rate. Offer yourself these phrases every morning, and you will be in great joy for the rest of the day. You need not hold on excuses for failing to achieve something. Be yourself and have the ability to struggle until you reach that success in life. It is through this that your mind will have settled, giving you peace of mind. Peace of mind will enable you to lead a stress-free experience. It will reflect in your body image.

Be control of your won happiness. Happiness is an aspect of life that will initiate your feelings and moods towards a positive experience.

It is like a gear geared towards your prosperous life. Staying positive here will be of great importance, and for you to realize this, you must take control of your happiness. Responsibility is a virtue and being responsible will make you bold enough to face all kinds of situations. Your joy is your key to success, and no one should tamper with it. Make happiness your priority and be responsible for it.

You must let no one make you angry. Angriness will only induce you with emotional feelings that will eventually affect your life more so your body image. Having seen this, you must now be in an excellent position to embrace this affirmation. Take it as an opener to your morning and employ it entirely in your life.

To achieve much in this process of weight loss, you need to embark on areas that give you a clear view of affirmations. Remember, affirmations are just phrases that are highly powerful and lead to positivity in life. By applying these affirmations, be sure that you will be able to stay focus, positive, and relaxed. There are several affirmations that you need to choose from. Try picking the ones you can manage and start your daily routine of making them permanent. Your weight will reduce tremendously.

We also aims at making you stay positive about yourself. That's, it indulges you in the world of motivation. Motivational affirmations, therefore, help you in achieving this ultimate goal, thus resulting in a more positive life with lots of happiness and relaxation. Stay tuned once more to these phrases, especially the way they been explained in this chapter. I hope you do prefer a perfect body image full of pleasure and positivity. Imagine a life full of happiness just because you have followed and fully implemented the principles in this book.

# Chapter 27 Spiritual Sound for Meditation

T his meditation is one of my favorites and I find that a lot of people feel in tuned with it. During this practice, we are going to imagine to be a rock-solid mountain, surrounded by nature and habited by animals, plants and trees.

Once the image is well painted inside our mind, we will add the element of time, allowing it to pass in a constant and smooth way. We are going to feel the different seasons, starting from the Summer, and we are going to experience different emotions. What it is important to notice is how the mountain remains still and solid, even during the most difficult times, offering a safe place for animals and plants.

By becoming self-aware of our mountain-ness, we can face daily difficulties with new energy and a rejuvenated spirit. Doing this practice once a week for a month is ideal to see the most benefits. Also, as you will see it is a pretty interesting and fun experience!

Let's get started!

Find a comfortable, relaxed and balanced position. Give yourself permission to be completely present for yourself, and let your body and mind calm down until they become soft and relaxed.

Breathe in, feel relaxed...

breathe out, feel calm...

Breathe in, feel relaxed...

breathe out, feel calm...

Breathe in, feel relaxed...

breathe out, feel calm...

Breathe in, feel relaxed...

breathe out, feel calm...

Allow the mind to distance itself from all thoughts and orientate awareness on your breath. Breathe naturally and do not force a specific rhythm. Let your breath come and go.

Carefully, now, drive your attention from the breath to the space in which you are.

Feel the energy and atmosphere of this space as it permeates all of your being. Notice the noises in the background. Maybe there is a clock ticking, maybe there are cars passing just outside your windows. Whatever you feel it is fine, let your attention rest on the external.

Breathe in, feel relaxed...

breathe out, feel calm...

Breathe in, feel relaxed...

breathe out, feel calm...

Breathe in, feel relaxed...

breathe out, feel calm...

Breathe in, feel relaxed...

breathe out, feel calm...

Now bring the attention back to the breath. Take your time and you will naturally reach a place of warmth and ease.

There is nothing to do here, nothing to think or to worry about. Just rest your attention on the breath, following each inhalation and exhalation with curiosity, falling into the rhythm of your very own body.

If you want, you can place your hands on your belly. This will help you enter in connection with the natural movement of the air entering through your nose and exciting trough the mouth.

Breathe in, feel relaxed...

breathe out, feel calm...

Breathe in, feel relaxed...

breathe out, feel calm...


Breathe in, feel relaxed...

breathe out, feel calm...

Breathe in, feel relaxed...

breathe out, feel calm...


Breathe in, feel relaxed...

breathe out, feel calm...

Breathe in, feel relaxed...

breathe out, feel calm...


Breathe in, feel relaxed...

breathe out, feel calm...

Breathe in, feel relaxed...

breathe out, feel calm...

I will give you a few more minutes to get into this zone, as we will than begin the actual practice.

Breathe in, feel relaxed...

breathe out, feel calm...

Breathe in, feel relaxed...

breathe out, feel calm...

Breathe in, feel relaxed...

breathe out, feel calm...

Breathe in, feel relaxed...

breathe out, feel calm...

Breathe in, feel relaxed...

breathe out, feel calm...

Breathe in, feel relaxed...

breathe out, feel calm...

Breathe in, feel relaxed...

breathe out, feel calm...

Breathe in, feel relaxed...

breathe out, feel calm...


Breathe in, feel relaxed...

breathe out, feel calm...

Breathe in, feel relaxed...

breathe out, feel calm...


Breathe in, feel relaxed...

breathe out, feel calm...

Breathe in, feel relaxed...

breathe out, feel calm...


Breathe in, feel relaxed...

breathe out, feel calm...

Breathe in, feel relaxed...

breathe out, feel calm...

Breathe in, feel relaxed...

breathe out, feel calm...

Breathe in, feel relaxed...

breathe out, feel calm...

Now start imagining a mountain, a big and rock-solid mountain. If you have a favorite one, you can picture it as well. Maybe it is a place where you go on a regular basis or maybe it is a mountain you have only see on video. Just take a few minutes to paint it as clearly as you can in your mind. Try to grasp every detail, from the height to the temperature. The more you can add, the greater the benefits.

Breathe in, feel relaxed...

breathe out, feel calm...

Breathe in, feel relaxed...

breathe out, feel calm...

Breathe in, feel relaxed...

breathe out, feel calm...

Breathe in, feel relaxed...

breathe out, feel calm...

Breathe in, feel relaxed...

breathe out, feel calm...

Breathe in, feel relaxed...

breathe out, feel calm...

Breathe in, feel relaxed...

breathe out, feel calm...

Breathe in, feel relaxed...

breathe out, feel calm...

Once you have the image in your mind, we can get started. It is Summer and all the animals are coming towards you, finding peace under the shadow you provide them. Tourists and hikers take pictures of you and their kids run up and down your trails. Trees and flowers are nourished by your soil and paint you in a dark green color. Everything is perfect, nice and cozy, and it seems that this beautiful feeling will never end.

Breathe in, feel relaxed...

breathe out, feel calm...

Breathe in, feel relaxed...

breathe out, feel calm...


Breathe in, feel relaxed...

breathe out, feel calm...

Breathe in, feel relaxed...

breathe out, feel calm...


Breathe in, feel relaxed...

breathe out, feel calm...

Breathe in, feel relaxed...

breathe out, feel calm...


Breathe in, feel relaxed...

breathe out, feel calm...

Breathe in, feel relaxed...

breathe out, feel calm...

Breathe in, feel relaxed...

breathe out, feel calm...

Breathe in, feel relaxed...

breathe out, feel calm...


Breathe in, feel relaxed...

breathe out, feel calm...

Breathe in, feel relaxed...

breathe out, feel calm...


Breathe in, feel relaxed...

breathe out, feel calm...

Breathe in, feel relaxed...

breathe out, feel calm...


Breathe in, feel relaxed...

breathe out, feel calm...

Breathe in, feel relaxed...

breathe out, feel calm...

Time goes by very quickly though and sooner than later fewer and fewer people come and take picture of you. The beautiful trees are now losing their leaves and the animals are seeking repair in the valley, leaving you almost alone. The last flowers are perishing, and your soil is not a good source of nourishment anymore. You think that this feeling will never end.

Breathe in, feel relaxed...

breathe out, feel calm...

Breathe in, feel relaxed...

breathe out, feel calm...

Breathe in, feel relaxed...

breathe out, feel calm...

Breathe in, feel relaxed...

breathe out, feel calm...

Breathe in, feel relaxed...

breathe out, feel calm...

Breathe in, feel relaxed...

breathe out, feel calm...


Breathe in, feel relaxed...

breathe out, feel calm...

Breathe in, feel relaxed...

breathe out, feel calm...


Now Winter comes and snow starts coming down, covering all your trails and rocks. There are no flowers popping up and trees are now completely brown. Their leaves are on the ground, covered by snow. The temperature is freezing, and all the animals are now far away, trying to survive this season as best as they can. People stay far away from you, because they are scared of avalanches. They look at you with a deep sense of respect but are not willing to visit you for the time being. You think that this feeling will never end.


Breathe in, feel relaxed...

breathe out, feel calm...

Breathe in, feel relaxed...

breathe out, feel calm...

Breathe in, feel relaxed...

breathe out, feel calm...

Breathe in, feel relaxed...

breathe out, feel calm...

Breathe in, feel relaxed...

breathe out, feel calm...

Breathe in, feel relaxed...

breathe out, feel calm...

Breathe in, feel relaxed...

breathe out, feel calm...

Breathe in, feel relaxed...

breathe out, feel calm...

Slowly things start to change, and you are noticing it with new hope. The snow is melting, the trees becoming green again and beautiful wildflowers are popping up all over you. Soon enough, the first hikers are taking picture of you again and everyone is telling how gorgeous you are. The sun is getting brighter, days are getting longer. Animals are coming back and are dancing for you on your beautiful trails. It is Spring at its finest and you think that this feeling will never end.

Breathe in, feel relaxed...

breathe out, feel calm...

Breathe in, feel relaxed...

breathe out, feel calm...

Breathe in, feel relaxed...

breathe out, feel calm...

Breathe in, feel relaxed...

breathe out, feel calm...

Breathe in, feel relaxed...

breathe out, feel calm...

Breathe in, feel relaxed...

breathe out, feel calm...

Breathe in, feel relaxed...

breathe out, feel calm...

Breathe in, feel relaxed...

breathe out, feel calm...

And in a blink of an eye, everything starts all over again. Summer, Fall, Winter, Spring and then Summer again, in a never-ending cycle. And no matter what happens around you, you are still there, feeling strong and solid as a mountain.

I would like you to bring this feeling with you for the rest of the week, as you are truly capable of amazing things, when you tap into the unlimited source of energy that is your soul.

Breathe in, feel relaxed...

breathe out, feel calm...

Breathe in, feel relaxed...

breathe out, feel calm...

Breathe in, feel relaxed...

breathe out, feel calm...

Breathe in, feel relaxed...

breathe out, feel calm...


Breathe in, feel relaxed...

breathe out, feel calm...

Breathe in, feel relaxed...

breathe out, feel calm...


Breathe in, feel relaxed...

breathe out, feel calm...

Breathe in, feel relaxed...

breathe out, feel calm...


Now bring the attention back to the body and start feeling your arms and legs once again. You can close your hands or move your fingers, just to take control of the space around you.


Please, keep the eyes closed for now and enjoy the beautiful moment you are living. You have given yourself the time to feel better and that is absolutely incredible.

Breathe in, feel relaxed...

breathe out, feel calm...

Breathe in, feel relaxed...

breathe out, feel calm...


Breathe in, feel relaxed...

breathe out, feel calm...

Breathe in, feel relaxed...

breathe out, feel calm...


Now become aware of the environment around you once again. Feel the different sounds, the temperature of the room you are in and once you are ready, open the eyes again.

# Chapter 28 Peaceful, Calming and Relaxing Music for Relief, Anxiety and Stress

Welcome to this guided meditation, it has been designed to help you feel happy and confident inside. To help you let go of any inner fears or doubts.

Everyone feels sad or worried at times.

Sometimes life is good and at other times, life is more difficult. At times, you may doubt your abilities. You may compare yourself to others.

You may worry that you are not as clever ....... or, as kind.

Perhaps you feel you are not as popular.

This can make you feel less confident.

Practice this meditation daily and your confidence will soar.

You will feel relaxed. Carefree and so contented.

Find a comfortable position in which to relax.

You can lie down or sit up if you prefer.

Make sure you have time to complete this meditation.

Just close your eyes and try to follow the sound of my voice.

Your mind may wander sometimes, don't worry, just try to pay attention again. Tuning into my voice as you continue this journey of pure discovery.

Breathe through your nose and feel your chest rising.

Breathe out through your mouth and feel your chest lower.

Try to feel a connection between the mind and the body.

Every muscle starts to relax.

You feel your muscles becoming heavier.

As if you are sinking...

Floating.

It is like daydreaming but not quite asleep.

Breathe in again, feeling the sensation as your lungs expand.

Now breathe out through your mouth and let your body relax and muscles go all limp.

You feel happy and this moment.

Very relaxed.

Calm and peaceful

You are going to transport yourself to the beach.

It is a wonderful hot day.

Not too hot but enough for people to go swimming.

Or to relax on the sand.

As you stand on the sand, you can see so many people lying in the sun.

Family groups. Young children creating sandcastles. Parents helping them shape sand into shapes.

You are so interested in what they are doing.

Gaining ideas for your own castles.

As you continue to look, there are people swimming and others playing in the water at the edge.

The water is a deep blue with frothy white tips as it hits the shore.

It ebbs and flows at a wonderful pace. In and out. It flows naturally and you feel drawn to play in the water, to splash about.

Feel the warmth from the sun on your skin.

The sun is a golden yellow ball in a beautiful clear blue sky.

There are no clouds to mar the view.

Everyone is so happy here.

You hear laughter and the sounds of the water breaking on the shore.

You are happy to be here.

You feel warm.

As you look down, you see that your bare feet are covered in sand.

It feels wonderful to have the warmth through your feet.

The sand between your toes.

Walk to the water and now feel the cool water over your feet, washing the sand away.

Even though there are so many people here, you feel that it is so peaceful.

There is happiness.

Laughter.

Seagulls fly noisily overhead.

White bodies against a blue sky. Large wings stretched out.

Soaring, dipping in and out of the waves.

Boats pass by, white sails a contrast against the blue horizon.

Someone is on jet skis.

There is so much happening. So much fun.

Take a moment to enjoy this beach scene.

*Music to fade 40 seconds.*

As you walk along the beach, you see amazing sand sculptures.

Wonderful works of art.

They exist in this wide expanse of sand.

Huge sandcastles take center place.

As if on show.

Self Guide Meditation For Beginners

They have turrets and towers.

One has a moat around it.

And a drawbridge.

So much detail.

You can see how much work has gone into it.

You are creative, and you want to build the same, but you don't know how to do it.

As you look at other sand creations, you see, people have shaped faces and animals. There is so much detail. All made from sand.

You have never seen anything like this before. You long to be shown how to do it.


The desire to build a big sandcastle fills your mind.

Yours will be better than ever.

If you feel doubts about your abilities, let them go.

Just enjoy the pleasure of creating an image from sand.

Of sculpting.

Of being a sand artist.

You are so in the moment.

Happiness washes over you.

There is so much pleasure.

You fill a bucket with water and add sand to it.

Scooping the first handful to create a base on the sand. You can feel the wet sand on your fingers.

It feels rough.

Course against your skin.

You add more wet sand but, you cannot shape it...the block falls apart.

As you look around, you see what others are doing. Filling a hole in the sand with water. Sending sand into the center. They drain the sand.

You are learning.

Through watching others.

You take these lessons on board.

Take a moment here to think of your design.

*Music to fade 30 seconds*

Feel the warm sand in your fingers as you scoop out a hole. Fill the hole with water. Now, with your fingers, feel the sensation of wet, gritty sand against your hands. Now, make your shapes. Using the bucket to create solid turrets.

You keep building.

Enjoying the pleasure of creativity.

You are an artist. ^

Not with paints but with sand.

You love being here.

Learning

Happy in this moment.

Confidence growing as your sandcastle takes shape.

Even when some sand does not stay in shape, you learn from the experience.

You realize what you must do.

You are driven to complete the castle.

It continues to grow. Shape upon shape.

Growing taller.

Reaching up out from the sand.

You draw shapes of windows with a twig.

Patterns in the wall.

And a moat.

Now, you fill the moat with water...

You know it will drain but, for a moment, you feel your castle is real.

Something you have created.

For all to see.

You are an artist.

This is so relaxed.

So peaceful....

Even now as people start to leave.

You feel happy in this moment.

You achieved more than you thought you could.

By learning, by listening, by thinking.

Know that you are capable of anything.

You believe in yourself.

You know you can do whatever you want.

You are not afraid to try.

Trying is part of the experience.

Each experience is important to you.

Breathe in warm air and breathe out...fully...

You feel relaxed and so peaceful.

You feel happy in this moment.

As you stand back to view your castle, you know it is time to leave. But you feel wonderful. The sun is setting.... you watch it sinking towards the sea. The sky is now red streaked. It looks beautiful.

The sea is calm.

Gentle.

Boats are sailing back to the port.

It is time for you to go home. But always remember, you can come back here at any time you like. You just need to close your eyes.

Breathe in slowly and breathe out fully.

When ready, you can open your eyes.

# Chapter 29 Short Stories Against Anxiety and Stress Helping the Adult Fall Asleep

D enmark is high up north, where Germany stops. There is still a king there today, but he is no longer there to govern, but usually visits kindergartens because his wife likes children so much.

But a long time ago, the Danish king was very powerful. As all kings used to do, he always wanted to increase his land so that he would become even more powerful. So, he also had to conquer another country. That was not easy. In the south of Denmark was Germany, then the kingdoms of Hanover and Prussia. He could not mess with them because they had many more soldiers than he. Likewise, the Swedes, whose country lies next to Denmark.

So, he looked north. Far behind the sea was Greenland. This is a huge country, but at the time it was very little known, and it was supposed to be very cold there. So, he had three ships loaded from the royal fleet. On each he put a brave knight and several soldiers, as well as horses and all kinds of war equipment.

Then it went off to Greenland in the terribly cold north. When the ships arrived, they first saw a lot of ice and snow. The knights put on their armor and went ashore to conquer it. But no one was visible, and the knights froze in their iron armor on the ice, so they could not move.

They kicked wildly, clawing their iron armor hard to free themselves from the ice.

A few of the other soldiers had to make a fire to get them released. As a result, of course, the armor on the feet were pretty hot and the knights burned their feet. They shopped around wildly until they were finally free and quickly disappeared on the ship.

Then one tried to bring the horses ashore, because one should conquer Greenland. The horses struggled hard, but after a few meters they also got stuck in the snow. The soldiers could not walk in the high snow and froze miserably, so that finally all went with their horses back on the ships and Greenland could not conquer first. When the knights sat around thinking and pondering, the lookout on the ship's mast reported "Enemy ahead !!"

And indeed, the knights saw in astonishment how a sleigh came with very small horses. They were astonished even more when they discovered that it was not horses but many dogs in front of a sled so effortlessly whizzing across the snow.

Everyone brought their rifles and lances and feared that they would have to defend themselves. But there was only one man on the sled, an Eskimo. He greeted them in a very friendly way and was happy to see so many people, because in Greenland not so many people live, and one is often quite lonely and alone. He welcomed everyone and asked them if they would not visit him in the evening, his wife would cook a nice soup of seal meat for them.

From whom you are greeted so friendly, you can fight badly against, and so put three of the knights on the dogsled, but without their heavy armor. Husch - you rushed over the landscape to a strange hut, which was made entirely of snow. It's called an igloo and it's round, but it's very nice and warm!

When they had eaten, they thanked each other, and the Eskimo drove them back to their ships by dog sled. Then it was decided to drive back to Denmark.

They then reported everything to the king. He held advice with his ministers how to conquer Greenland. They also asked a wise old man named Count Johannsen. The count whispered his suggestion in the ear of the king, and he was thrilled!

He sent his steward to the city to buy whatever vanilla powder he could get. Then he equipped a ship again, but this time the knights should put on thick fur coats and take sledges with them. In addition, the whole load compartment was full of vanilla powder!

Arrived in Greenland, they were greeted by Eskimos again, it was already known by now. The soldiers from Denmark brought a lot of fresh snow and made it with their vanilla powder from delicious vanilla ice cream. They gave it to the Eskimos.

They had never eaten anything like that! They were crazy about it and still wanted to have more. The knights, however, kept everything under wraps and first wanted to speak to the eskimo leader, who was quickly brought for them. With him, the knights made a contract that now

Greenland would belong to Denmark and for that the Eskimos would get as much vanilla ice cream as they could eat.

Then the knights sailed home with their ship and told their king that Greenland would now belong to Denmark, without there being a war!

And that's how it is today, so you can ask every Dane.

# Chapter 30 Short Stories to Help Adult on Meditation, Relaxation and Fall Asleep Quickly

Visiting Paris in the spring is the ultimate in luxurious travel, and I plan to submerge myself entirely in the authentic Parisian experience. This is why I recruited a friend who recently relocated to the city of lights to host me for a few days and give me a tour of the favorite places they had discovered.

The plan is to meet at a cafe near my hotel, and I decide to dress my best. Comfort and style are needed to blend in with Parisians, so I wore my most fashionable ensemble. I know we will be walking all day, so I finish my outfit off with stylish, white sneakers. For good measure, from the souvenir shop in my hotel, I purchase a delicate silk scarf with a dash of orange and pale blue in the sizeable geometric pattern. I loosely tie it around my neck the way I've seen movie stars do and feel like I fit the role entirely.

My enthusiasm for the day is like a child on Christmas morning. I am ready ahead of time, so I walk to the cafe early and begin my Parisian experience. As I walk, the city comes alive through its residents going about their weekday routines. My hotel is on a corner. When I exit the lobby, the narrow street is populated with a few cars, and some cyclists squeezed into the even more narrow spaces for the bike lane. There is limited space to travel, but the morning commuters are peaceful and do not seem to be in a rush to get anywhere.

I walk through the neighborhood and see shopkeepers open their doors and windows to let in fresh air. The sky is a lovely bright blue speckled with the lightest dusting of wispy white clouds. It's a picture-perfect spring day. I cross a street and see the cafe already filling with patrons. A few people are outside reading the newspaper. Someone is sitting with their eyes closed, and their face toward the sun soaking in what I can guess is the first beautiful day this season. A woman is having a conversation with a person who has a small, fluffy, tan-colored dog who is not interested in chit-chat. The dog gently tugs on the leash to encourage their owner to move on to the exciting thing around the next corner.

Inside, the cafe is bright and welcoming, with plants spilling over the edges of their pots and colorful chairs tucked into wooden tables. In my best French I order a cappuccino, a croissant with jam and a glass of orange juice. The woman who takes my order repeats it to me in English, and we share a knowing glance of appreciation. She tells me to find a seat, and she will take my breakfast for me. On the patio, the woman talking to the dog walker has left, so I seat myself in her place. A few moments later, my server deliveries my first Parisian breakfast, I say merci and pause for a moment to take in the enjoyment of this moment.

The croissant is warm with a crisp golden exterior. When I pull it apart, I can see the steam release, telling me this pastry was freshly baked just moments ago. I savor each buttery bite in between sips of my creamy, dark, perfectly smooth cappuccino. With half of the decadent pastry gone, I spread a generous amount of the fresh strawberry jam onto my next bite. The tartness of the jam with the richness of the croissant is possibly the most delightful breakfast I've had in a long time. I feel very much like the natural Parisian of my dreams.

As I sip on the last of my freshly squeezed orange juice, my friend arrives. I rise to give them a long hug, we express how long it's been, and they complement me on my silk scarf. We tidy up my table, and I bring the empty dishes inside and wave goodbye to my lovely server. My friend links their arm in mine, and together, we walk through the streets of Paris, catching up on each other's lives since the last time we saw each other a few years back.

We pass through the Palace De La Bastille with its tall pillar celebrating the three-day revolution that saw the fall of one king and the rise of another. The tall post is topped with a golden statue of a man, perched delicately on one foot, and a hand raised into the sky in victory. The sun gleams across the flame is his raised hand and floods the plaza with its warmth.

After a short stroll, we come to the main attraction of our walk, the Le Viaduc des Arts, a collection of artisan shops built into the remnants of the old Paris-Bastille railways.

The brick structure is tall and stretches as far as I can see in a series of wide arches closed in with floor to ceiling windows and filled with unique creations in each different arch. The top of the bridge-like structure is a raised park filled with trees, water features, and an almost secret pathway that covers the entire length of the bridge. I can smell the roses blooming atop the building and struggle to decide which splendid sight to take in first. My friend and guide suggest we browse the workshops for half of the walk and enjoy the park for the rest of the journey.

Each archway holds a different treasure, from art restoration to custom made jewelry, perfumers, and jam makers to artists and craftspeople of all genres happily go about creating their work. Many are focused on their craft.

Those who are not busy smile as we press our faces close to the windows for a better look at the delicate nature of their work. Filled with awe and inspiration, we make our way up the stairs to the raised park and continue our walk surrounded by the early spring blooms of this secret garden.

We walk silently, content in the moment, and with each other's presence.

Near the end of the park, my friend asked if I was ready to see more of Paris. There is the Pantheon a few blocks up, the stunning Jardin du Luxembourg and all its statues, and of course, the Eiffel tower was not that far away. I gently rub the silk scarf I purchased that morning as I think and reply, "while in Paris my love," and we turn to make our way toward the exciting place around the next corner.

# Conclusion

J ust like using medication, you will want to do these meditations consistently in order to get the best benefits possible. It took a while to create your pain. It doesn't always happen so quickly, so just as it took some time to create the mentality you have, it will take some time to reverse it.

If you stay dedicated to the healing process and focused on finding peace within yourself, you will discover an incredible ability to actually heal yourself. Don't wait around and simply hope that things will eventually get better. Take power back over your mind and let yourself become fully healed in this process.

We offer a plethora of other meditations that you can do for specific reasons. Whether you want to get a better night's sleep or are interested in losing weight through the healing process, you can find a meditation directed specifically at your needs. The only way that you will be able to enjoy a fulfilled and happy life is to let yourself be free from the things that cause so much anguish and pain.

Meditation has been a way of life in many cultures for centuries. It has helped millions of people in conducting their life in a meaningful way. It is a peaceful way of life that focuses on being mindful and aware.

Modern life has become so fast-paced that people have stopped rationalizing over the need for the actions they take. Everyone is following someone or the other. However, one solution fits all don't work when it comes to human beings. This has led to numerous problems. The biggest problem is that people are finding it increasingly difficult to focus and find a purpose in life. Meditation doesn't dictate a path to you. It is a way to develop the abilities to find the right path. It is an important tool using which you can become more successful in life.

Meditation has always been liked by monks who had no love for the material world. However, it is not the way of leaving everything out. It is the way in which you can get the most even while you don't have much. It teaches the most difficult art of being content.

We will prove to be your primer for meditation. It will tell you everything about meditation. From the right way to begin meditation to the various ways in which you can practice meditation as a beginner.

Meditation should not distance you from people, especially from your loved ones. Although many people these days meditate to relieve stress and feel better, the true effects of meditation are not really just for yourself, but also for others. Meditation should lead you to be kinder, express more love, and exercise compassion at all times. You must do so sincerely. The fact remains that even among those who meditate for years, only a few reach enlightenments in one lifetime. Therefore, although enlightenment may be your goal on why you meditate, never allow yourself to be obsessed with the idea of enlightenment. If you want to have less stress and live a happier life, then make peace with the people around you and show your love, even to your enemies.

Meditation will give you the strength that you need to do so. All forms of meditation also develop the heart chakra, which will allow you to be more compassionate and exercise universal love. Daily meditation practice can make you healthier, happier, and more successful than ever. Only a few minutes of meditation practice daily can help you lower stress, improve your mental and physical health, boost your focus and increase work productivity. If you heard about meditation but don't know how to begin – or you have practiced meditation in the past, but need help to get started again, this beginner's meditation guidebook is for you.

You may find benefit in learning to be a better-rounded individual with emotional intelligence, hoping to defeat your anxiety through learning social skills that can benefit you. You may find benefit in becoming more skilled at the techniques brought to your attention within this book. You may even prefer a book dedicated solely to cognitive behavioral therapy that can teach you the steps necessary to complete cognitive restructuring in detail.

You deserve to live a life that is one you can enjoy, free from worrying about what your friends think of you. Through spending the time and effort necessary, you can achieve that life that, up until this point, may have seemed like impossibility. It will not be easy, but it is possible for you. If you want it, all you have to do is reach for it and practice the steps provided within this book for you. With the effort necessary, you will begin to find relief from the symptoms, and if you do not, you are not out of options—a therapist or licensed medical professional can help you further. Just remember, there is always hope of getting out of this situation. All you have to do is ask for the help that is out there.

Meditation will help you become more disciplined and focused in everything you do. It will help you relax and take a break from all your troubles. It will help you to improve your physical, mental, and spiritual health over time.

The best part is that you will only have to give 10-15 minutes of your day just to reap all these rewards. So, find a quiet place and take the time to practice meditation from today forward. You will notice positive changes if you start sooner rather than later.

This has been "Self-Healing Power And Relaxation Meditation: Beginners Guide To Mindfulness Therapy. Stop Anxiety, Live Stress Free And Declutter Your Mind. Bedtime Stories: Fall Asleep And Awakening Better" Written By : Peace of Soul & Brain Foundation.

# GUIDED MEDITATION FOR MINDFULNESS AND RELAXATION

## HOW AND TO CHANGE AND CALM YOUR MIND. STRESS FREE WITH SELF HEALING. UNDERSTANDING AND PRACTICING BUDDHISM. YOGA AND ZEN MADE PLAIN FOR BEGINNERS

**"PEACE OF SOUL AND BRAIN" FOUNDATION**

# TABLE OF CONTENTS

# Introduction

Meditation is the way to quieten the mind for a bit. It is a simple activity that can give you better control over your mind and your thoughts. You will be able to practically empty your mind for some time and then refill it with positive things. The time you get through meditation helps you in objectively selecting the thoughts you want to work on. You can single out each and every negative thought in your mind and choose to discard it forever. Meditation can give you great control over the thought process and effectively over your life.

It can prove to be an effective cure of the sorrows, fears, anxieties, feelings of hatred and general confusion that plague your life. It is one of the best ways to completely transform the mind. You will be able to achieve a state of thoughtless awareness. This will not only make your mind clear but also relaxed and inwardly focused.

Meditation is the way to understand the cause of the problems plaguing the mind. It is the deep state of thought where you are able to view things objectively and make a better judgment.

The best thing about meditation is that you don't need anything extra to do all this. You only need to sit, stand, or walk quietly. Once you get fairly acquainted with the process you can do it anywhere. You will have amazing control over your life and would be able to feel the bliss you have been longing for. You'll become more joyful, satisfied, and peaceful.

Modern life has become a race in which we all are running without a goal. In this race, no one can be victorious as there is no finish line. Meditation will give you the required understanding to enjoy the race.

You'll be learning everything you need to know from learning how to be aware of the present moment to learning how to become aware of your own thoughts and feelings. These are important building blocks to meditation as often time we don't want to take the time for ourselves. Many of us spend a good chunk of time worrying about others and trying to get as much done as possible. In fact, I would bet that as you read this introduction, you may be holding your breath trying to get to the next point. Take a moment to release that breath, inhale deeply, and try to calm your mind.

As you'll soon be learning, meditation is not about rushing to the next task. As we work our way through several different meditations, I want you to remind yourself that this is not a selfish practice. Much like we nourish our bodies with nutritious foods, it's important to give your mind some peace and quiet. Peace for the soul is just as important as health for the body. When you put both aspects together, you'll be granted the gift of life as you have never experienced before.

Once we have gone over the benefits of meditation and how to create the perfect environment for your practice, you'll learn how to begin your first meditation in chapter four. Here, you'll learn some basic induction skills and how to get the most out of your practice. From breathing exercises to a full-body scan, we'll make sure you are comfortable before furthering your practice into the visualization meditation scripts.

It should be noted that you should not enter this practice with any expectations. The most important factor is that you are taking steps to help relieve your stress and anxiety. There will be moments of frustration when you are unable to quiet the chatter of your brain, but I promise that as you practice more, you'll be able to enjoy the benefits meditation can bring into your life.

# Chapter 1

# What You Should Know About Hypnosis?

Hypnosis is susceptibility of the mind to suggestions. Despite this state, a person under hypnosis subconsciously knows what is being done except that he/she allows these things to happen.

A common application of hypnosis is hypnotherapy, which aims at improving a well-being. You cannot inflict damage to a person in a hypnotized state. Even in such a state, a person can react to danger. The mind has defense mechanisms that are hard to understand.

The practice of hypnosis has been around for so many centuries. Lately, scientists devote time to study and explain how and why it is possible. Many theories arise regarding the different practices of hypnosis. Here are the truths about hypnosis.

Hypnosis is a natural, inherent trait.

It happens to everyone, in some form or another. You may not recognize it or may even deny that you witness at least once or maybe more. Every person may drift in and out of the hypnosis state.

For example, you are reading a novel. You are so engrossed with the story you do not "hear" your significant other asking you a question. Your conscious mind may not register the question, but you know you are being asked. In some way, it resembles hypnosis. Others do not call it that way.

Since it is a natural trait, a hypnotized person is not at risk of getting stuck in one state or another. They naturally drift to wake state or deep sleep. Thus, hypnosis is not dangerous. The experience is like listening to a boring speech and zoning out until the speaker finishes. Some may feel disoriented, but such feelings do not last.

Hypnosis is not a sleep state.

Although the word hypnosis comes from the Greek word, Hypnos, which means sleep, it does not constitute the normal sleep state. Hypnosis state seems like you are asleep, but your mind is aware, awake and responsive. You hear everything. Your senses heighten.

Hypnosis does not make a person weak-willed.

A hypnotized person is susceptible to suggestions, but it does not mean they are weak-willed. They remain in control. In fact, they can stop hypnosis anytime they want. If hypnosis makes a person weak-willed, hypnotists could abuse such power over a hypnotized person. A lot of hypnotists could command a person to do everything they say. Fortunately, a hypnotized person remains in control despite his/her highly susceptibility to suggestions.

Relaxation is not a prerequisite to hypnosis.

You can hypnotize a person anywhere, anytime, provided that person is willing. You may even do it during a strenuous activity. Hypnosis can bring relaxation, but relaxation is not a prerequisite.

Hypnosis does not cause permanent amnesia.

A hypnotist can command a person to forget, for the time being, what has transpired. This allows the mind to process the events subconsciously. In the long run, a hypnotized person can remember of the hypnosis in great detail.

Hypnosis is different from a trance state.

Many hypnotists have difficulty identifying the difference between hypnotic and trance state. Most of the times, these two words are used interchangeably. The only similarities between the two are the heightened senses and highly efficient mind.

Hypnosis deals with heightened susceptibility of the mind, most likely the subconscious part. Trance state targets both the conscious and subconscious.

Concept of Hypnosis

The human mind is a complex mechanism. Learning these concepts enables you to hypnotize anyone, anytime. Understanding these hypnosis concepts helps you recognize which technique to use.

## Power of Suggestion

Sometimes, people act based on someone else's suggestions. This power of suggestion is what advertisers use to convince consumers to buy a product. Hypnotists also use this power of suggestion to induce hypnosis.

The most common example of the power of suggestion is the placebo effect. This is a suggestion during the waking state. Doctors, nurses, pharmacists apply this power of suggestion to patients. The doctors would sometimes give an ordinary pill to patients. Believing that this pill cures their diseases, the patients feel better. Why? The doctors suggested that the particular pill can heal them.

Combined with the power of language, the power of suggestion creates expectations. It creates a powerful way of making the hypnotized person's move towards his or her dominant thoughts.

## Power of Imagination

The human mind is capable of unlimited imagination. Together with the power of suggestion, you can create endless possibilities with your hypnosis.

Visualization scripts include the power of imagination. This power helps people achieve something or anything close to their physical limitations or beyond their normal capabilities.

Conscious vs. the Subconscious

In psychology, the mind can function on conscious and subconscious levels. The conscious part is what you can control. The conscious mind makes decisions, thinks logically, and performs cognitive functions. It is the origin of willpower and the recorder of short-term memory. It dwells in the past, present and the future.

On the other hand, the subconscious mind controls body functions and automatic reactions and reflexes. It does not think in executing an action. Like a computer program, once hitting the run button, the subconscious automatically executes whatever actions a body part or organ has to do. Examples are breathing and blinking.

The subconscious mind is the seat of habit and long-term memory. It does not change so easily. Embedded memories, actions, and reactions in the subconscious take time (or years) for newer ones to replace them. The subconscious controls self-preservation mechanisms. This is the reason hypnotists cannot make a person to something bad while hypnotized.

The mind generalizes and filters events, actions, objects or anything seen, felt, heard, tasted, and experienced. Generalization is the ability of the mind to think in blocks or concepts. It makes thinking quicker especially in times of danger. Filtering is the ability to block sensory inputs and delete negative mental images.

## Language Patterns

Hypnotists use language patterns to hypnotize other people. These patterns include dissociation, supposition, double binds, metaphors, embedded commands, exploration, and anticipation.

## Use of Metaphors

Metaphorical language pattern is an excellent way to make other people trust you. They can relate to what you are saying without the feeling of intrusion to their personal lives. With metaphors, you can speak about the lives of your targets and still be confident that you can hypnotize them.

## Double Binds

This language pattern offers choices, usually two, to your subjects or targets. Whatever the answer is, the outcome is the same. Most of the time double binds language pattern is only answerable with a yes or no.

## Embedded Commands

In this language pattern, you are commanding other people do what you want them to do. It is usually used in an authoritarian method of inducing hypnosis. However, scrutinizing closely induction scripts, all induction techniques, except non-verbal method, use embedded commands to deliver suggestions and ask permissions.

## Dissociation

This pattern uses an out of the body experience. Many people fall into a dissociation state when they experience stress and traumatic events.

This dissociation seems to be a natural response of most people. Dissociation happens naturally during hypnosis. You can utilize this natural occurrence to hypnotize other people.

The Laws of the Mind

Thoughts affect the body. If the mind thinks you are strong, the body seems to follow. This is the reason constant emotional stress weakens the body. You can use this law to induce hypnosis. If your targets think that hypnosis is possible, they are more susceptible than those people who are skeptical.

Concentrated attention

The more you think of something, the more it becomes a reality. For an instance, constant, repeated imagination of wanting to become more sociable or efficient in work will make your conscious mind believe it. As a result, you find ways to achieve it.

However, for people who have difficulty separating between reality and imagination, concentrated attention has a negative effect. These people sometimes live in a world of protected cocoon.

In hypnosis, you can use this law of the mind to hypnotize anyone and strengthen your suggestions to your subjects. Concentrated attention makes your targets believe in anything you suggest them to do.

Dominant effect

People create habit over time. They hold on to this habit to rationalize behavior and thoughts. Once an idea is embedded in the mind, it takes time for this to be replaced a new one. For new ideas to replace old ones, people need strong emotional connection or consequences.

Association

The opposite of dissociation, people sometimes feel when they can relate such emotions with something. For example, classical music relaxes the mind while metal rock music evokes harsh and negative vibes.

Reverse Effect

This law proposes that the conscious mind cannot force the subconscious to follow. The greater is the effort of the conscious mind to understand or remember something the harder it is for the subconscious to response.

Negation

The mind does not know how to compute negation. When you say do not think of this or that, the first thing the mind does is to think of this or that. For example, do not imagine that this elephant is colored in violet. The mind interprets it as "see the elephant, it is violet."

Compounding

This law utilizes the compounding effect of repeated suggestions. Every time you make same suggestions over and over again to the same person with only slight variations, you are creating a pattern. On the succeeding hypnosis, induction is easier than the first to third sessions.

Core Beliefs

Core beliefs are created early in life. These beliefs determine who you are and what you are in life. However, every core belief does not define all aspects of your life. One core belief may define how you deal with your social life but not how you manage your work environment.

These core beliefs are consistent with the rest of your life but can be altered through hypnosis, will power and by other life changing events. These beliefs play a big role in retaining long term problems in your life.

Understanding these personal core beliefs will help you in knowing exactly how to hypnotize anyone.

# Chapter 2
# Relaxation Techniques

## Technique 1: Meditation

When the body and mind are stressed, you need to slow down. It is best to commence a relaxation response. Studies have shown that daily meditation and prayer not only eases one's anxiety, but it also helps modify the neural pathways of the brain making it more resistant to stress.

You should practice meditation and prayer every single day, especially during stressful situations. It will help you focus on better things and keep your mind off stressful conditions. When your mind is relaxed and focused, you can go back to challenges and obstacles with a clear thought and course of action. Even if you will not be able to solve the stressful situation you are facing now, meditation will keep your body from releasing bad hormones that can damage your health.

Mindful meditation is important when quieting your mind. It is the art of becoming heedful or attentive to your thoughts and feelings, your surroundings and your bodily responses.

Reducing stress levels may be the first benefit when you meditate. It has long-term effects such as increased self-awareness and lesser bouts of depression. You will find that you will easily be content with life, you will be more confident with yourself and stressful situations will not bother you as much in the future.

A simple meditation exercise you can try today is to simply sit in a comfortable position and focus your attention on your breathing. You don't need to alter your breathing in any way, simply focus on it. Your mind will wander many times, each time it does, simply forgive yourself and have some humor about it, and return to your breathing.

## Technique 2: Relaxed Breathing

You can practice the art of breathing deeply at regular intervals, which will calm and soothe you deeply. This will help improve the air and blood circulation in the body and produce calming effects.

You need to make yourself feel comfortable.

Here are some things you can do:

- Go to a quiet place with less distractions.

- Loosen tight clothing or remove your shoes, jewelry and jacket.

- Get a comfortable chair that will support your head. Make sure that your arms are placed on the arm rest and your feet are firmly planted on the ground. You should not cross your legs.

- You can also lie on a bed or on the floor. Place your arms away from your body with your palms facing up. Stretch your legs out making sure they are apart.

Once you are comfortable enough, you can now focus on your breathing. To start, inhale and exhale slowly in a regular beat or rhythm.

## Technique 3: Laugh Out Loud

Laughter is the best medicine is such an old saying but still rings true. It is no joke that laughter is one of the best techniques for stress relief. Chuckles and chortles, giggles and guffaws – they may not cure all illnesses, but they sure can lighten your load.

So go ahead and try to laugh. Even if it is forced, laughter can do wonders to your body and mind. Turn up your mouth and smile and start with a chuckle. You will feel that your body will be less tensed, and you will feel lighter.

## Technique 4: Improve Your Sense Of Humor

Having a positive outlook will help you deal with stressful situations effectively. Having a good sense of humor will increase your chances of getting over something stressful quickly.

Finding something humorous in your own situation and laughing about it will help you fight stress. It will do your body good to chuckle in the face of challenges.

If you feel that you don't have a funny bone in your body, don't fret. You can learn to have humor and it can be developed.

When you are trying to be funny, it is important to exercise discretion. There are some things that aren't meant to be laughed at. There are forms of humor that is out of place and hurtful such as laughing at the expense of other people. So always be socially intelligent, which I'm sure you are.

Laughing with your friends and family is especially bonding. If you find yourself alone a great deal, try to take some time to watch or read something funny. The effects of humor are amazing and can-do wonders for your spirit and counter stress very quickly. Research has shown that using humor to respond to stress can help you live longer by an average of four years!

## Technique 5: Decompress

If you are feeling stressed, your body will tense up and your muscles will become sore. You can feel this particularly on your neck and shoulders. There will be a heavy feeling as if you are literally carrying a weight.

To soothe the muscle tension, you can use a warm compress or heat wrap. Place it around your shoulders and neck.

After you put the warm compress around the tensed muscles, close your eyes to relax. Sit or lie down in a way that your neck, chest, back muscles and face will be relaxed. The heat from the wrap will cause your muscles to loosen up. After 10 minutes, you can gently massage the muscles on your neck and shoulders to ease the tension. It is best if someone can do it for you so you will not strain your arm muscles.

## Technique 6: Eat Stress Busting Foods

Foods can relieve stress in different ways. There are comfort foods that improve the levels of serotonin in your brain. It has a calming effect on the body. Other foods help lower the levels of adrenaline and cortisol to counter the effects of stress.

You need to have a healthy diet so that your body becomes strong enough to combat stress, improve your immune system and lower your blood pressure. And you need to know which foods to eat when you are in a stressful situation, so help your body fight off stress and not add to it.

## Technique 7: Exercise

You can change your diet or munch on stress busting foods to relieve your stress, but it will also help if you get moving and start exercising. If you are not active, chances are, stress eating will make you overweight.

When you move your body, you increase the circulation of oxygen in your blood and help your brain release endorphins.

You do not need to be too athletic, but it is best to do some aerobic exercises at least three times a week for 30 minutes. You can do all kinds of exercises as well such as walking, jogging, biking and yoga to help ease your anxiety. You can walk up and down the stairs and do some stretching as well.

## Technique 8: Incorporate Music In Your Life

Integrate music into your life to help you blow off your steam. Music can lower your heart rate and blood pressure and help decrease your anxiety. Music has the power to soothe your soul because it has a unique and effective link to your emotions.

You need to create a playlist of songs that will help you focus and relax. Slow, classical music is known to have a calming effect, but different people have different preferences. The choice of music is really up to you. It can be nature sounds or different melodies and instruments. It can be a variety of songs and singers. It can even be upbeat tunes.

Music will help distract your attention away from stressful situations and quiet your mind. It is a good aid when you are meditating. When your mind is relaxed and focused on things that are not stressful, you can be effective at finding solutions to what you are facing. You can explore your emotions so you can better deal with situations at hand.

## Technique 9: Reach Out And Relate

We may have saved the best for last. Just as you physically reach out during an exercise or internally reach out during meditation and listening to music, reaching out and relating to other people will help you deal with your stress levels.

Your social network is a great tool for managing stress and it this doesn't mean social media. It is not about ranting on Facebook or Twitter. It is more than posting your emotions on a mood board. It is about actually relating to people.

Talking with others will help your mind relax and sort things out. It can be done face-to-face, or it can be done over the phone. You can pour out your emotions and share your problems with family and friends.

241

# Technique 10: An Attitude Of Gratitude

There are people who can deal with just about anything and still stay happy. They can enjoy the good times and tough it out during the bad. Their focus is on the positive side of everything and they always see the best in people and situations.

To be able to maintain a positive outlook in life, it is vital that you appreciate what you have. When you have an attitude of gratitude – a thankful spirit – then you will not be beaten down by any storm or stressful situation. Emotional resilience can be improved by gratitude.

You can cultivate this attitude regardless of your personality or temperament. With a little practice, you can go from stress to optimism and maintain a good mood. Think about what you have now and be thankful. Do not compare what you have with what others have.

Do not worry about tomorrow's concerns or yesterday's regrets. Live in the present. Be grateful for the little things and the big things in your life. Meditate on the goodness of God in your life, His blessings and favors upon you. When challenges come, be grateful that you have the ability to overcome it or that you have friends who can help you go through it.

People who have a grateful attitude develop stringer relationships and are generally happy. They have a greater sense of purpose in life and become content.

Positivity will help lower cortisol levels that cause your body to feel anxious. And positivity comes when you are grateful. With gratefulness, you live life with more purpose, you appreciate the people around you, the job that you have, the roof above your head and all the other things that are part of your life. You will live happier, sleep better and be healthier.

Gratitude will help you stay focused on all that's good in your life and stop the stressful habit of ruminating on all your worries. Keep a gratitude journal (but don't stress about getting it perfect and writing in there every day!) and write in there one or two things you're grateful for, once or twice a week.

# Chapter 3

# Causes of Anxiety And Panic Attacks

U nderstanding anxiety and panic attacks can't be complete without looking at the causes. The aim is to ensure that we treat the root cause of anxiety and not just focus on symptoms. Understanding the cause of anxiety makes it possible for us to address the issues related to the conditions. There are two broad causes of anxiety

I)  External Causes

II) Internal Causes

External causes mainly refer to daily life circumstances that may lead to pressure. The external causes of anxiety may be social or environmental. These causes may lead to anxiety and panic attacks all alike. The internal cause of anxiety refers to factors that you may have control over. These are inbuilt emotions and ideas that may lead to anxiety.

External Causes of Anxiety

- Stress at work and Stress from school: Social stress imposed on a person by work and school expectations may lead to anxiety. Although this is not common, it happens. If a person feels that they may lose their job or fail in their exams, they may start experiencing anxiety. It is important to learn and handle the job pressure. If things are not working well at your workplace, you need to find a way of handling the situation. Poor management of stressful situations will in one way or another lead to anxiety or panic attacks. If you cannot talk with your boss or explain your situation to another employee, the pressure might get to your head leading to constant fear, worry, and intense nervousness even in a situation where there is no alarm.

- Stress in a personal relationship: Stress from personal relationships such as marriage, courtship, and friendship may also lead to anxiety. This is very common for individuals who are in abusive relationships. Narcissistic abuse victims are known to suffer from anxiety and panic attacks many years after getting out of such relationships. If you realize that a close friend is showing any of the above symptoms after getting into a new relationship, you have the responsibility to help him/her. You should help such a person get out of an abusive relationship or at least, make them open about the situation. If a person who is in a stressful relationship speaks out, he/she may be able to find the needed help. In most cases, individuals who are in stressful relationships lose their sobriety. Their thinking gets clouded by the relationship. They are unable to make decisions or choices that are beneficial for their life and are vulnerable to more abuse. External help from friends and family may go a long way in helping such individuals.

- Financial stress: Lack of finances is also another situation that may drive a person to the wall. This often occurs to men, who are deemed as breadwinners in most families. If a person feels that they are being devalued due to a lack of money, they may plunge into depression. It is important for all of us to be watchful and helpful of any individuals who may be suffering from financial stress. Such individuals can be helped via financial counseling and financial advice.

- Stress from an emotional trauma such as the death of a loved one: This is a common cause of anxiety and panic attacks. If you lose someone so close to you, it may take long before you attain full healing. Individuals who have lost dear family members have to spend a lot of time thinking about their past experiences with their loved ones. They are constantly lost in their thoughts thinking about the good times they shared with their loved ones. It is important to ensure that we all pay close attention to friends who suffer such loses. If we can stay close and show love to such individuals, it is easy for them to heal and recover from the psychological trauma. For such individuals, they only suffer due to denial. Refusing to come to terms with reality and living in a false world may cause a victim of such traumatic events to stay in anxiety for a long time. However, if the victims can be helped to come to terms with the occurrences, healing is easily achieved.

- Stress from a serious medical illness: Medical conditions can cause stress and anxiety to some people too. This is common when a person is diagnosed with a chronic condition. Some diseases are associated with death or excruciating pain. It is also such diseases that are associated with stigma. For instance, individuals diagnosed with cancer or HIV are likely to suffer from anxiety. If you realize that a person who is close has been diagnosed by such conditions, the best solution is to offer a helping hand. Most people diagnosed with chronic conditions end up dying not because they were unable to handle the condition but because of stigma. If you can keep your friends who suffer from deep conditions close, you may help reduce anxiety and panic attacks.

- Side Effects of Drugs: There is no doubt about the fact that some drugs affect the normal functioning of the brain. If you are undergoing medication, your body must experience changes. The same applies to anxiety. Some drugs may cause nervousness and anxiety. Some of the common drugs that may cause anxiety include alcohol, caffeine, and cocaine among others. The same case applies to some prescription medicinal drugs such as Ritalin and amphetamines. These drugs may lead a person to feel light-headed and as a result, lead to panic attacks and anxiety.

- Symptoms of medical illness: Individuals who have suffered from panic attacks are always afraid of suffering from the same. This may lead to fear and constant worry, especially if the patient suffers from illnesses such as stroke and heart attack. Since the symptoms of heart diseases are like panic attacks, the patients of such diseases may suffer panic attacks when the symptoms of the illness show up.

- Lack of oxygen in circumstances as diverse as high altitude: Oxygen or lack of it may lead to panic attacks. When a person is in a place where there is no enough supply of oxygen, the breathing mechanism of the body is distorted. At high altitudes, a person has to breathe heavily and randomly. Due to the low supply of oxygen, the victim also must experience an increased heart rate. All these factors contribute to the feelings of fear and worry. If a person has experienced a panic attack before, these symptoms may be too familiar and may lead to another panic attack right away. It is common for persons who have suffered from panic attacks to associated accelerated breathing and increased heart rate to panic attacks.

Generally, any person who fears or worries about something or the future will experience panic attacks. The things we worry about are not threatening. If you examine the reasons why you are afraid, you will realize that there is nothing alarming. If you suffer from anxiety or panic attacks, chances are that you have build up the fear within your mind. This leads us to the other cause of anxiety.

Internal causes of anxiety

The internal causes of anxiety are factors that are built within your mind. There is a close relationship between your mind, your emotions, and your behavior. If you show symptoms of anxiety, chances are that your mind has been corrupted by factors that you have allowed to grow internally. Some of the internal causes of anxiety include

Bitterness: Internal bitterness occurs when you choose to hold on to a situation that caused you pain. Bitterness is a state of emotion where an individual is constantly bitter due to events that occurred many years ago. Bitterness may stay within a person either consciously or subconsciously. If you harbor bitterness subconsciously, you may never know the causes of your anxiety. You will find yourself treating people around you as suspects, without knowing that your actions are informed by past life experiences.

Anger: Anger is another situation that may cause anxiety and panic attacks in a person. This is especially true if you let anger stay within your heart and mind for a long time. Through life circumstances, we all come to situations that may cause anger and bitterness. However, the way you deal with such a situation will determine whether you will live a free life or not. If you allow anger to stay within, it will eventually breed negativity, leading you to live a negative lifestyle. Living your life with a negative perspective will lead to anxiety and panic attacks. When you build up a negative perspective of life, you will never see any positive in any matter. You associate everyone and everything around you with negativity. This may be a dangerous place for anyone who wishes to live a happy life and enjoy love, success, and prosperity.

Fear: Fear is an emotional situation where an individual is constantly worried about the future or the past. The fact that you are worried about the future or the past is entrenched within your personality. Fear is mainly caused by past life experiences. The human brain creates an emotional association to past events. If you experience a positive event in your life, the brain will naturally associate such an event with positive emotions. If you experience a negative event or an event that caused negative emotions, you will naturally associate such an event with negativity. It is, therefore, important to ensure that you clear your mind of any events that may be associated with negativity. Negativity may mess up your normal thinking process and infiltrate your mind with fear or such like occurrences.

Beliefs and stereotypes: The human brain works in such a way that, whatever you feed it accepts it as the truth. When you tell your brain that something is bad and it believes it, it becomes impossible to overturn the situation. This is the reason why the world suffers from racism and tribalism. When most people are growing up, they are made to believe that a certain race or a certain tribe behaves in one way or another. Such beliefs are entrenched deep within a person, making that person a stone believer. Beliefs and stereotypes may lead to anxiety and panic attacks. If you believe that a certain person is dangerous based on their gender, race or tribe, you may experience fear in their presence.

Your intense fear and worry are not based on the fact that the said person is a threat, but it is based on the fact that you have allowed beliefs to take control of your mind. Allowing beliefs to take over can mess up the way you think and cause you to live in constant fear of the unknown.

# Chapter 4
# Understanding Anxiety

Anxiety is classified as an emotion; yet unlike love or joy, we tend to see it as something negative that is not supposed to be a part of our lives. However, since the earliest days that humans walked the earth, anxiety has served a purpose. It is a sensation that is intended to call us to alertness. It triggers the fight or flight reaction that has guided us for millennia in making our decisions when under stress. Yet, today, we tend to see it only as a negative and useless emotion. The question is why?

Despite us having changed the equatorial jungle for a concrete jungle, we are still in need of that early warning system that kept primitive humans safe. Anxiety can let us know when we don't feel comfortable in a situation or with a certain person. It can alert us to aspects of our psyche that require further development, and in small doses, it improves our mental functioning–allowing us to score better in tests and tasks that require heightened focus. Despite these valuable functions of anxiety, we want to stunt it today by medicating ourselves into fallaciously flavored bliss. What a loss this is to the human race, if we remove our ability to create awareness of our inner self and the world around us! For most of us, anxiety is that friend that we don't really want to play with, but they tag along with us, despite our best efforts to shoo them away. What if you turned back and decided to really look at anxiety, measure it up for its worth, its impact on your life, and begin to negotiate with it?

Unfortunately, some of us really struggle to face that uncertain playmate on our own, and when we lack the skills, and are not born with the talent to wrap up anxiety with a neat bow, we can succumb to depression and anxiety-related psychological disorders. When you don't know how to adequately address your anxieties, you could succumb to panic disorders, Post Traumatic Stress Disorder (PTSD), and other mental illnesses. When you feel unable to deal with your anxiety and your worries on your own, there is no shame in reaching out for professional help.

Why Do We Get Anxiety?

Psychologists will all tell you that anxiety is a normal emotion. It only becomes a problem when it goes into overdrive and begins reducing your abilities to cope with life. This can be best seen in extreme cases such as people who are so anxious about the world around them that they become reclusive and shut themselves off from society completely. For these people, the things that trigger their anxieties are simply more than they can face.

We can recognize the symptoms of anxiety quite easily. We have all, at some stage and to differing degrees, suffered the hyper-tension, pounding heart, raised blood pressure, and gnawing worries of anxiety that seem to dominate and destroy your life. If you continually suffer from anxiety in a certain setting or with certain people, you will likely begin to see these as triggers that set off the flood of anxiety. In turn, you will begin to fear those triggers and do everything in your power to avoid them. Sadly, this does not cure the anxiety, and you would be better served to start really looking at those triggers and what your anxiety is trying to tell you.

In the past, the triggers were situations or creatures that threatened us, and we had to decide whether we would fight off the predators, or if we would run from the stronger clan that moved onto our terrain. Today, the triggers may look different and instead of facing a saber-toothed tiger, we may be facing a vicious boss who dominates us or a relative that abuses us. Anxiety is the warning sign that something is going on, and it needs your attention (and decision-making skills) right now.

We commonly tend to say that we are stressed when we are actually feeling anxious, but whichever term you use, anxiety can have positive benefits to you in small and controlled amounts. The benefits can even outweigh the potential negatives of anxiety (Star, 2019).

- Self-Growth

Anxiety can help you learn about yourself. It can make you more aware of people, places, and situations that make you uncomfortable. We are often in denial about what we feel throughout our day, and if we keep avoiding an inconvenient truth about how we feel, anxiety tends to crop up to draw our attention back to that avoidance. Next time you feel anxious about someone, take the time to ask yourself why. You may have been conditioned to be polite to someone when actually there is something about them that sets your warning bells ringing. Feeling anxious may be a result of loads of tiny stimuli that you have not even consciously been aware of noticing. You may find a certain look that someone gives you to be disturbing, yet you try and avoid thinking of this observation since it goes against how you are preconditioned to treat that person. Unease, disquiet, and suspicions are all derivatives of anxiety that help you evaluate whether people can be trusted or not.

- Motivator

You can use the energy of anxiety to become more motivated. Like the early humans were able to get that extra boost of energy to run away from predators, you can use the energy to increase your mental awareness, physical alertness, and thinking skills. However, if you let anxiety overwhelm you, it will lead to draining your motivation and can trigger depression. That energy has to go somewhere, so it's better that you channel it constructively. In a mentally trying situation such as writing a test, a small amount of anxiety helps you focus and recall all that you have learned. However, in a social setting such as going on a date, the energy may present as being nervous and could end up costing you a pleasant evening. In this case, you would need to channel that energy into a positive direction such as a mindfulness task, a distraction, or even physical movement. This is why dancing is such a great icebreaker for those who are prone to feeling a little anxious.

- Safety

Healthy amounts of anxiety keep us alert to potential dangers in life. It is what makes us look before crossing a road, and it helps us to avoid situations that could cause us harm. Being utterly fearless would lead us into situations and places where we will likely be injured and seriously harmed. In this sense, small amounts of anxiety are equivalent to common sense. It helps us realize that something is dangerous before we are hurt.

- Fosters Empathy

If you know anxiety, and you have learned to look it in the face, you will have developed a much treasured and often rare skill–empathy. You will understand that people are not always feeling up to a challenge, and that it's okay to be scared. Instead of telling people (and yourself) to suck it up, you will be able to help them (and yourself) live peaceful and self-embracing lives.

- Makes for Good Leaders

Healthy amounts of anxiety can lead to being cautious, considering what happens, and what could happen. This stimulates effective planning and responsible decision making. In excessive amounts, anxiety can make leaders act obsessively and take decisions based on unrealistic fears, though many highly passionate leaders throughout history have displayed the traits of anxiety, which might explain some controversial decisions that they made.

Anxiety may have many positives to those who are able to tame their inner fears and develop the skills to conquer and use it. However, if you do not learn how to manage your anxiety, you will fall subject to its whims, and like a fickle ruler, it can ruin your life.

## You Are Not Alone

One of the biggest challenges to you if you suffer from anxiety is that you probably believe you are the only one who is dealing with those nagging worries, negative thoughts, cold sweats, sleep deprivation, numbness, nausea, and a whole list of other embarrassing and painful symptoms. You probably feel like a massive failure and a loser. News flash—you are not alone.

Since anxiety is a normal emotion, we all "suffer" from it from time to time. Suffering from anxiety is, however, your choice. You can choose to think of it as the enemy; or you can accept that it is normal, we all have it, and you can learn to control and use it. It may be painful to initially make that mind shift but once you do, it will vastly improve your approach to life, and the way in which you think about your fears.

In the digital age that we live in with information at our fingertips, we are constantly surrounded by fear-inspiring news, overwhelming and often fake standards that are promulgated on social media, and the pressure of staying connected and online. The fear of missing out (FOMO) can be hugely detrimental to our existence, and we become anxious when we're not able to be online or participate in Internet-driven activities. Oddly, in being "connected" in the age of technology, we have become very disconnected from ourselves. In knowing yourself, making peace with your feelings, and accepting your needs, as well as meeting them holistically, you can overcome the fear-driven behaviors of anxiety.

# Chapter 5

# What is Buddhism?

Buddhism is more popular today than it was half a century ago. Many people have realized that they would like to pursue this way of life, especially because of the amazing benefits it provides for the mind and body. When you decide to pursue Buddhism, your main goal is to obtain a state of lasting, unconditional happiness known as enlightenment. Every Buddhists goal is to reach enlightenment and to be able to reach this, you must use practical tools like meditation to gain your insight and develop compassion and wisdom. Every single person is able to tap into their potential and realize that the ultimate goal is enlightenment.

Buddhism is a way of life that will lead to the discernment of what true reality is. Its focus is to help you develop the ability to be mindful and be aware of your actions, thoughts, and surroundings. All of these will initially lead to a life that is fully in tune with nature and your true self within. It may be hard to get a grasp on at first, but everything that happens in your life is dictated by your thoughts and emotions and when you meditate, you will get a clearer look at what needs to change in your world, as well as discovering more about who is in relation to the bigger picture that you are apart of and the world that you live in, as well as the body that you inhabit.

One of the most important teachings in Buddhism is the understanding that where you are in this exact moment is exactly where you are supposed to be. As every event comes and time passes, you are following your own course throughout life and enjoying everything that comes to you. Each moment plays an important part in creating a path of wisdom and understanding just for yourself. Take in each and every sentence and take the time to fully understand what you are doing. Every teaching can pave the way to a more joyful, enlightened, and open path in your life.

Buddhism is actually not a religion technically, at least not in the sense that there is an institution that dictates how somebody should believe in specific higher power. Many people make the mistake of believing that Buddhism has that characteristic and they end up avoiding it because they don't want it to be contrary to the teachings they experience in a church. But you can, in fact, practice Buddhism at the same time as your personal beliefs and/or religion, and it will only compliment it.

In Buddhism, there isn't a god to be worshipped, although there are worshipping statues called Buddhas, Buddhist just pay respect to the memory of the Buddha. It always helps as a guide to what you are doing. Buddha is neither worshipped nor prayed, too. He is simply a guide and teacher for those that seek the initial path to enlightenment. The altars you may see while exploring Buddhism are simply an inspiration and are there to remind people to practice the path they have chosen to walk.

Many people that wake up in the morning intending to practice Buddhist teachings often find inspiration from the image of Buddha. It is not like finding your motivation from the words of a successful figure. His peaceful and meditative image can help you understand the teaching you are following when life becomes stressful and your mind begins to run off course.

The main practices of Buddhism include yoga and meditation. They are meant to help you unlearn and break away from your past preconceived notions of yourself and the world. They will serve as your guide towards fully embracing qualities like love, wisdom, kindness, and awareness. Over the course of your youth, you are taught the values of your society and they may not be in tune with true values which is why the reminder is needed. Look at all of the uncertainty that resides in the world, and at the bottom of it all, you will always a find a line of thought that leads you to the unhappiness that you experience in your life.

Those who continue to participate in the path of Buddhism often find themselves achieving the state of enlightenment. In other words, they become a Buddha. A Buddha is simply being someone who has been able to see the nature of life for what it truly is. An enlightened being will then continue to live life fully, all while holding onto the principles that are in line with this specific vision. Since your philosophy of Buddhism may question your current values, you need to stay open-minded enough to learn the teachings because they are very direct. To reach the ultimate goal of enlightenment, you will need to let go of the values that may, at the current time, be essential to who you are.

In other belief systems, these are given names, often known as the soul. Although you can give it any name, it is important what you decide to name it for yourself. It is important that you recognize that these two parts of you exist. If you are unhappy in your life, your balance and harmony are essentially missing and that is where Buddhism can help you align your values so that both parts of you are in harmony with each other.

Every human being has the opportunity to become enlightened in whatever life they decide to live, there is no set course for your life. Karma plays a major part in deciding the circumstances of your life, especially in which you will be born from life to life. Your own spiritual and mental ambition and how you embrace it is what drives each person to take the step closer to enlightenment. When you follow the path of Buddhism, you do not have one big goal for the end. It is a paradox for someone to declare they are using Buddhism just to reach enlightenment.

# Chapter 6

# Who is Buddha?

The word "Buddha" translates back to "enlightened one" or "awakened being." It refers to any person that has reached this state, however, here are some things you may want to know about the real Buddha.

According to ancient legend, the first Buddha was named Siddhartha Gautama. Most people believe that he was born in the B.C. time era, in a land that is now found in Nepal. It is said that the Buddha was born a royal and shielded from the suffering of the kingdom that his father build, a grand palace that was full of religion and suffering. Buddha had an entire world created within that walls of the castle, and as Buddha grew, he was led to believe that the world outside was one made of empathy, joy, and happiness. The king was told by fortune tellers that when his son was born, he would be a great spiritual leader and a warrior.

Later in Buddha's life, after he was raised and has been married, he ventured out into the real world and saw everything that his father had been hiding from him. He saw the truth of humanity and met an old man, which he then gained the knowledge that all people age and eventually die. After figuring all of this out, he then decided he wanted to go out into the world and explore as many religions across the world as he could to find the answer to the questions we would all ask ourselves such as "where do we find happiness?" He tried many ways including fasting and when he found that fasting was irrelevant, he decided to meditate on the problems he faced. While others still decided to fast, he decided to go about finding another route, one that would lead to enlightenment.

Several years into his spiritual adventure, Buddha encountered something called "The Middle Path" while meditating under a tree. This path was a way of balance without using extreme measures which he found only through many trials and much error. Buddha sat under the tree for days seeking the answers he had set out for. During this meditation, Buddha had to face a demon known as Mara who had threatened to stand in the way of his Buddha status. He looked to mother earth for answers and the land answered by banishing Mara and allowing Buddha to reach complete enlightenment. After this life-changing experience, while meditating, Buddha lived the rest of his life trying to inform and share with everything that he had discovered. People began to follow his ways and eventually named his principle the Dharma, which translates back to "Truth."

When you hear the word suffering, you instantly think of pain and anger, but in Buddhism, they believe that all of life is suffering. As humans, we feel the pain of life which includes loss, happiness, sadness, disappointment, and so on. These emotions are manifestations of our mind, and they don't come from our inner self. Because they do not come from one's inner self, they are depicted as suffering. These are initially false feelings that were created by our brains and programmed into us by what our society has taught us. The way forward was believed to be the Noble Eightfold Path and this allowed people to get closer to reaching enlightenment.

In this day and age, Buddhism is increasingly becoming a popular way of life for millions of people all around the world. People generally like the concept of Buddhism just because what they find speaks to their heart and that is how it should be. Regardless of what your views and values are if Buddhism speaks to you, it is encouraged that you explore the teachings and try to pursue it, but only if you want to and if you feel it is right for you. Scientists and researchers have explored the relationship between the Buddhist teachings and the way that the brain operates, they found that Buddhist monks were able to use the creative side of their brain and the calculating side of their brain at the time, therefore, more open to creativity.

In a world where everything is in constant motion, always forcing us to move forward at a quicker and more rapid pace, many people lose their connection with nature and the connection with themselves. Though nature is all around us, what we have done as human beings to change the pure form of the earth creates a disconnection from our minds. In Buddhism, you are reminded to be constantly connected with every natural thing in the world, and by practicing the teachings of Buddhism, you are brought back to a connection with the earth. Think of it as connecting back to your original roots.

If you are unsure of what this means, you only have to go back to nature to get inspired. The feelings you experience don't just come from your external stimuli. They come from your inner self recognizing the joy that lies in the ever-moving thing called nature. Go up to the mountains and ground yourself with the beauty this world beholds. Another reason why Buddhism is so widespread around the world is the fact that the Buddha never claimed to be a god. Instead, he wanted to be seen as a teacher and somebody that helped others with his wisdom based on his own experiences in life.

Buddhism can be found in every natural effect on mother earth, from the worms in the soil to the leaves on the trees. They are the story of the past, but you don't need to look to the past to find enlightenment. To find enlightenment, you have to look at all of the moments that you experience. Buddhists never seek to convince others of a certain belief. Instead, they only provide an explanation of it if they are asked. Buddha encourages one to be curious through awareness, therefore, Buddhism can be seen more as a way of life that is based on discernment rather than faith like most are.

Mindfulness forms a very important part of the philosophy of Buddhism. You are losing the opportunity to enjoy when you are not present at that moment that you are in. Regardless of how many problems you encounter in life, being mindful can help you to overcome any obstacles that are placed in your way and to get beyond those problems in healthy ways.

Buddhism is an awareness of self, awareness of your surroundings, and awareness of others. Without this awareness, you lose out on a lot of benefits. By having awareness, you are able to empathize with others and encourage them to do the same. You are also then able to control the way that you interact with others and keep your negativity to a bare minimum. Whether you decide to realize it or not, all of your unhappiness stems from you. Although you may feel the need to blame others for any negative feelings you are experiencing. Buddhism helps you to understand this impact and to work on lessening the impact it has on you.

# Chapter 7

# The Teachings of Buddhism

The Way of Investigation

The very first teaching of Buddha is to investigate everything and not accept anything that is based on blind faith. He advised people to discover the truth of everything and anything that they encounter. He pointed out that most of the problems were induced by believing in things that are not based on tradition. The right way to accept things is to have an open mind and dig a little deeper into the development, origin, and characteristics of things, just so that you know the whole truth about everything. Similarly, he said that people should only explore Buddhism after investigating meditation and thinking about Buddhism while using meditation.

Four Noble Truths

During the course of Buddha's life, especially while working towards reaching enlightenment, Buddha discovered the four noble truths. These are the truths you need to accept and understand if you want to reach complete happiness and peace in your life.

The first truth of Buddhism is the 'Truth of Dukkha', which states that each of us is affected by some sort of suffering in this world. There are two types of suffering: physical and mental. Mental problems are the emotional disturbances we experience after going through a traumatic experience or difficult time in life and physical suffering refers to the physical harm, pain, and injury we experience.

The second truth in Buddhism is 'the truth regarding the creation of dukkha'. This truth explains that the main cause of suffering is your ignorance and desires. Ignorance is not being conscious of the reality of things and just completely living a life of delusion. Desires refer to all of your wants that make you indulge in practices that bring different kinds of harm and pain to your life.

The third truth in Buddhism is 'the truth pertinent to the ending of all suffering'. This truth states that by working on eliminating all of the things in your life that are negative or bring negativity from your mind and life, you can rid your life of all sufferings and reach the state of complete peace, serenity, and happiness.

The fourth truth to Buddhism is 'the truth of following the middle way that ends all dukkha'. This truth is said to contain complete peace and happiness. You need to follow the middle way, also known as the eightfold noble path. By following this path, you can live a more balanced life, which is neither careless nor too difficult. It is just perfect and helps you live a perfectly happy and beautiful life.

Eightfold path

The eightfold noble path is known as the middle way that sets out the guidelines you need to follow to deal with every type of hardships and sufferings. This way of life compromised of eight rules that you follow when you are following Buddhism.

Samma ditthi or right view/understanding: You need to reevaluate your understanding of things and view things the right way so that you can gain complete insight into them. This means correcting your view of this life and not getting attracted to the worldly pleasures and desires because when this happens, you become very involved in this world and strive just to obtain those pleasures that will eventually result in suffering. Try to mentally understand what you really desire in your life that will ultimately bring you the absolute happiness in your life and not just temporary happiness that is brought to you by the worldly possessions and desires. Secondly, you need to understand that you inflict suffering on yourself with or without knowing it, so end it and correct your vision of things.

Samma Sankappa or Right Thought: Next, you need to focus on correcting your thought process, which can be accomplished if you correct your intention. For that, you need to reject the pleasures the world tries to dangle in front of you and instead bring love, kindness, and compassion for others in your thoughts.

Samma Vacca or Right Speech: You need to work on correcting your speech and the way you speak to people, which can be done if you practice abstinence from bad grammar, gossip, cruel speech, arguing, and idle chitchatting.

Samma Kammanta or Right Action: You must improve your actions and correct them by giving yourself a cleansing and ridding yourself of all sorts of sexual misconducts, destructive, and illegal actions.

Samma Ajiva or Right Livelihood: You need to work on the way that you make a living and must not do anything that will harm any other living being. Buddha instructed that you absolutely cannot practice these five professions: dealing in ammunition and arms, dealing in the flesh (butcher), dealing in sex and human trafficking, dealing in any sort of drugs, and dealing in any poisonous substances.

Samma Vayama or Right Effort: You need to correct your efforts. For that, you need to think in the right direction which may be a different direction. The sixth, seventh, and eighth factors are interlinked and closely related.

Samma Satti or Right Mindfulness: You need to work on reaching the state of mindfulness, which means you need to be aware of everything that is happening inside you and around you. This can be reached by practicing the eighth factor.

Samma Samadhi or Right Concentration: Lastly, you need to work on your concentration and focus. You must be fully concentrated on a subject to be aware of it and to understand it better. Right effort, concentration, and mindfulness can only be reached with meditation; hence, meditation is a very important tool of Buddhism.

By following these eight factors, you can live a more balanced, smooth, and composed life that is free of all sufferings.

## Karma

Karma refers to actions that humans make and the law of action. It states that every single action has a reaction. If you do bad things, bad things consume your speech, body, and mind and harm you, then you will get painful results that you may not like. If you are living a life full of hardships, then it is a reflection of the bad things you chose to do.

## Rebirth

Buddha believed in rebirth. He states that the reason why some people are born rich or poor is because of the good or bad things they did in their lives. According to Buddha, a person is born many times and rebirth goes far beyond the human realm and into the spiritual realm. He believed that people could be born as an animal, a bird, or even a spirit. The different realms that exist within are the human realm, grim and lower realms, ghost realm, animal and bird realm, and heavenly realm. Human beings can come or go into any of those realms if they desire.

# Chapter 8
# The Four Noble Truths

When Buddha started teaching about his enlightenment, he started with the Four Noble Truths. In these truths, Buddha is teaching about suffering, its cause, how there is an end to suffering, and what to do so you can end suffering.

## Dukkha

Dukkha is the truth that states that suffering exists. Dukkha is real and universal, and there are several causes of suffering. Some of these causes are sickness, the impermanence of pleasure, and pain. Dukkha states that our suffering often starts because we have a desire that we can't fulfill.

No matter what we want, we continue to suffer because when we reach one goal, we want more. This is human nature, and Buddhists feel that in order to fully reach the path of enlightenment, we need to understand dukkha and take control of it so that we can control our suffering and take the next step toward entering the pure state of mind. An example of this is money. How often do we state that if we just had more money, we could buy a nicer car or a bigger house? However, once we attain this level of wealth, we still want more money because we want more things.

## Samudaya

Samudaya states that there is a cause for suffering, which is the desire to control things. Some people refer to this as the cravings or thirst for things that we can't have at the moment. There can be many forms of samudaya, such as the desire for fame, craving of sexual pleasures, and the desire to avoid unpleasant sensations, such as anger, jealousy, and fear. Buddhists also state that this craving creates karma, which is what makes you want more. When we suffer, we are ignoring karma because we are too worried about our own selfish desires and wishes.

When we let suffering take over, it's because we've let go of what really matters and started to focus on our wants. For instance, we start looking toward our neighbors to see what they have in life, and we begin to want that. We want the bigger car, the bigger house, and nicer clothes. We work on trying to impress others instead of focusing on compassion, understanding, keeping our minds clear, and karma. We also start blaming others for our own problems instead of looking inside ourselves to see if we can find an answer and cure for our problems.

In the eyes of Buddha, anything that made you unhappy or took away your peace was a cause of suffering. When the word suffering came to Buddha, it didn't just have to do with seeing people become sick, die, or get physically hurt. It also had to do with allowing ourselves to become unhappy, clouding our minds with unwelcome thoughts, such as "I have this, but it's not good enough, so now I want this."

# Nirodha

Nirodha gives us the realization that there is an end to suffering, and this comes when we finally reach the liberation of nirvana. In Buddhism, the only true way to end suffering is to end your wants and wishes and your selfish desires. You need to become free of those thoughts. In order to do this, you need to understand the right view from the Eightfold Path. Only then will you be able to realize that suffering can end if we let go of what we want and find happiness within ourselves. Once this is attained, we let go of all the cravings we have and are truly free of our suffering.

# Megga

Megga is the fourth Noble Truth, which states that the only way we can work toward ending our suffering is by following the Eightfold Path, or the Middle Path. To end suffering, you need to follow a path. One of the best ways to understand this path of ending suffering, along with the Four Noble Truths, is to look at this as if you had an illness. For example, dukka is the diagnosis. This is the part where the doctor tells you what illness you have, and you come to realize that you have this illness. The next step of the process is finding the cause. What caused this illness? In other words, what caused this suffering that you've realized is inside of you? The third step, which is nirodha, is the treatment phase of the process. Now that you have observed you're suffering and you've found the cause, you can come up with a plan to help treat the suffering. The final phase, which is megga, is the recovery phase. This is the part where you've been able to get through the suffering and you're liberated.

Of course, it's important to realize and remember that no matter how hard we try, we can't get rid of suffering in the world. It's just part of life, and we need to learn to deal with it and, at times, overcome it. We suffer when we are born; we just have no remembrance of it. We also suffer when we are growing up and growing old. We also suffer because of death and other situations that happen in our lives, such as heartaches. Buddhism isn't about getting rid of suffering or finding ways, so you don't have to feel like you are suffering; it's more about working to ease the suffering. Buddhism can work to try to give you an understanding of your suffering and why suffering exists in this world.

# Chapter 9

# Karma, Nirvana, Reincarnation

## Karma

As indicated by the British savant Alan Watts, Karma in Buddhist and Hindu way of thinking shows "The related origin of the considerable number of structures and periods of life." You can't just credit an Eastern way of thinking to a Western perspective without having a nearby take a gander at its cause. You need to think about that Karma is a piece of a greater roundabout, profound picture. It includes rebirth and realizing that everything is associated. Western thought doesn't give space for us to imagine that we are the texture of the universe. Be that as it may, we are.

Buddhism instructs us that we are not minor, unimportant bits on a desolate little planet. We are, in certainty, a piece of everything around us, and everything that happens is occurring as it should. It isn't dependent upon us to control our general surroundings. We need to control what is inside ourselves, and this way, we become some portion of everything.

Karma includes the possibility of congruity with a pattern. Individuals search for designs all over the place. It is a piece of our characteristic make-up and a central explanation behind the endurance of our species. At the point when history rehashes itself, it will, in general, do as such with great karma or terrible karma. Karma rises above numerous cycles of life, so you won't receive the rewards of what you sow in this lifetime.

Karma isn't a momentary reward framework. It is a lot of qualities that are intended to encourage all of us to improve. The greater individuals do, the greater will happen to it. You shouldn't be in it for yourself, yet for the development of more noteworthy benefits. The individuals on the planet will continue evolving. They will travel every which way. Be that as it may, the more individuals cling to the lessons of karma, the better the world will become for everybody.

Consider a war that has been continuing for a considerable length of time or hundreds of years. The individuals battling the war today are not the individuals who began the war. On the off chance that you think negative musings and perform damaging activities, the karmic cycle of antagonism and decimation will proceed. Individuals need to settle on a cognizant choice to change dangerous examples of conduct. They have to spread cherishing consideration and sincere goals to break the unlimited cycles of war. It requires more significant levels of reasoning and comparable profound qualities. Everybody needs to make an individual commitment to achieve the undertaking of realizing harmony known to humanity.

Karma directs; in case you plant an oak seed, an oak will develop. The oak will deliver oak seeds, and the cycle of development will proceed. In the event that you plant a spoiled seed, nothing will develop. That is karma.

Karma as activity and response: if we show goodness, we will procure goodness.

Karma is the all-inclusive standard of circumstances and logical results. Our activities, both great and awful, return to us later on, helping us to gain from life's exercises and become better individuals. In religions that incorporate resurrection, karma reaches out through one's present life and all past and future lives also.

Karma, in itself, is basic energy. One individual tosses out energy through considerations, words, and activities, and it returns, in time, through other individuals. Karma is the best educator, compelling individuals to confront the outcomes of their behavior and along these lines improve and refine their conduct or endure in the event that they don't. Indeed, even brutal karma, when looked in insight, can be the best flash for profound development. The triumph of karma lies in clever activity and dispassionate reaction.

Supporting any activity, with the case, "I am doing it," is karma. Affirming any activity ties karma, and then, the binding karma supports the action with the conviction 'I am the practitioner.' In the event that you realize that you are not the practitioner and know about who the genuine practitioner is, 'I am not the practitioner' and 'who is the practitioner' at that point, the activity won't have any help, and the karma will be shed.

## Nirvana

The term Nirvana in Buddhism is mostly used to show the definitive spiritual objective of accomplishing a condition of enlightenment which discharges one from the cycle of rebirth. The term alludes to the dousing of three flames inside oneself, every one of which speaks to ravenousness, disdain, and daydream, with the goal that one can arrive settled and profound satisfaction. Present-day elucidations recommend a "nirvana in this life" is conceivable reliant on a changed condition of the character described by empathy, harmony, profound otherworldly delight, and a nonappearance of negative mental states and feelings, for example, question, stress, tension, and dread.

## Reincarnation

According to the Buddha, we all will pass away in the end in the regular procedure of birth, mature age, and demise and that we ought to consistently remember the fleetingness of life: The existence that we as a whole appreciate and wish to hang on to.

To Buddhism, death isn't the end of life, it is simply the termination of our body in this world, yet our soul will, in any case, remain and search out through the need of connection, connection to another body, and new life. Where they will be conceived is an aftereffect of the past and the amassing of positive and negative activity, and the resultant karma (circumstances and logical results) is a consequence of one's past activities.

This would prompt the individual to be re-awakened in one of 6 domains, which are; paradise, people, Asura, hungry apparition, creature, and hellfire. Domains, as per the seriousness of one's karmic activities, Buddhists accept in any case, none of these spots are perpetual, and one doesn't stay in wherever uncertainly. Therefore, in Buddhism, life doesn't end; it simply goes on in different structures that are the aftereffect of gathered karma. Buddhism is a conviction that underlines the temporariness of lives, including every one of those past the present life. In light of this, we ought not to fear to pass as it will prompt resurrection.

The dread of death originated from the dread of the stop to be existent and losing one's personality and a dependable balance on the planet. We see our passing coming sometime before its appearance, and we see fleetingness in the progressions we see about us and to us in the appearance of maturing and the enduring due to losing our childhood. When we were solid and lovely and as we age, as we approach our last snapshots of life, we understand how short-lived such an agreeable spot really was.

The idea of resurrection or rebirth has gotten increasingly prominent in the west as of late because of the impact of Tibetan Buddhism. Normally individuals worry about life past death was animated by the thoughts contained in such methods of reasoning and convictions.

The incomparable point of Buddhism is to acquire nirvana or illumination. This shows a condition of freedom or brightening from the impediments of presence. It is the freedom from the push of resurrection through incalculable lives here, and there the six realities. It is gotten through the termination of want.

Nirvana is an express that is realistic in this life through the correct yearning, immaculateness of life, and the disposal of narcissism. This discontinuance of presence as we probably are aware of it, the achievement of being, as particular from turning out to be. The Buddha discusses it as unborn, un-began, uncreated, unformed, standing out it from the conceived, started, made, and shaped the extraordinary world. The individuals who have acquired the province of Nirvana are called Buddhas. Gautama Siddhartha had acquired this state and had become a Buddha at 35. Anyway, it is currently accepted that it was simply after he had passed away that he arrived at such a position of immaculate serenity since some buildup of human pollution would keep on existing as long as his physical body existed.

# Chapter 10

# Uncovering the Secret of Zen

## What Is Zen Meditation?

Zen Meditation is an outgrowth of Buddhism. Zen is primarily a Japanese development of Buddhism, but it does not have to be linked to that religion and can be practiced by anyone, anywhere. The word Zen is derived from "Chan," a Chinese school of Buddhism or possibly from the word dhyana, which simply means meditation. Whole books have been written tracing the development and etymology of the word "Zen," but you don't actually have to know any of that in order to be able to practice Zen meditation. Later on, you might want to read some of the extensive literature that is associated with Zen and with Buddhism as inspiration, but for right now our concern is simply what is meditation and how to do it.

Meditation can actually be a lot of different things. It can be a focused practice of mindfulness while doing repetitive manual tasks, such as shelling peas, washing dishes, digging ditches or mopping floors. It can be concentration on a candle flame, mandala or repeated syllables that are spoken out loud. It can be meditation-in-motion, such as is practiced by martial artists who learn a set of movements called forms or a set of asanas such as might be practiced in Yoga. But Zen takes meditation down to its very simplest and sometimes most difficult form: sitting meditation.

Sitting meditation is difficult because it does not give the body any way to distract and occupy the physical system while the mind is meditating. It is not sleep or daydreaming—although both of those things have been known to occur during meditation times. Those who have attended a Meeting of the Society of Friends of Jesus (otherwise known as Quakers) might have observed those times when some of the Elders in the meeting doze off while observing silence. Polite members of the Meeting will ignore the sonorous snores that sometimes punctuate such a gathering.

Sitting meditation can be exceptionally difficult for those who are accustomed to nearly constant movement, such as those whose work is physically active or demanding. It is equally difficult for the Millennium generation because they must unplug themselves, as it were, and cease data input for a span of time. But sitting meditation, or zazen, is the heart of Zen.

Sitting meditation has several steps, and it can be part of a more elaborate system of exercises such as yoga, ordinary exercise workouts or as the beginning or closing of a day. But it can also provide a time-out during a busy day that provides clarity and stills the busy mind that can become a distraction. These are actually simple steps and do not require elaborate preparation or extreme dedication. One follower

Chinese disciple of a follower of Buddha is said to have sat zazen so long that his legs fell off, and he is said to have later cut off his eyelids to keep from falling asleep.

Frankly, as a modern person who practices meditation, this writer classes these stories in the same category as the Paul Bunyan or Davie Crockett legends of the American west. Such tall tales are supreme exaggerations of real situations. Perhaps the original person sat so long that his legs fell asleep—not unusual once one is used to meditation; or perhaps he had a habit of going to sleep while supposedly meditating. Or, more likely, these were cautionary stories told to young monks by older ones who wanted appropriate action by the youngsters without extreme behavior.

One method to avoid sitting in meditation for an overly long amount of time or to gauge whether one has sat long enough is to invest in a timer that has a soft, bell-like chime. The regular kitchen timer with the annoying buzzer will keep track of time just as well, but the harsh sound can jangle nerves and partially defeat the serenity you might hope to achieve through meditation.

Let's face it: humans are not naturally serene. They are an argumentative, competitive, emotional lot that are more prone to rationalize than to think rationally. Meditation won't cure all of that, but it can help the practitioner hew out a space in his or her day to let the brain cells stop being busy with the tumbling thoughts that live in each of us. Once the chattering monkey mind is stilled, then inspiration, solutions to problems or just a wonderful sense of peace can rise to the surface.

Deeper in, even those things are stilled, and the self-perception stops, merging into a perception of Self as part of everything, and then simply perception of the Deep Stillness. Out of that stillness comes real Inspiration, the life-changing revelations—or not. Sometimes all that comes of it is a sense of peace, which can in and of itself be life changing.

Unless you are a very exceptional person, you won't get there the first time you try meditation; you might not even get there the fiftieth time. Leo Babauto, author of Zen Habits, writes that most people do not understand the art of doing nothing. While meditation isn't actually doing nothing—it is doing something—getting past the need to Do Something is one part of learning to meditate.

Robert Anson Heinlein, in his science fiction novel Glory Road wrote that Americans are a busy people. He went on to say that a Frenchman could easily sit at a café and wait, while the empty coffee cups piled up around him, but that the American culture is one that encourages industry-in-motion.

Perhaps that is why the early Zen movement in the United States overlapped with the drug counterculture. The whole idea of simply sitting down, sitting still and doing nothing was foreign to the mainstream American mind in the 1950s and 1960s. The 1970s showed a little promise, coming out of the consciousness raising sessions and communal experiments of the 60s, but the falling economy of the 1980s and continued budget crunch of the 90s through many people back into the "keep moving, make some money, survive" mode of living and thinking.

But no historical event is without the ability to teach; and no decade is without its gems of wisdom that can be passed on to the next generation of learners and thinkers. Zen entered Japan sometime around the 7th Century CE (Common Era) but did not fully develop until around the 12th Century. This was about the time of the ending of the Pax Romana in Europe and around the Mediterranean, and the beginning of what is sometimes referred to as the Dark Ages. In actual fact, the Pax Romana sort of whimpered its way out over time and never quite totally died, and the Dark Ages were actually a time when a number of new ideas and concepts emerged—but that is quite a different story, although one that is interesting. I digress.

Back to the topic at hand: Zen Meditation. Not all Zen masters fully agree on what constitutes Zen meditation, so it is no wonder that other people are a bit confused by it. The truth is that the practice is highly individual, although learning how to do it is facilitated by the presence of an experienced teacher. While there are a number of YouTube videos available currently that purport to instruct in the art of meditation (and some of them are not bad), there is no experience that is quite like being face-to-face with an experienced Zen meditation instructor. Which is not to say that one cannot learn to meditate without an instructor; but instruction can keep the new practitioner from chasing red herrings down mental rabbit holes, as it were.

For example, out in central Missouri in 1962 there were not a lot of Zen instructors available for a twelve-year-old girl who wanted to explore the concept. In fact, she fell into the practice quite by accident thanks to having ordered an illustrated book about Yoga. Yoga is made for the twelve-year-old body, which is still flexible enough to turn into a pretzel without days or even weeks of steady practice to stretch joints— although a spotter would have been nice when she was learning headstands.

Part of that Yoga book was devoted to meditation—sitting, standing, and lying down—meditation was something that a farm girl who spent a lot of time alone could easily do on those lazy afternoons when all of the adults were taking a siesta.

Now, let's fast forward that young woman about six years to her first year in college. She went to a Midwestern United States college that provided the opportunity for students to earn their tuition by working four hours every day. The girl's first job was in the college's candy kitchen—a hot, sticky place to work during the summer. One afternoon, the power went out and the supervisor and her crew were left sitting in an overly warm sub-basement while waiting for the air conditioning, lights and power to the stoves to come back on. The girl knew that one way to handily pass time and to block out physical discomfort was to pass that time in meditation. What she had not counted on was the panic her stillness and ability to ignore her surroundings would create in those who were not experienced in meditation. The supervisor actually shook her by the shoulder to bring her back up from deep meditation. This left her disorientated for several minutes, while she brought the real world back into focus.

Needless to say, this was a lesson learned. She never, after that, meditated in an area where there were inexperienced people about who would not understand that a person who is meditating needs to be brought back up to the real world gently. It is probable that the supervisor suspected that she had taken some sort of drug the year was 1970, after all but the girl had taken nothing. Having had eight years of sporadic, but frequent sessions of study and practice, she was very good at meditation. It should be noted here that for the beginner, sitting too long in meditation is far less of a problem than being able to judge how long one has been meditating. Humans just are not geared toward doing nothing. Really, they aren't—especially not these days. They are in the habit of always doing something—texting, playing video games, watching television, working, playing face-to-face games, talking, even exercising. Sitting down to meditate just might be one of the hardest things that a busy person can do. Setting a timer for the amount of time to be spent in actual meditation helps diminish the habit of meditating with one eye on the clock to see how many more minutes one is supposed to be continuing the activity. Clock watching is a distraction that no beginning meditator needs. In fact, one suspects that clock watching was one of the functions of a meditation teacher—although there are certainly others. For directions for how to get started with Zen Meditation if you do not have a teacher and anticipate having to practice alone for some time to come. That still, small place that is so huge when you get there is available to everyone, and does not require special equipment, special instruction or special anything. It is yours; now, let us go look for the path to find it.

# Chapter 11 Preparing for meditation

While meditation can be undertaken virtually anywhere, at any time, there are certain guidelines to follow if you want your meditation to be as effective as possible. However, keep in mind that meditation is meant to be flexible. The idea is not to create a rigid system that you will have a hard time following. Meditation aims to be easy and adaptable to suit your specific needs.

## Sitting And Posture

We start by discussing the five basic meditative postures. Your job is to determine which attitude works for you in most situations and stick to it. Although you have to follow a specific meditative posture for certain meditative exercises, most can also be adapted to alternative postures.

## Chair Meditation

Since most of us tend to have 9-to-5 jobs, we realistically tend to sit in some office chair for most of our time. Chair meditation is a great way to break through your afternoon monotony without ever having to leave your station. For seated meditation, you want to straighten your back and make sure you hit the floor with your feet. Ideally, your knees should be bent at a 90-degree angle and your back should be as straight as possible. If you're not sure what to do with your hands, just rest them on your knees.

## Standing Meditation

Sometimes you want to get out of your chair and it may be more pleasant to try a standing method. You will want to start standing so that your feet are shoulder-length apart. Bend your knees slightly and relieve pressure throughout your day down to your feet. As you do this, adjust your hands so that they are gently placed over your abdomen so that you can feel every breath moving through your body as you embark on your personal mission.

## Cross-Legged Meditation

Another pose that you can explore if you feel comfortable is the traditional Indian cross-legged. This particular posture is actually the most recommended posture of meditative activities, the idea being to keep your legs crossed, hips slightly higher than the heels of your feet. If you are new to meditation, it is generally recommended to try this pose with a pillow or towel or some kind of soft surface underneath so that you don't hurt yourself as it can be difficult to hold when that are not used to it. If you feel there is too much pressure on your heels, try bringing one of your legs over the other so that the ankle is one above the knee of the other leg. You can also bring full heels over the thighs of the other leg in what is commonly known as the Lotus position.

The Burmese pose is slightly different because you don't cross your legs. Instead, you can position your feet so that the ankles of each foot are bent inward and facing the pubic area - this pose is generally preferred by people who have a hard time crossing their legs.

## Kneeling Meditation

If you want to keep your back straight but don't feel comfortable crossing your legs, another great alternative is kneeling. Traditionally this is known as the Virasana or the Vajrasana. Here you start by bending your knees and resting your body weight along the length of your shins. Your ankles should be tucked under your buttocks. For convenience and comfort, you can choose to place a rolled-up yoga mattress or some type of tube between your buttocks and your knees.

This particular position is usually easier than sitting cross-legged and is also generally pain-free, so your ankles will thank you.

## Horizontal Meditation

However, if none of these positions suit you, or if you try a sleep-inducing meditation, you will find that the chosen posture is generally the horizontal posture. When laying down, make sure that your feet are shoulder-length, similar to the standing meditation position, and that your arms are at your sides instead of being folded over your body. If you find this position uncomfortable, you can bend your knees and lift your hips slightly to help yourself adjust.

## Tuning Into Physical Sensations

The physical world around you affects your mind. This is a fact we all know. What we don't necessarily notice is that just as the physical world affects our mind, so does our mind in turn affect our physical form. In the world of meditation, this form of comprehensive concept is called body sensation.

Think about the last time you were happy. In addition to being mentally excited, how did you feel on a physical level? Were you in pain? Did you find it difficult to move? Or did you feel uncomfortable for some reason?

Chances are you don't feel this - why? When you're happy and relaxed, you don't feel physically unwell. In fact, you feel lighter and more physically relaxed. At the same time, the exact opposite happens when you are dealing with some sort of emotional upset. For example, you may feel nauseated or uncomfortable if, for example, you panic before a major exam. Or you may feel listless when you are depressed or dealing with massive amounts of mental stress. Your body is a reflection of your mind. When you feel happy, your body is also happier, and you have more rest. While, when you are upset, your physical form tends to manifest in a way that reflects that negativity.

As you prepare to practice meditation, one of the things you want to make sure is that you are working on your ability to understand what your body is saying to you. The easiest way to do this is by practicing body sensation. Body sensors not only allow you to control your central nervous system and allow your mind to achieve a deeper form of mental and physical relaxation, it is also known to increase your body's natural resilience. This work will help you develop your ability to experience a more solid and constant sense of wholeness and well-being, in a way that is not attached to your external obstacles.

## Emotional Focus

As you prepare for your meditative journey, another factor to consider is Emotional Self Focus. One of the main goals of meditation is to promote self-care. It is even known that meditation itself has extremely therapeutic properties. Emotion-focused therapy is actually a short-term psychotherapy approach that is usually included in most meditative guides. The logic applied here is simple: emotion-focused meditations are designed to identify and clear the participant's innate emotions. This form of elimination of a specific emotion can be problematic for a person's growth and development, because eliminating a specific emotion in its entirety can cause people to develop mental blocks.

Research has shown that emotion-focused therapy helped participants identify with their own self, helping them better manage their emotional experiences. Mental health problems such as depression, complex trauma, etc. have been improved when associated with emotion-oriented meditations, therefore it has been specifically used to help individuals with the internalized stigma of sexual orientation, for example

As you practice using the meditative guides provided, it is important that you focus on trying to achieve a specific goal during the meditative process. This ensures that you focus on self-care and self-awareness. As you get older, you will find that it is much easier to focus on other people's needs than your own. But while this is very common, it just isn't right. Remembering your own needs and feelings is just as important as caring for others. In addition, it is equally important that you make sure that your self-sacrificing mindset does not result in you suppressing your own emotional needs and depriving yourself of the help you need.

## Identify And Deal With Physical Pain

Another important factor in preparing for a meditative lifestyle is clarity about where you are working. Let's say you work on dealing with physical pain. You will need to know specifically what type of pain you are trying to deal with. Understanding the basics and depth of your pain will help you choose which meditative guides are most effective for you.

When it comes to dealing with physical pain, it is important that you make a point to understand which pain management technique is best suited for your condition. Body scanning allows a person to mentally 'X-ray' their body, identify their pain points, and then address or heal them.

Another important form of pain management meditation is the mindful movement technique. This technique teaches individuals to use mindful movements, such as standing in a specific pose and then continuing to go through a list of physical actions, including turning your hands and shoulders, stretching your arms, and moving in and out. exhale at specific intervals. This type of targeted breathing is another common pain treatment technique that can help people with relaxation problems and chronic pain.

## Physical Distraction

In addition to all this, there are also a multitude of problems that you want to avoid if you want your meditation to run smoothly. For starters, you want to make sure you have the right set-up. This starts with the space where you have chosen to practice your meditation. Other factors to consider are the ambient noise or your point of view from that physical space. So always make sure to choose a quiet, empty space where you can minimize interruptions and let yourself relax. If you can, try to spend some time outside, or at least make sure your space is well ventilated, so you have fresh air before or during meditation. The fresher air you let in, the easier you'll find it to project yourself outside the four walls you're constantly crammed into.

Soft, quiet beats and musical rhythms, such as ambient music or simple instrumental songs, work well to create a relaxing space. There are also meditative songs and music selections available online on popular streaming sites. These are specially formulated to add an extra level to your meditative depth.

# Build Focal Points

Another extremely important part of the meditative process is finding the true meaning of your mind. In general, meditation practices ask you to establish an intention before starting a session. This allows you to fully appreciate and use your meditative time. You can pre-program your meditative focus or intention by using a mental questionnaire process. Start by asking simple questions, such as' Why do I meditate? ',' What do I hope to achieve by meditating? ',' What is my goal? ',' Who am I? ',' What do I want to be? How do I get where I want to be? 'Etc.

The idea here is to use the question to center yourself before you start meditating so that your meditation focuses on that specific point. This is similar to how compasses show you the real north, with a magnet constantly bringing the arrow back to it. Keep in mind that meditation doesn't have to be religious. While certain people meditate to experience God and build upon that consciousness, belief in a higher power does not increase your meditation ability.

Meditation can also be about finding the right wavelength for your thoughts and experiences. However, it is important to keep in mind that although focused meditative instruction seems unnecessary, your meditative energy depends on the mentality with which you begin the meditative guide. Taking time to focus on your intent will not only help increase the efficiency of your meditative guide, it will also help you maximize this time that you take for yourself.

# Chapter 12

# Creating an Environment for Meditation

Before we jump right into your practice, it's vital that you set yourself up for success. When it comes to meditation, your surrounding is going to be very important, especially if you are just starting out. Remember that as you practice, you'll want as little distraction as possible. You should work on finding a safe space to get started with your mindful meditation. I'll be providing you with some simple tips and tricks to create a space that you can feel relaxed and at peace in.

## Step One: Find A "Feel-Good" Space

The very first step for setting yourself up for successful meditation is to choose a room in your house that always makes you feel good. What I mean by this is that you are able to step into this room, take a deep breath and smile to yourself because it brings joy to you. This room should be slightly secluded and quiet. By doing so, you'll be able to limit the amount of traffic that passes by and noises that could potentially distract you.

When thinking about your space for meditation, mood lighting should be a factor. An example of this would be a room that has a good amount of natural light. It has been said that natural light has the ability to enhance one's mood almost instantly. With that in mind, try finding a room that faces the sun during the time that you decide to meditate. You could also find a view with the sunset or sunrise for a gorgeous backdrop for your meditation.

With your natural light in mind, you don't want the sun blazing on you while you are practicing. If you are indoors, consider dimming the lights to help create a calm sensation within the room. You could also place a sheer fabric over your window to help defuse some of the harsh sunlight if it's shining directly on you. No matter which you choose, you'll want to be able to have options depending on the day.

To take it one step further, you may want to consider a serene paint palette for your room. While the sensory and physical elements are important to consider, you may be surprised to learn how much color can affect your mood. While some say pastel shades are the most soothing, dark colors help individuals feel as though they're returning to the womb. If you have the ability, choose a room color that makes you feel relaxed and calm.

If you feel there is no room in your house that can fit your needs, you could always consider meditating outside! Whether you be on your deck, in your garden, or perched beside a pond; simply find a place that you'll be able to relax your body and soul without too many distractions.

## Step Two: Clear Your Mind And Clear Your Space

When you hear distractions, you may instantly think about noise and people talking to you. Having a cluttered area can also be very distracting when you are trying to relax. Once you have chosen your space for meditation, I always suggest having minimal "extras" in the room where you are trying to practice. An example of this may be your office. Often times, we have piles of papers stacked on the desk, filing cabinets that need some attention, and other stressful distractions that can happen in an office such as bills and work.

If you do feel that you need something more in your meditation room, you can always bring in some natural elements. Some people find that they're able to connect better to their mind and body when they're surrounded by nature. If you aren't outside, consider touches of nature that can infuse balance and harmony into your practice. For some, that means jars filled with sand, and for others, it could be a simple vase filled with their favorite flowers.

One of my favorite natural elements in my studio is a water fountain. An indoor waterfall can create soothing sounds that grant the ability to drown outside distractions. Instead, you can close your eyes and pretend you are meditating at the beach. I enjoy matching my breath to the sound of the rushing water; it's something you could consider for your space if you are looking to enhance your meditation area.

## Step Three: Aromatherapy And Music

One of the best parts of meditation is that you can create a space that makes you feel joyful and relaxed. A major element to consider for your room of practice could potentially be aromatherapy. There are many different essential oils such as peppermint, chamomile, or even lavender, that can soothe the body, the mind, and the soul.

If essential oils aren't really your thing, there are always incense and candles to burn. These scents have the ability to boost the immune system, eliminate stress, reduce muscle pain, and help create a sense of overall relaxation, too. There is a reason that this form of therapy is becoming more mainstream and gaining momentum. Of course, it's okay to practice without aromatherapy; this is just merely a suggestion as you decide how to begin your practice.

Another element to consider could be music for your space. While it's relaxing for some people, it may not be for you! I find that music can be beneficial for those who live with sirens constantly going off and traffic in general.

As you concentrate on the gentle tones, it can help gain a sense of peace and tranquility. I always recommend music that does not have lyrics. There are sounds such as birds chirping, waves crashing, or wind blowing that you could give a shot. There are many meditation tracks that you can time with your meditation. It may take a few tries, but you are sure to find something you can enjoy during your practice.

## Step Four: Fresh Air

While you could include aromatherapy in your meditation room, fresh air will always be the number one factor. There are so many incredible benefits to fresh air that can help you feel refreshed and may help boost your brainpower. If you are meditating indoors, be sure to find a room that has good ventilation. If you find yourself in a room that does not have any windows, you can always consider a standing fan or an air purifier. If this is the case, be sure to find a gadget that is quiet so that it does not interfere with your train of thought.

## Step Five: No Technology

I feel is the most important factor to take away when you decide on your space for meditation practice. While of course there are no hard rules when it comes to meditating, you should really consider ditching the technology when it comes down to your time. Aside from your music player, there should be no phones and no computers. There is absolutely nothing more distracting than getting email and text notifications on your phone when you are trying to relax.

What it comes down to is that you are simply taking several minutes to yourself. It's okay to get away from it all for a few minutes. More than likely, those phone calls and text messages can wait a few moments while you spend time meditating and connecting to yourself. It's healthy to unplug from these electronic devices. It may seem difficult at first, but I promise you'll live and may even learn to enjoy some time without being glued to your screen.

With all of this being said, it's finally time to get started on learning your very own meditation practice. We'll be going over everything you need to know about your first meditation. Before you begin, remember to choose your space carefully. The more you practice, the more you'll know how to fine-tune your space for maximum happiness and joy.

# Chapter 13

# Tips for Meditation

W
e will share some more suggestions and tips to allow you to continue with your meditation practice. These are not aimed at making you an expert but just to assist you on the journey. It is not necessary to try all of these tips at the same time. You can try one or two at a time to see if they help you. There will be some that work better than others. Find what's right for you.

## Begin Your Practice With 2-Minute Sessions

It may sound like it's pointless to meditate for just two minutes but trust us when we say it's anything but. It's simple to do this and is the easiest way for a beginner to learn to practice meditation. Just dedicate two minutes of each day to meditation. Continue this for a week. It's easier to follow through with these two minutes than pressuring yourself to sit still for half an hour. Once you get used to these two minutes, you can add more minutes the next week and so on. You will soon see that you easily meditate at least 15 minutes daily after a couple of weeks, and that will be more than enough time for most. So don't worry and don't make excuses about not having time. Everyone has two minutes to meditate.

Practice Your Meditation Every Morning

A lot of people say that they will meditate every day in the beginning, but most of them fail to follow through with this claim. Don't assume that you will always remember or be inclined to do it. Commit yourself to meditating every single morning after you wake up. After you wash up, just set aside a few minutes for this and you will see how much better your day goes. Early mornings are considered the best time to meditate.

# Don't Worry About The Process And Focus On Beginning The Practice

When people start meditating or think about starting it, they often waste a lot of time and energy on worrying about how they should go about it. They waste time in looking up too many methods, finding the perfect mat to sit on, learning chants, etc. All of these are a part of the practice but not the essence of it. You need not spend so much time on this and should try to go with the flow. Just find a comfortable place to sit where you won't be disturbed or distracted by anything. Sitting right on the ground is completely fine and so is sitting on a chair. To begin with, focus less on all this and more on spending two whole minutes just meditating. The stress of these trivial things will hinder your meditation. So try to get more used to meditating itself and worry about all this later.

# Pay Attention To How You Feel

Once you begin meditating, you need to try being more attuned to your personal feelings. Pay attention to how you feel and how this practice is affecting your body. Tune in to the thoughts that pass through your mind. Don't focus on them but notice them as they flow past. Be accepting of all the feelings and thoughts that you experience during meditation. Nothing is wrong or right; so, don't judge yourself for any of it.

## Count as You Breathe

Breathing is an important aspect of meditation. Find the right place to meditate and then close your eyes as you sit comfortably. Start concentrating solely on your breathing. Focus on your breath as you inhale and exhale. Notice how you take in air through your nose and into your lungs. Pay attention as it leaves your body. When you take in a breath, count one. Count two when you breathe out. Continue the counting as you keep breathing and focus on this alone. It will help you focus more.

## It Is Okay For Your Thoughts To Wander

The human mind tends to wander a lot, and you need to be more accepting of it as you meditate. You don't have to assume that you are not allowed to think anything when you meditate. This can be impossible to avoid, at least at first. When you meditate, try not to think but be accepting when thoughts come in. When you notice your concentrating wandering off from your meditation to your thoughts, push back your mind slowly. It can be disappointing, and you might feel like you are doing it wrong, but it is all right. Just slowly come back when your mind wanders away.

Be More Accepting

Like we already said, it is natural for thoughts to appear as you meditate. Don't be defensive and try to push them away all the time. Instead, be more accepting and allow them to come and pass. Take note of these thoughts, and you can focus on them later. But as you meditate, allow them to come and go naturally. Your thoughts are a part of you, and you need to accept and forgive yourself for everything that you are.

## Don't Stress About The Method Of Meditation

You might be worried that you are meditating the wrong way at first. A lot of people get stressed about this and think it will be ineffective if they don't practice the right method or do it the right way. The truth is, there is no perfect method of meditation. You can try the various methods we have mentioned and use them as guidelines, but ultimately, you need to do what feels best for you.

## Your Mind Doesn't Have To Be Empty While Meditating

Some people think that meditation means getting rid of all thoughts and clearing the mind completely. However, this is not true and can be almost impossible for most people. It can be possible to clear your mind out sometimes, but for the most part, it's not what is essential for meditation. It's normal to have thoughts, and you don't have to force yourself to push them all out. Just be more accepting of them and let them pass without focusing on them. Work more on your concentration, and you will see that it gets easier to reduce distracting thoughts over time.

## Take Some Time To Accept Your Thoughts And Feelings

As we mentioned repeatedly, having thoughts while meditating is totally normal. When a thought passes through your mind, it is okay to take a moment and pay attention to it. In the beginning, we recommend to just let the thoughts pass and focus more on breathing. But over time, you can try noticing more of your thoughts too. You should avoid focusing on anything negative and try to bring in more positive thoughts. When you notice your thoughts, you will be able to learn more about yourself. But only allow yourself a moment for this before continuing with your meditation.

## Learn A Little More About Yourself Every Day

Meditation is not just about improving your focus or being better able to concentrate. It is about helping your mind develop too. When you become more accepting of your thoughts and feelings, you will learn a lot about yourself. Don't push yourself too hard to think or feel a certain way. Be accepting and learn about yourself. No one can know you better than yourself.

Be Your Own Friend

You need to try learning more about yourself, but this should not be done with a mindset of self-analysis and judgment. Instead, be kinder to yourself. Think of it like learning more about someone you like. Accept who you are and be your friend. Don't be cruel and judgmental towards yourself.

## Pay Attention To Your Body

After you get better at counting breaths and meditating, you can try something else. Now you should try focusing on your body. Do this with one body part at a time. As you meditate, focus on a specific body part and try to pay attention to how it feels. Start with the lowest point in your body and move on until every part of your body has been acknowledged. This will allow you to pay attention to your body and learn more about it. You will be able to notice if something feels wrong too.

### Be Truly Determined

You cannot say you will meditate regularly and then fail to follow through. It is important to dedicate yourself to this practice. Don't take it lightly. Make sure you stick to this resolution for at least a few weeks. Motivate yourself to follow through with it every day. It will soon become a habit, but not if you lack determination right from the beginning.

## Meditate, Regardless Of Where You Are

It doesn't matter if you're on a trip or have to work overtime on some days. Don't skip your meditation practice. You might reduce the amount of time you can dedicate to it, but you should still meditate. You don't necessarily need that meditation corner in your home for this. It can be done while sitting in a car or even while you sit in your office chair.

Use Guided Meditations

It may seem hard to meditate when you first begin. Guided meditations can be instrumental in this case. Use these audio or video files to help you get started. They are very simple and accommodating regardless of whether you are a beginner or have practiced for some time.

## Have Someone To Be Accountable To

If you keep your resolution to meditate to yourself, you are less likely to follow through with it. It will be easy to give up because there is no one to berate you over it. This is why you need to have someone that will hold you accountable. It could be a friend or family member. Just keep checking in with them, and they will help you stay on track. You can also find someone to practice it regularly. This could be someone you live with, work with, or even someone who will go to lessons with you. Finding a network of people who are interested in meditation will help in reinforcing your new good habit. These people can help support you through your journey. You can find online forums or communities of people who practice meditation too.

# Chapter 14

# 15 Minutes Guided Meditation (Transcript)

Take your position at the place of your meditation

Be seated

Sit in a completely relaxed manner

Don't do anything immediately

Ground yourself first

Just sit completely relaxed for a few minutes

Get into a comfortable position

Keep your back straight

Ensure that your shoulders are also straight

Your back and neck should be in a straight line

Now, close your eyes

Lean slightly forward and then backward

Lean-to your left side and then to your right

Now, bring yourself to the center and find the best and most comfortable position

Feel your head positioned on your neck

Raise your chin slightly upwards

This will help you in placing your focus between your eyebrows

Try to feel your whole body

Notice if there is tension anywhere

If you feel any part tense, release the tension

Adjust your body to release the pressure

Focus on your breathing

Inhale from your nostril

Hold your breath for a few seconds

Exhale from your mouth

Breathe in

Breathe out

Feel all the tension getting diffused with each exhalation

As you exhale, all the negative energy goes out of your body

It also takes away all the stress

You are feeling joyful and blissed

Simply focus on your breathing

Live in the moment

Remain aware of the things happening around you

As you breathe in your focus on the breath is getting deeper and deeper

You are feeling more and more calm and composed

You smile with every inhalation and feel relaxed with every exhalation

You are feeling blissed out

Now, start paying attention to your breathing

Pay very close attention

Closely observe the path of the breath you take

Become aware of the way it causes your chest to expand

Air is filling your lungs

Then it travels to your gut

It causes your stomach to inflate

You are amused by this act

But you can't release the breath yet

You need to control it

This is your dominion

You are in control

You hold it for a few seconds

Then, release it slowly

Watch the air go out through your mouth

Observe the sound you are making through your mouth

The air is taking away all the tension with itself

The stress in your body is also going away

There are some thoughts in your mind

They don't concern you

But you are drawn to them

Observe those thoughts

Don't get involved with them

Don't interrupt or intrude

Don't judge those thoughts

Simply observe them

Become aware of them

If you run from them, they will come after you

Embrace these thoughts

Accept their presence

Don't be afraid of them

It is time to expand your awareness

Look outside the body

Try to feel the surrounding

Feel the air around you

Become aware of the fragrances

Become aware of the sensation the air is making

Listen closely to any kind of noise being made by the air-conditioning

Expand your awareness even further

Go beyond the realms of the eyes

Look far beyond the limit of your eyes

Try to imagine first snowfall of the season

You are sitting in a comfortable cottage

It is the first snowfall of the season

It is evening now

You are completely relaxed

There is nothing to do

You are looking at the falling snow

You are sipping your coffee

You are in comfortable clothes enjoying the weather

There is nothing to fear

You have the supplies

You have nowhere to go

The family is with you

There is no one to worry about

You can easily sit back and relax

The snowfall has just begun

There is a thin layer of super white snow on the cars

The floor and the roads are not yet fully covered by snow

There is a thin layer of snow on the trees, branches, and leaves

It is giving it a romantic look

You feel a bit of chill

There is a blanket on the chair

You cover your shoulders for more comfort

You are thinking about making a snowman in the morning with kids

You are thinking of the games you'll play with the kids in the morning

It would be a really wonderful sight

The night is approaching

There is a warm bed waiting for you now

You have a book which you are still reading

You start reading the book

But you are drawn to the snowfall

It is the first snowfall of the season

You want to observe it a bit more

You want to cherish this moment

The life is in the moment

Tomorrow this moment would be a past

There would be no way to live it

You leave the book aside

You are now standing firmly in the balcony of your cottage

You light a small bonfire

You want to fill this sight in your eyes

The bonfire is keeping you warm

Some more family members have also joined

They are talking among themselves

But you are lost in the beauty of the snowfall

You want to explore this snowfall further

You go to the back of your cottage

Now, you are watching the snowflakes falling through the window glass

Snowflakes are falling on your windows

You can see them clearly

It is time to sleep

You close your eyes

You fall asleep immediately

It felt like you slept just a few minutes ago but it is morning now

It is a beautiful day

There has been a heavy snowfall whole night

The roads, houses, cars, trees, everything is covered by white snow

Everything is looking mesmerizingly beautiful

You watch is through the window of your room

The kids are not awake yet

You get out to explore the snow

There is a piping hot mug of coffee in your hand

You are standing at the same place you were standing yesterday

A thick layer of snow all around

This is the beginning of the new season

It is a weekend

There is no rush to go anywhere

So, there is no need to clear the snow

No one is shoveling the snow

Everything is calm

There is great serenity in the environment

It is getting complimented by the white blanket of snow all around

The white color is very soothing to the eyes

It is even soothing to the soul

You want to remain in the moment

You want to live this moment forever

It will remain in your eyes now

It is an indelible memory

It is time to become aware of the moment

It is time to feel the breathing

Feel the falling and rising of the stomach

Breathe in

Breathe out

Don't stretch your breathing now

Let it come to a natural pace

Don't put any effort into it

You have been effortless at the moment

You have enjoyed the moment completely

Now it is time to become aware of the surrounding

Feel the warmth or chill in the room

Feel the sensation of clothes on your skin

Experience the air around you

There is no need to open your eyes immediately

You can enjoy the moment a bit longer

Or choose to open the eyes

You are in control.

# Chapter 15

# Mindful Breathing and Mindful Movement Meditation

Mindful Breathing Meditation

Mindful breathing meditation is the most basic form of meditation for beginners to start their meditation journey. However, basic doesn't mean shallow or easy. Meditation of breath is a powerful and effective tool.

The exercise:

    1.    Choose a straight sitting position that is comfortable for you. Sit comfortably in a chair or on the floor. Keep your spine straight, but not stiff, and keep your back away from the back of the chair. If it makes you comfortable, then close your eyes. Sit in a place with a comfortable temperature and ensure you won't be disturbed for the next 10 minutes or so.

    2.    Keep your attention on your breathing. Remember, if your mind wanders off to other thoughts, don't judge or criticize yourself. Let go of any ideas of

achievements or success. Whatever happens, allow it to happen.

3.      Focus on your breathing. Feel your breath as it enters your body. Feel your out-breath as you exhale. Feel your belly or chest falling or rising. Feel the air moving in and out by placing your hand on your belly. When you have accurately found the place where you can feel your breath comfortably, focus there, and allow your hands to rest. Let the breath flow at its natural depth and speed. Just breathe normally, your breath may gradually deepen or slow down, or may remain steady – either way is fine.

4.      Slowly bring your mind back to your breathing: When you are trying to focus on your breathing, your mind may drift off into different thoughts, fantasies, dreams, feelings, plans, and ideas. This is totally normal, and when this happens, observe where your mind went, don't try to judge it or analyze it, and gently guide your mind back to your breathing. Your mind drifts off and you bring it back to your breathing is an integral part of your meditation. If you start to get annoyed or feel frustrated, take a deep breath and smile. Then refocus your attention to your breathing, just like turning a car into another direction.

5.      After 10 -20 minutes of practice, open your eyes and notice how you feel after the meditation. Avoid negative thinking such as 'I am doing it wrong, ' or I can't get it.' Each mindful practice and experience is different.

Stay with the things and events just as they are, from moment to moment.

Practice daily for 10 -20 minutes. Practice different times of the day and see what effect it has on you.

Practice Mindful Movement Meditation

Unlike popular belief, your body doesn't have to remain still to exercise mindfulness meditation. Some meditation practice requires you to stay still for a few minutes. However, almost everybody enjoys and comfortable mindfully moving their bodies. Practice this simple mindful movement meditation and see how you feel afterward.

The exercise:

1.     Start with mindful standing: Just stand up straight and place your feet about hip-width apart. Keep the knees a little loose, chest comfortably open and the shoulders back and down. Allow your hands to hang by the side of the body. Make sure your head is perfectly stable in your shoulders and neck. Picture a balloon is on the top of your head, and it gradually drags you upright. If it makes you comfortable, and help you to maintain balance, then keep your eyes closed.

2.     Observe the sensation of your breath, feel the sensations in your body, and feel the weight of your body on your feet. Notice the spot on your body that feels uncomfortable, stressed, or tense without trying to relax them.

3.     When you are ready, move the arms up and down with your breath. As you inhale, move the arms upwards in front of you and back down again as you exhale. Focus on the sensations in your hands and arms while you repeat 10 times.

4.     The next time you inhale, lift your arms in front of the body, then as you exhale, open the arms outwards. As you inhale, bring your arms together in front of your body again. Bring your arms to your sides again as you exhale. Practice for 10 times.

5.     Now lift your arms above the head and feel the stretch. See how far you can stretch yourself without difficulty. Stay with the stretch until you start to feel uncomfortable and see if you can stay with the feeling of uneasiness and for a few moments before returning to the pose. Repeat the practice if you feel comfortable with the pose. Keep breathing normally, and no need to hold your breath.

6.     Rotate the shoulders slowly a few times in both directions. Notice if you can feel any tension. Simultaneously, feel your inhales and exhales if you can.

7.     Gradually switch your head from side to side. Slowly lower your left ear towards your left shoulder.

8.     Then gently turn your head in front of your body. Make sure your right ear is aligned with your right shoulder, then go back to the center pose again.

9.    Shake your arms and legs for about 30 seconds and finish. Stand and feel the sensation all over your body.

# Chapter 16

# Mindfulness Meditation

When you enter mindfulness meditation, you become like a mountain. You are surrounded by movement and changes, but you remain just as still and strong. Your thoughts would then be like clouds that float over you. They are there but you do not interact with them; they merely pass you by until they fade away into the distance.

Mindfulness meditation in the formal sense can be practiced daily, but just like exercise and eating you need to set aside specific time for it. However, unlike the first two, you do not have to change into a different set of clothes or prep some ingredients to practice. You can start anywhere and anytime.

How to Apply the Right Meditation Posture

It is important to make sure that you follow proper posture while being still for several minutes. Here are the steps on how to properly position yourself for meditation.

Sitting on a chair

Sitting still for a certain period requires good posture not only for health, but for comfort as well. Slouching, after all, is the surest way to cause long term damage on your spinal cord. Here are some tips on how to improve your sitting posture for meditation:

- Make sure to sit on a chair that will enable you to put your feet flat on the ground. If the chair is too low or high, you would be better off sitting on the floor.

- If you have a slouching problem, you can place wooden blocks or old magazines beneath the two back legs of your chair to allow it to tilt forward slightly. This slight tilt will compel you to maintain a straight back to keep balance.

- Visualize that you have a string pulling your stomach forward until your spine is naturally straight without any feeling of strain. Allow your head to lift naturally until all the discs in your spine are naturally aligned.

- You may place your hands on your knees. They can be facing downwards, upwards, or to the side. You can also place a cushion on your lap and place your hands on top if you feel tension on your shoulders.

Sitting on the floor

The more traditional and formal sitting practice for meditation is on a cushion on the floor. There are two basic postures for that: the kneeling posture and the Burmese posture. It is best to invest in a good quality meditation stool with a flat cushion (called a zafu) on top so that it can absorb the pressure of your weight instead of the back of your legs.

To properly do the kneeling posture, here are some tips:

- Always shake and stretch your legs as well as rotate your ankles before you go to the kneeling posture. This will minimize feelings of tension or strain.

- Prepare the kneeling stool and cushion on the floor, then carefully sit back down on it. Shift your weight until it is evenly distributed.

- Gently straighten your back and place your hands on your knees or lap.

To do the Burmese posture, here are the steps:

- Do some stretching exercises for the legs to prepare them for the position.

  - Lay out a mat or blanket on the floor. Over it, place a firm, flat cushion on which you will be sitting.

  - Carefully lower yourself over the cushion into a sitting position. Try to let your knees to touch the floor; if they do not, you may need to add more cushions until they do.

  - Let your left heel touch or be as close to your right inner thigh as possible. Let your right leg be in front of your left leg with its heel directed at the lower left leg. You do not have to position this perfectly, so adjust according to what is comfortable and stable for you.

- Gently allow your back to become straight, but with your shoulders relaxed. You may then place your hands on your knees or on a cushion on your lap.

Aside from following proper posture, it is important to make sure to meditate during the times when you are not hungry or too full. Otherwise, you will be too distracted or sleepy.

That said, let us move on to one of the most fundamental mindfulness meditations, mindful breathing.

Mindful Breathing Meditation

Mindful breathing meditation is the core of all mindfulness meditation exercises. It is in fact the first thing you usually do to enter the state of mindfulness before you proceed with walking mindfulness, eating mindfulness, and other mindfulness exercises.

Beginners are highly encouraged to practice this every day for at least two weeks so that they could get into the habit of meditation.

If you do not want to get lost in time or be worried about how long you are meditating, you can set a timer on your phone or alarm clock to signal you when to come out of the meditation. It is best to set a gentle tone on the alarm instead of a ringing one, as you would want the reminder to be gentle rather than a disturbance. You can start with 10 minutes, if you like.

Here are the steps to mindful breathing meditation:

Step 1: Get yourself into a comfortable sitting posture, be it in a chair or on the floor. Give yourself time to become stable and comfortable.

Step 2: When you are ready, announce to yourself and the universe that you are ready to focus on the present moment. You may start by saying out loud, "I am in the present moment. I am ready to meditate." Invite an attitude of kindness, curiosity, and acceptance.

Step 3: Shift your focus towards your nostrils. Notice the feeling of your natural breath as you inhale through your nostrils. Then, trace the sensation of the breath as it flows down through your windpipe into your lungs, causing your belly to expand. Notice how it flows out of your belly, causing it to deflate, and then goes back up through your windpipe and nostrils. Continue to focus on this sensation for as long as you like.

Be careful not to change how you are breathing as your purpose here is not to judge how you are doing it. Rather, it is a mere observance of your natural breath, the core of your present moment.

Step 4: As you continue to focus on your breath, you may soon notice your mind wandering off. This is completely normal and should not cause you to worry. All you need to do when you notice this happening is to draw your focus back towards your nostrils.

Each time you start to entertain thoughts unrelated to the sensation of breath, call to mind the word "thinking…" You can also make it more specific, such as "worrying…" or "planning…" or "ruminating…"

After the thought floats away, ground yourself back towards your breath.

Once you hear the timer go off, you can either gently come out of the meditation but bring the state of mindfulness with you throughout the rest of your day. Some like to shift their focus from their breath towards their surroundings after mindful breathing meditation. They focus on the colors, textures, and shapes, the sounds they hear, and so on. This enables them to become more in tune with the present moment than ever.

Guided meditation

The mindfulness meditation practices may be difficult at first. It is recommended to try one of the apps or programs listed in the resources to introduce you to meditation and help you with your posture, breathing and techniques. This will allow you to build a meditation habit with less than 10 minutes a day.

Try practicing mindful breathing meditation right now. If you don't have much time or can't sit down, just pause and take a few breaths in and out focus on your breath.

After you are finished, you might like to learn another type of mindfulness meditation called Walking Mindfulness.

Mindfulness Exercise

Mindful Breathing

You can try short meditation and mindful breathing anywhere; you don't have to be sitting down to try it.

To start focus on breathing in through your nose and focus on the air going in at your nostrils, just focus on this point. Then breath out through your mouth, focus on the air just as it leaves your lips.

Count 1 when you breathe in and 2 when you breathe out, keep counting until 10.

You can also try the full mantra from the smiling meditation mentioned earlier or just the first 2 lines as you breathe in and out:

As I breathe in, my mind becomes calm.

As I breathe out, my mind becomes clear.

Let go of thoughts, worries and things you need to do and just focus on your breathing. You don't have to do this for very long but if you found it helpful, you can try for longer or do it a few times during the day as you feel you need to calm your mind a bit.

# Chapter 17

# Meditations with Stones and Crystals

Meditation is a simple matter. Have you ever tried it? If you haven't tried it, rest assured that these guided meditations will be very accommodating and straight forward. A tip for effective meditation is to find your center. What this means is that you have to resolve distractions that may be occurring outside of your body and focus your energy and intentions inward. You may hear a variety of thoughts, checklists, reminders, and so forth, emerge in your mind during your relaxation process and that's okay. It won't matter eventually and as you relax, the thoughts will begin to dissolve as you push past them and continue to find your center.

In the same way that crystals and stones can have an impact on the transformation of your energy, so can meditation. When you enter a meditative state, you are giving your body, mind, and spirit an opportunity to hit the reset button and recalibrate. It doesn't take long to accomplish this and as little as ten minutes a day is enough to powerfully shift your energy into a better balance and healthier state.

Meditation is a powerful tool for healing and alignment, just like crystals and stones, we will bring the two together for an even more impactful healing journey. These guided meditations are step-by-step instructions to help you feel rested, rejuvenated, relaxed, and refreshed. You can use them as often as you need to and each one will use one or more crystals for a specific healing purpose.

Once you have a general overview of simple meditations you can do with these wonderful tools, you can begin to create your own meditations for whatever your needs might be in your everyday life.

Healing Heart Meditation

You will need one or more of the following crystals or stones for this Mediation:

- Clear Quartz
- Jade
- Kunzite
- Malachite
- Rhodochrosite
- Rose Quartz

I recommend using Rhodochrosite or Rose Quartz if you are only using one stone for this meditation. You can use all of them if you are able and adding a piece of Clear Quartz will enhance the power of all of the other crystals and stones used in this guided healing meditation.

This meditation is all about opening the heart and protecting it at the same time. We don't want to be subject to being hurt by being overly compensating. This meditation opens you to living openly from the heart while still maintain a strong capacity for loving the self and standing strong in your ability to be graceful and serene in how you express love to everything and everyone around you.

Find a comfortable position lying on the floor or on a bed or mattress. Make sure that you will be undisturbed and can focus for about 30 minutes for the length of the meditation. Have your crystals and stones within reach so that you only have to reach your hand out to pick them up and place them where they need to go. They should be right next to you when you are beginning your meditation.

1. In your lying position, begin by taking some deep inhales and exhales. As you breathe in, count to ten slowly. Hold your breath for a count of five, and then exhale for a count of ten. Repeat this cycle ten times.

2. After you have connected to your breath, continue breathing normally. Starting at the top of your head, notice any tension that may be stuck around your neck, your forehead, and your ears. Make sure your eyebrows are relaxed. Relax your eyelids, your chin, and your jaw. Let your tongue relax as your breath in through your nose, and out through your nose.

3. Move slowly down the body, looking for more tension to release. Release the shoulders, the chest, and the elbows. Release the arms, hands, wrists, and fingers. Notice any places that you are holding onto and let them melt into release.

4. Continue through your belly, your hips, and low back. Release any tension in your thighs and knees, your calves and ankles. Let go of anything that is tense in your feet and your toes until you are fully released and relaxed into the floor and just breathe in this position for a few moments.

5. Now that you are fully relaxed, pick up your crystals and stones and lay them over your heart chakra. Try to maintain your relaxed state while you do this. You don't even need to open your eyes. Move slowly and gently.

6. Align the stone, or stones at the heart center and encircling it. If you have multiple stones, arrange them all around a large, central stone. It doesn't need to be fancy or pretty, and you should try to keep your eyes closed if you can.

7. With the stones in place, you can now begin to use your original breath cycle to connect with the energy of the stones. Breathe in for ten, hold for five, and breathe out for ten. Repeat this cycle five times and let the energy of the stones connect to you. Feel their vibration as you lift them up on your chest with your breathing.

8. Imagine as you are doing this that the stones are radiating soft pink and green light that is gently swirling around your heart. See the light filling your heart.

9. As the light expands in your heart, let it fill your chest. Continue breathing and see the light extending and growing int your head and through your whole torso. Watch the light fill your hips, legs, and feet.

10. As this colorful light fills you, see it reaching outside of your skin and enveloping you, like a soft, warm blanket of pink and green hues. Hold this image in your mind as you continue to breathe and relax.

11. Bring your focus back to the stones and feel their weight on your chest. Since the healing light of the crystal energy all around you and repeat the following mantra in your head, or aloud if you feel comfortable doing so:

"I am open to living a life of love and compassion.

I am strong and capable of loving all of myself, no matter what.

I will always give love to others who are in need, as well as to myself when I am in need of love.

I am open-hearted, caring, and tender and will offer my kindness and support whenever I can if it is a feeling I am inspired to offer.

I have the right to love and be loved.

We are all in need of love and put the energy of love into the Universe with my heart open."

12. Allow yourself to smile softly and bring your focus up to your crown chakra. Feel the light surrounding your body collect inside of you and begin to leave your body through the crown chakra, infusing the Universal energy around you with healing love and light.

13. Take a few more deep breaths and meditate for as long as you need to with their energetic feeling. When you are ready, you can begin to remove the stones from your chest and breathe a few more times before getting up.

14. To enhance the energy that you have just shifted inside of yourself, continue to do tender and loving things for you and others throughout the day. Take a day off of work and go for a walk in the park. Make a soothing cup of tea and enjoy your garden. Talk to an old friend or loved one over the phone or in-person and have a nice connection. Take a soothing and relaxing bath.

You can modify this Heart Healing Meditation as you get more comfortable and experienced with it. You may find new ways to creatively visualize the healing experience. Have fun with it and open your heart every day!

# Chapter 18

# Morning Affirmations Meditation

Are you looking to start off your day on the right side of the bed? If you want to wake up energetic and ready for any day ahead of you, I highly suggest starting your day off with a morning meditation, topped off with some positive affirmations to get you in a positive mindset.

Of course, you can listen to this meditation at any time of the day, but it is a perfect start to your morning and will only take a small amount of time to energize you and get you started!

As we start this meditation, I now invite you to go ahead and take some deep breaths. With each breath you take, allow the airflow to begin to energize you. Inhale deep into your lungs and exhale everything out.

Breathe in…and exhale. Allow for your breaths to be slow, deep, and calm. Each breath you take brings in the air that your body needs to help get you started. Allow your breaths to fill you with energy and let go of any fatigue you may be feeling at this moment. For the next few moments, this is all I want you to focus on. Just concentrate on your breath. It does not matter what tasks you have for the rest of the day. All you need to think about is breathing in, breathing out, and getting your energy set up for the day.

(PAUSE)

You are going to be ready for this day ahead of you. Breathe in positive energy and allow all positive thoughts to enter your mind. With your next few exhales, let any negative feelings go. If you feel any tension built up in your body, let that go too. You do not have the time nor the energy to waste on negativity. There is only energy and positivity right now. Breathe and remind yourself to be positive.

(PAUSE)

Now, I want you to squeeze your hands into fists gently. As you do this, feel as the muscles strengthen in your arms and your shoulders. Feel now as the strength and energy begin to flow through your veins. You are powerful, and you can accomplish anything you want to. You are capable of accomplishing anything that you need to get done today. You can do anything you put your mind to. Now, relax your fists, and allow your muscles to relax.

(PAUSE)

As your body begins to awaken, feel how warm and energetic you are starting to feel. If you would like, try to open and close your hands a few times. I want you to become mindful of how wonderful your body feels as it wakes up, ready to tackle anything that comes at you today. Allow yourself to become excited for the day, ready for anything that can happen today; there are so many possibilities. Feel now as this positive energy waves through your body and allow your mind and soul to become alive.

(PAUSE)

If you are feeling up to it, I now invite you to enjoy a gentle stretch to get your muscles going. Go ahead and place your fingertips together and gently stretch your arms above your head. Reach for the ceiling and feel the soft pull down your shoulders and into your sides. If you want, gently lean from side to side and feel as your muscles begin to warm up. When you are ready, bring your arms back down and bring your awareness to your toes. Take a deep breath and allow the energy to surge through you.

(PAUSE)

Next, I want you to start to wiggle your feet a little. As you flex your feet, feel as the muscles in your legs enjoy a gentle stretch. Go ahead and spend some time waking your legs up. They are well rested from the night before and are ready to be put to work! Now, hold your feet still and enjoy the sensation of energy tingling through your toes, into your ankles, and up your legs. Take another deep breath in and allow for these sensations to wash over your whole body. The more you move, the more energetic you begin to feel.

(PAUSE)

Now that your body is awake and feeling energetic, it is time to open your mind to positive thoughts to carry you through the day. In the next few moments, we will go over some self-esteem affirmations to boost your confidence and get you excited for the day ahead of you. If, at any point in your day, you feel your stress and anxiety start to take over, I invite you to take a few moments to breathe and repeat the following affirmations to yourself.

As I say the following affirmations, I invite you to continue to focus on your breathing and stretch; however, you feel fit. If you still feel tense in some areas, go ahead and stretch these areas out. This is your time; use it to your advantage. If you start your day off on a positive note, it can get better from there, even if you hit a couple of rocky patches. Feel free to repeat after me or simply listen to the following; it is completely up to you.

I am capable of achieving anything that I work hard for.

(PAUSE)

When times get tough, I have the ability to work through them.

(PAUSE)

I deserve to be happy.

(PAUSE)

I am a strong individual, and I am in charge of my life, even when I cannot control the circumstances.

(PAUSE)

I am worthwhile, even when people make me feel like I am not.

(PAUSE)

I accept myself for who I am.

(PAUSE)

I am proud of all of my hard work and accomplishments.

(PAUSE)

I deserve happiness because I work hard for it.

(PAUSE)

I have many wonderful qualities.

(PAUSE)

I love myself.

(PAUSE)

I am grateful for my life.

(PAUSE)

I am grateful for all of this energy I am feeling.

(PAUSE)

I am ready to tackle this day and anything that comes my way.

(PAUSE)

I will handle everything with as much grace as possible.

(PAUSE)

In tough times, I will remember to breathe and remain calm.

(PAUSE)

I am in control of my thoughts and my body.

(PAUSE)

I choose to be calm and peaceful throughout the day.

(PAUSE)

I am ready to get started with this day and will remember to be at peace.

(PAUSE)

Fantastic. As we draw this meditation to a close, take a few more moments to breathe on your own time and focus your thoughts and intentions for the day. When things become overwhelming, remember to find your breath, and you can work through just about anything. At the end of the day, it all comes down to your mindset, and by starting with this meditation, you are ready to overcome anything with positivity. Now, breathe and get ready to start your day.

(PAUSE)

Meditation Time: 40 Minutes

Breathing Awareness Meditation

Before we begin this meditation, I now invite you to find a position that is comfortable for you. As you settle in, take a few moments to make sure all distractions such as your cellphone and laptop are closed. For the next few minutes, I would like you to just focus on yourself. As you meditate, there is nothing else that matters. If you are feeling anxious right now, that is perfectly okay. We all go through these feelings. What matters right now is that you do something about it.

(PAUSE)

As you settle into position, go ahead and take a nice, deep breath in. If you would like, allow for your eyes to begin to flutter closed. If you are not comfortable with this, simply keep them open and start to soften your gaze. When you are comfortable, all I would like you to do is find your breath. With each breath you take, simply become mindful of how it feels to breathe in fully and exhale everything out. When we feel anxious, we often forget the very basic concept of breathing. Our thoughts begin to move quickly, and our breathing patterns begin to match. Perhaps you are mindful of this, but most likely, you had no idea because you were so focused on being anxious, and that is okay! Just breathe and tune your focus in on yourself.

(PAUSE)

Right now, all you need to focus on is the air entering through your nostrils. It does not matter why you feel anxious, and it does not matter what tasks need to be completed once this meditation is finished. Allow for all of the thoughts in your head to exit and focus only on your breath.

(PAUSE)

On your next breath, I want you to become mindful of how the air travels into your lungs and allow for your belly to expand fully. As you breathe out, feel how your belly gets smaller, and the air moves peacefully back out through your mouth or nose. You may notice that you inhale, feels different from your exhale. Breathe in and feel the comfort of the cool air as it enters your body and how warm it feels as it leaves.

(PAUSE)

If you ever become distracted during your practice, that is perfectly okay. We all get distracted sometimes. If you find yourself getting distracted by noise or thoughts, allow these to pass without judgment and bring your focus back in yourself. There is no need to change anything right now. All you are doing is relaxing and breathing. Simply bring your attention back to your breath and continue a few more moments to breathe on your own.

(PAUSE)

If you would like, you can count with me as you continue to find your breath. On your next breath, I invite you to hold the breath for a few beats. Allow for the air in your lungs to nourish your body and your thoughts. I want each breath to relax you and clear your mind of all worry. When you are ready, we can begin.

Breathe in softly…and hold for one…two…three…and slowly release. Excellent.

Let's do that two more times together.

Breathe in softly…and hold for one…two…three…and release.

(PAUSE)

Breathe in…and hold for one…two…three…and slowly release.

(PAUSE)

Wonderful. At this point, you are probably already feeling much better. Go ahead and take a few more breaths on your own time.

(PAUSE)

During times of anxiety, I want this to be the first practice that pops into your mind. While breathing is a simple task, it can be highly effective. We all experience anxiety in different ways. If you start to become overwhelmed with tasks or emotions, take a step back and find your breath. With each breath you take, gently remind yourself that these feelings will pass, and as long as you are breathing, you are going to be okay. When you are ready, we can continue to the next meditation to keep working through overcoming your anxiety.

# Chapter 19

# Meditation for Anxiety Under Pressure Script

While there are many different reasons people experience anxiety, being under pressure can be one of the major culprits. Through meditation, you can teach yourself how to remain focused and calm; even when placed in a high-pressure environment. Whether you are giving a presentation, being tested, or even attending a job interview; you will be able to stay calm, cool, and collected when you need to be the most. Next, you will be provided with a meditation script to help you build your relaxation skills for moments you need to be calm.

For this meditation, you will only need to set a few minutes aside. This is a great aspect as you can remind yourself of this script when you only have a few moments to get your mind back into a calm headspace. In the following script, you will be provided with three different ways to help calm your thoughts, relax your muscles, and become mindful of your breathing. All three of these aspects are important so that you can get back to business without the distraction of any panic or anxiety.

To begin this exercise, be sure that you are comfortable. Wiggle your body a bit and loosen everything up. Once you feel you are mindful of your comfort, bring your concentration to your breathing. How does your breath feel right now before you change anything? Allow yourself to take note and gently let go of that thought without judgment.

Right now, I just want you to focus on your breathing. Breathe in softly and let it all go. Breathe in nice and deep, take all of that oxygen in, and then let it back out. When you can, try to slow your breathing down. With each breath you take, try and count it out to the number of four and then hold that breath for three before letting it out on the same count. When you are ready, try this with me.

And, breathe in…4.3.2.1

Brilliant. Try that a few more times until you feel you are completely in control of your breath.

Breathe in…4.3.2.1…hold…and exhale…4.3.2.1

Very good. Focus on your breath. I don't want you to think about anything else in the moment. It's just you and your breath, nothing else.

Breathe in… …and exhale…

With each breath you take, you can feel a sense of calmness washing over you. Each breath is bringing the focus back into your brain. You are relaxed and comfortably alert. With each breath, you are teaching yourself that you can, and you will be relaxed under pressure. There is nothing that can shake you. You are strong and one with yourself. There is nothing that can take that away from you.

Great.

Now, I would like to invite you to bring your new-found focus to your muscles. How is your body feeling right now? I want you to be mindful of how your jaw feels; how your shoulders feel; and now how your hands feel. When we are under pressure and stressed, we often hold all of our tension here.

Now that you are aware of the tension, allow yourself to unclench your teeth. Allow for your jaw to fall slightly slack into a comfortable position. Remove the tongue from the roof of your mouth and take a nice, deep breath in. Feel already how relaxed you feel now that your jaw isn't clamped shut.

With that in mind, lower your shoulders from your ear. If you would like, gently roll them forward and back; allow for the muscles to fall loose. Again, feel how this new position is already helping you feel much calmer and relax. Your body appreciates when you become conscious of putting yourself in a more relaxed position.

Finally, bring your attention back to your hands. Are they clenched and tight right now? Allow them to fall open and relaxed. Your arms can rest by your side with no tension. There is no need for any of that right now. You are in a safe environment. You are being mindful of making yourself calmer. You are using your skills to relax under any type of pressure thrown at you.

Now, bring your focus back to your breathing. On your own time, run a body scan that you learned earlier. Are there any other spots of tension you are holding onto? If yes, direct your calm energy toward those areas and release the tension. There is no need for it. It's just you and your breath right now; nothing else.

Relax your body. Relax your mind.

Whenever you are under pressure, remind yourself to breathe. When you have power over your mind, you have power over any event that is thrown at you. As long as you stay calm and remember to breathe, you can get through anything.

Relax your body. Relax your mind. Remember to breathe.

When you are ready, take a few more deep breaths before returning your thoughts to your surroundings. Remember that you are in control. Just remember to breathe.

# Chapter 20

# Positive Body Image Script

L et's face it; there is always something that we don't approve of on our bodies. I 'm here to tell you that you absolutely need to stop being so hard on yourself! Everyone else out there is judging you, stop being mean to yourself. You have a heart in your chest, you have lungs that keep you breathing, and you have a body that allows you to get through life. It's time to appreciate everything that you have instead of fretting over the things you don't.

In the following meditation, we will focus on self-image and self-acceptance. Now is the time to learn how to love yourself. When you are ready, we can begin.

As you settle into your meditation space, I want you to find the most comfortable position possible. It doesn't matter what has happened before this moment nor what is going to happen after. Right now, there's you and this moment. Make yourself comfortable and allow for your mind and body to relax.

Before we begin, take a moment to take note of how you are feeling right now. How are you feeling? How is your body feeling? Take another few seconds and scan your body, starting from your toes and gently bring your focus up your feet, over your ankles, up your legs, and continue scanning up over your stomach and your chest, take that focus over your shoulders and neck and face.

Where are you feeling tense? Where are you feeling relaxed? Remember, there is no point in judging yourself right now. You are simply just becoming mindful of your body; there is no need to change anything right now. Notice as you become aware of the areas of tension, you are able to relax them with little to no effort. By simply being mindful, you allow your body to relax. Your muscles are becoming less tense and loose all on their own. All you have to do is sit there and relax. You're not even trying. With each passing moment, your body realizes that you are safe, and it's okay to let down your guard.

If you are feeling up to it, I would now like to open a conversation about your body image. The question here; what is body image? Perhaps the first thing that pops into your mind is what you feel your body should look like. Maybe you want a bigger butt or smaller hips or a bigger bust. That is okay. But, what does body image mean to you? Consider all of the ideas and thoughts you have about your own body. Take a second to take note of how those ideas and thoughts make you feel. Perhaps you are accepting of your body or maybe even comfortable. Some may feel dissatisfied and unhappy, and it's perfectly okay to feel however you are in this moment. There is absolutely no judgment, just a sense of being mindful of your body and mind.

Now, I want you to take a moment to consider accepting your body for everything that it is. What if you stopped wasting energy on hating aspects of your body and feeling perfectly okay about your physical self?

351

Bring your focus to your breath and think about what that would feel like if you could finally accept yourself. When was the last time you felt happy about your body? What part is the easiest for you to accept?

I want you to picture your body as a whole. You're not a collection of different parts. I want you to picture loving your mind, your body, and your soul. You are a collective person, and it's healthy to love yourself!

True, these thoughts can be difficult, but you can take a step back from facing these ideas head-on and take a few moments to relax. If at any point you feel overwhelmed, go ahead and breathe in deeply and allow all of the negative energy out with your next breath. Relax your mind, notice your breath, and center your thoughts.

If you feel tense anywhere in your body, allow the muscles to relax. With each breath you are taking, you can allow your body to relax and let go of tension. You are perfectly safe in this moment. No matter what your thoughts are on your body right now, it's okay.

Once your body is relaxed, and you are ready to start up again, I would like to go over some positive body image affirmations. If you would like, you can listen or repeat them to yourself. All you need to do in this moment is relax and allow yourself to be mindful and calm. When you are ready, we can begin.

It's okay for you to accept yourself the way you are.

Your body is beautiful.

Your soul is beautiful.

Your mind if beautiful.

You are wonderful the exact way you are.

There is nothing you need to change about your body.

You are a fantastic person.

It's okay to love the skin you are in.

Any imperfections you have make you, you.

You are healthy.

You are whole.

You are human.

It's okay to accept your imperfections.

You are human, and imperfections are a part of life.

You do not need to judge yourself.

You can use your energy to be positive.

It's okay to accept yourself for who you are.

You love your body.

You love your mind.

You love your soul.

Great. Now, after a deep breath or two, I would like for you to repeat after me.

It's okay for me to accept myself the way I am.

My body is beautiful.

My soul is beautiful.

My mind is beautiful.

I am wonderful the exact way I am.

There is nothing I need to change about my body.

I'm a fantastic person.

It's okay to love the skin I'm in.

Any imperfections I have make me, me.

I'm healthy.

I'm whole.

I'm human.

It's okay to accept my imperfections.

I'm human, and imperfections are a part of life.

I do not need to judge myself.

I can use my energy to be positive.

It's okay to accept myself for who I am

I love my body.

I love my mind.

I love my soul.

Go ahead and repeat these until you believe them. Once you do, take note of how these positive affirmations make you feel. What does it feel like to believe in your own self-worth and to accept yourself for how you are? Allow these thoughts to pass and kindly return your thoughts to your breath. Remember that there is nothing to worry about right now. All that matters in this moment is you and your breath — nothing else.

When you are ready to return to your day, gently bring your focus back to your surroundings. You are becoming aware of your body, relaxed in position. Listen to the world as it gently begins to buzz around you. I hope that you now feel centered and relaxed. Remember to love yourself and accept yourself for who you are. As you repeat these affirmations, you will begin to believe in yourself and lead a happier life.

# Chapter 21
# Self-Healing Scripts

I n short notice, sometimes, all we have is ourselves. If you need a few moments to step back and breathe in times of emotional and physical pain, the following meditations are going to be perfect for you. We will start out with simple healing and relaxation meditation and end with a guided morning starter complete with some daily affirmations. When you are ready, we can get started on learning how to self-heal.

Healing and Relaxing Meditation

Before we begin this first meditation toward self-healing, I invite you to create a comfortable space for yourself before we even begin. Go ahead and set yourself up in a safe space with zero distractions. For some, this may involve your favorite yoga mat, some peaceful music, or even a relaxing candle burning. I want you to create your space; however, makes you feel the best. Once this is complete, we can begin our meditation.

As you settle into your practice, go ahead and find a comfortable position. I want you to allow yourself to relax in this position, whether you are sitting or lying down. Now that you are feeling your body begin to relax go ahead and bring your awareness to your breathing. I would like to go ahead and just spend a few moments doing this. All you have to do is breathe.

(PAUSE)

With each breath, I want you to imagine that you are breathing in cleansing air. Allow for each breath you take to wash away the tension you have been holding in your body. If you feel some areas are tenser than others, go ahead and take a gentle note. From this point on, we will address these areas, and work on healing our body, healing our soul, and healing our mind. Good. Just breathe and let it all go.

(PAUSE)

Now, with your next breath, I invite you to close your eyes and begin to imagine a wave working its way toward you. This is a comfortable wave, filled with healing powers and gentleness. The water is warm and comfortable as it gently makes its way over to you. Now, picture the wave beginning to kiss your toes and gently washes over your feet. Perhaps this wave gives you a tingling sensation or how it feels to step into a warm bath. Allow for the relaxation to softly wash over your feet and up over your ankles. Take a deep breath in and enjoy this feeling of relaxation begin to take over your body.

(PAUSE)

Picture now that the wave is slowly working its way up your lower legs, over your upper legs, and begins to spread its way further up your body. How does this relaxing wave feel? Allow for it to rise up over your hips and gently caresses around your stomach and lower back. Take a few moments here to note how your core is feeling at a time like this. If it is in knots, take a few deep breaths and let it all go. You are in a safe space. This is a time to heal and forget past issues. They do not matter right now. There is just you and the healing power of this wave. Allow for it to wash up over your arms and your chest. Take a deep breath and focus on the healing powers.

(PAUSE)

While this may seem overwhelming for some, remember that this wave is filled with healing powers. I want you to give in to the feeling of relaxation and picture that this wave is now washing over your shoulders, up over your neck, and finally spreads over the top of your head. At this moment, your eyelids may begin to feel relaxed and heavy. I want you to relax and allow your body to let it all go. Notice now how wonderful your body begins to feel as you calm your mind and your body. You are relaxing completely from the crown of your head to the tips of your toes. Allow for the relaxation to spread down from your neck to your spine and into the bottom of your tailbone. You are in a very safe space right now, and you are doing a wonderful job with this meditation.

(PAUSE)

Fantastic. Before we finish up with this meditation, go ahead and take a few moments on your own to breathe. If there is any tension left in your body, picture the healing wave, and allow for it to wash over these areas to take away any stress you may be holding onto. After this meditation, I hope you enter awareness feeling better than before. You have the power to heal your mind and your soul. If you are ever at a loss, tune in to yourself and ask what you need. Sometimes, it's just a few moments of peace and quiet. Now, breathe and let go.

(PAUSE)

Meditation Time: 15 Minutes

Pain Management for Self-Healing Meditation

If you are feeling mental or physical pain right now, realize that you are moments away from finding peace and pain relief. When you are able to relax, this can be a very effective skill for pain management. For individuals who are able to relax through pain, they typically have a higher tolerance for the pain and feel it less. In the next few moments, we are going to go ahead and work through some exercises to help you relax and make that pain go away. When you are ready, find a comfortable position, and we can begin.

As you settle in, I now invite you to begin to become mindful of how you are feeling right now. As you make some mental notes, I do not want you to change anything of how you are feeling or what you are thinking about. Right now, all you need to do is observe your pain, your thoughts, and how these things feel to you. Our pain management begins with becoming aware of these feelings.

(PAUSE)

Now, I want you to take a deep breath in and let the tension go with your next exhale. Where is your body holding onto your tension? For each person, this is going to be different. Some of us hold our stress in our jaws, and others hold it in their shoulders. On a different note, I want you to become aware of the parts of your body that are relaxed at this moment. Where there is bad, you can always find good. Go ahead and take a few moments to take mental notes of where you are tense and where you are relaxed.

(PAUSE)

As we move through the next part of the exercise, I want you to continue to breathe slowly. A major part of pain management is to simply be passive with your attitude. We are not trying to make anything happen right now; it is all about taking notice of how you are feeling. Go ahead and breathe on your own for a few moments and try to let that tension go.

(PAUSE)

Pain is something we all experience. I want you to gently become aware of the pain you have experienced or are experiencing right now. Our bodies are constantly moving and changing. The way we feel in our bodies can change from morning to night. At the end of this meditation, you will feel different than how your body felt in the beginning. All you have to do right now is simply observe how you are feeling and take mental notes.

(PAUSE)

Now, I want you to begin to accept how you are feeling. While pain can be difficult and intolerable, I want you to accept how you are feeling both emotionally and physically. Accept the way you are, whether these feelings are positive and negative. We must accept ourselves for who we are, even in the hard times. Allow your mind and body to be exactly how they are. There is no good or bad; just allow yourself to exist. Breathe.

(PAUSE)

When you are ready, I would like to go through some self-healing affirmations together. You can repeat after me or simply listen to the words I am about to say. This is your practice; you can complete this meditation; however, you see fit. Take a deep breath, and we can begin.

(PAUSE)

At this moment...I am choosing to accept myself.

(PAUSE)

I accept myself...and I accept the pain that I feel.

(PAUSE)

I feel pain...but I will not let this pain define me.

(PAUSE)

I choose to let this pain go...I can be relaxed.

(PAUSE)

I accept myself for who I am and what I feel.

(PAUSE)

Wonderful. With these thoughts in mind, it is time to return to your awareness. I want you to carry these words with you through your day. Any time you feel pain, go ahead and repeat these affirmations to yourself. As you learn to breathe and relax, you will be able to let this pain go and accept yourself the way you are. To finish this practice up, go ahead and take a few more breaths on your own time. Allow yourself to release your pain and return to your day feeling more at peace.

(PAUSE)

Meditation Time: 20 Minutes

# Chapter 22

# Color Visualization Meditation Script

D o you have a short moment to meditate? This script is perfect for those who just need to take a few minutes out of their day. By visualizing calming colors, you'll be imagining each color of the rainbow so you can take a few moments to relax. Remember to focus your mind and allow yourself to relax into this moment, even if it's only for a few minutes.

Before we begin this script, take a few deep breaths on your own time. As you breathe, begin to draw your thoughts to how your body feels in this moment. Perhaps you are having a stressful day, or it's not going according to plan. That is okay. Try your best not to change anything in this moment. All you need to do is notice how your mind is feeling, how your body is feeling, and accept yourself for how you are in this moment.

As you continue working through your breath, carefully notice that your body is already beginning to relax a bit. Breathe in…and allow for your shoulders to drop from your ears. Exhale and release your teeth from being clenched together. As you become more and more relaxed, your eyelids may even begin to feel heavier.

Good…Now I want to invite you to begin to paint a picture in your mind. To start off, I want you to begin to imagine a shade of red. Once you have the color red in your mind, try to paint your mind with different shades of red. What does the color red remind you of? Try to think of red objects such as sunsets, delicious apples, romantic roses, or anything that comes to your mind. Take note of how the color red makes you feel and allow yourself to relax into this color.

When you are ready, bring awareness to the color orange. Notice how the orange blends from the red and fills your vision. How does the color orange make you feel? As you work through your breath, try to picture some of your favorite orange objects. There are festive pumpkins, delicious carrots, and beautiful orange flowers. Try to envision different shades of orange and enjoy the feeling this color brings to you.

Next, we will bring our awareness to the joyful color of yellow. Take a deep breath in and allow for your vision to be filled with different shades of yellow. Imagine fresh lemons, bright flowers, and the sun warming your skin. There are so many different levels of yellow to imagine, allow it to cleanse your mind with pure joy. Imagine the color yellow filling you up and making you happy.

Now, the yellow is gently going to shift into a green color. Green is often associated with joy as well. There are many different shades of green, especially in nature. I want you to think about beautiful green leaves and grass and plants that you find out in the world. There are gorgeous shades of green; allow the color to fill your vision. As you inhale, take note of how this color makes you feel.

When you are ready to move onto the next color, begin to fill your vision with the color blue. The sky above us is blue, the water in the ocean and the streams and the lake are blue, perhaps your favorite person in this world has blue eyes. Think of what the color blue means to you and allow it to fill your senses. Inhale and exhale; allow this color to fill you with a sense of calm.

Purple is the next color that should begin to fill your mind. There are many beautiful shades of purple that you can find in the sunrise, in flowers, and other objects. Immerse yourself into this color and gently find your breath. Notice now how much calmer your breathing has become now that you have let go of your stress. In this moment, there is just you and your favorite calming colors.

If you would like, return to your favorite color out of the ones we just covered or perhaps select a color that makes you the happiest. No matter what color you choose, allow it to fill all of your senses, and remind you to be relaxed. No matter how bad things get, there is always a different way of looking at it. If you are stressed, close your eyes and remind yourself of your favorite color and the objects associated with that color.

When you are ready, I now invite you to bring awareness back to your surroundings. As you gently open your eyes, notice now how your mind is clear, and your body feels so much more relaxed. Give your muscles a little stretch and jump back into your day with a better sense of peace and joy.

If you enjoyed any of these meditations, you most likely have a very creative mind. Visualization meditations can take practice if the concept is something you're not used to, but it can be incredibly rewarding!

I suggest starting with more basic meditations before moving onto some of the more advanced scripts to follow. Being able to visualize your journey is an important aspect of meditation. When you are able to paint yourself a picture, this means that your mind is open and free to explore spiritual possibilities.

If you feel silly at first, you're not alone! Remember to focus on your breath, and that your practice is your own. Please feel free to customize any of these scripts to your liking. At the end of the day, the only thing that matters is that you are comfortable with what you are doing. As long as you are able to relax and calm yourself, you can benefit greatly from meditation.

# Chapter 23

# Guided Meditation - 30 Minutes Mindfulness Training

(to be read quite slowly. Increasingly slowly to help bring the more rapid state of waking in line with the rhythmic and slower cadence of breath and sleep)

Welcome.

This meditation is to be experienced lying down in a safe, comfortable and uninterrupted place you can remain asleep once the meditation plays through.

(PAUSE)

Lying down now, give yourself the space to breathe deeply and fully. Allow the breath to enter through your nose, descend along the length of your body and reach your belly which rises in response to the fullness of oxygenated air. It feels SO GOOD to let in this fresh new breath.

As you exhale, let the parts of the day you no longer need rise up and out of your body with your breath, gently breathing out through your mouth, lips shaped into a small "O". Feel the weight of the day leaving your body as you exhale, your belly flattening as the air leaves and pause here in this open space of release.

Good.

Now, breathe again in through your nose, imagining the breath has a color to it, any color of your choosing, the first color that comes to mind. Allow this color to permeate your entire body as you breathe it in through you nose, as the air travels to every single cell, bringing light and warmth, oxygen and peace to your being. You are a being filled with this colored light and infused with the newness of the atmosphere around you, a system of molecules and vibrations always regenerating with its own wisdom. All you must do to be a part of it is to breathe it in. Let it fill you.

Wonderful.

As you exhale, allow everything that no longer serves you to simply rise up and float out of your body through your rounded lips in a nice long exhale. Find yourself noticing the lightness that comes with each breath and release. Feel the peace of letting go the day. The week. The elements in your life you no longer need. How easy it is to simply let them go. How good it feels to breathe in the atmosphere. To take part in the universe. To discover the grace of breath.

Continue now, breathing in through your nose, bringing in light and color and newness and exhaling through the mouth, releasing all that is ready to release.

[1 minute of silence or light music]

Beautiful.

You find yourself feeling lighter by the moment, releasing everything that no longer serves and embracing the expansive wisdom that continually surrounds you, allowing the regenerative nature of the universe to become part of you through breath and rhythm. Through the simple act of breathing. This communion with life all around you. And it feels so good to be part of this rhythm.

Notice also how your body becomes more grounded, more connected to the substrate beneath it, to the earth itself. How you are at once light as air and part of the earth. How you are right where you need to be, in the most perfect place for you right now in this entire universe, supported and free.

And allow yourself to deepen further into this peace. Let any tension remaining in your body, your mind, flow down into the ground, into the core of the earth itself to be transformed and used for other purposes. You do not have to hold onto it any longer. The earth itself knows how to best use the excess energies we do not need.

Feel yourself melt right into the place you are, becoming fluid, becoming more sentient, becoming grace. Movement and light, breath and air. Every part of you now, every cell in your body breathes in the universe around you and breathes out in communion. Breathing becomes– you realize it IS– a conversation. It is a connection. Breathing is BEING life.

You are being. You are life. You are in the perfect place at the perfect time. You are everything you need to be right now.

Your body is pleasurably connected to the fibers beneath you. You notice the pleasant heaviness that comes from the safety of sinking into a warm space, a space you can trust, a space in which you are completed connected, held and supported. With every breath now, you sink deeper and deeper into a state of peace, of ultimate comfort, of knowing your place in the world. It is as simple as this, a noticing of the way you are part of everything around you and the beauty that comes from breathing in the atmosphere and breathing out the colors of your breath to create a resonance that holds and supports you right where you are at; just as you are now.

Every time you exhale now you create a field of light and color around you. Every time you inhale, the light and color become part of you. Every time you inhale, you feel yourself fill with lightness of air. Every time you exhale, you deepen into the fibers below you and the support of the earth itself.

Allow your noticing to grow larger.

Notice how the room around you becomes filled with this positive light and energy that you are breathing in and out. How the energies of the entire universe, how the support and grounding of the earth infuses the space in which you find yourself, and how this changes the space itself. Fills it with more peace, more safety, more comfort, more life and love.

Allow this to expand even further. Notice how this beautiful energy also infuses the entire house or building, the larger area in which you find yourself. How your very nexus, your very center of breathing and imbibing the universe is helping the entire space around you, large and small, near and far, become more infused with loving, peaceful and serene energy. How you create a larger sphere of radiance that surrounds as far as you can see, as far as you can feel, and breathes with you, within you.

(1-minute music/silence)

Ahhhh (sigh type of voice, in order to engage this response in listener, like a long deep exhale). This is the majesty of the living world as it becomes part of you, responds to you, emanates from you. This is the magic of breath and grounding. This is your deepest nature, your connected being, your beautiful soul. At once a part of everything around you and helping to create that which is around you.

Each breath continues to deepen your state of peace and harmony, rest and relaxation, trust and security in the communication you have with the particles of air, the elements of nature, the energies of the universe.

As with a cradle, you are held and supported, loved and carried and can allow yourself to sink deeper into a state of bliss and union, comfort and support.

You notice the colors shift and change, the sounds soften and swell, the concrete pieces of waking life fall away. The world blends and melds with your larger sense of being, with the larger consciousness of the earth, with the wisdom of the universe at large. Your body softens and stretches, settles and soothes. You are fluid and warm, bathed by the universe itself as you drift into a restful state of existence.

Let the rhythm of your breath soothe you. Feel its rise and fall in its most natural state massaging every cell in your body. Massaging the musculature surrounding your skull, releasing the tensions on the bones, your jaw, your eyes, your sinuses and tongue entirely. Feel the sweet release of open space for your mind to flow freely, your head itself swoon. Let your head sway side to side as you continue to unwind down into the neck, releasing even further any aches or pains, any stiffness and tightness, becoming fluid, light, air, becoming oxygen itself flowing through the body, connecting to the space around you.

Let your shoulders drop into the surface beneath you, releasing every bit of weight they carry, and your chest rise and fall easily in the softness you create with your breath. It is as though effortless, your breathing, your releasing, your increasing sense of peace and comfort. This restful state of bliss.

Notice your abdomen soften, with each and every breath, your belly is massaged from the inside out, your entire body can sense the renewed vigor of the cells, so full of oxygen and the softness this release brings. Even your hips roll wide open, released into the rhythm of the breath, the flow of blood and openness of your state of being.

Your low back and legs follow suit, settling into the most comfortable state of repose, rocking slightly with each intake of breath and settling with each outtake until your exhale reaches the very tips of your toes, the base of your feet and sends itself out into the air around you, out into the universe to be recycled, regenerated, and transformed into new energy or matter. You exhale all that you no longer need and inhale the freshness of new breath, the lightness of being, the fluidity of an ever-nourishing universe.

When you inhale again, you revel in the lightness of your body, the sense of being water itself, the motion of being still. You find you are everything that is peaceful about this universe, that you are so satisfied in this state of being. That you have become peace itself.

Your body knows how to best support you. It knows how to hold the attention of deep relaxation while being alert to the world around you. Your mind knows how to heed the call of the body, the need for rest, the ability to transition between states. It knows that when it is needed it will be called upon again, but for now, everything is just fine. There is nothing but this space, nothing but this peace, and a certainty in the wisdom of dreams.

You float and absorb the energies of the womb of life and allow yourself the regenerative nature of sleep knowing that anything important will gain your attention as it needs to, you need not hold onto any ideas or thoughts, they will find you again when it is time.

And in this you drift and know this is a type of home. A connection to the cosmos inside of you and all around you. A colorful and flavorful connection to life that blends with your cells, blends with your neurons and leads you into a blissful form of serenity conducive to sleep.

Breathe now, in and out at your own pace, while the energies of the universe move through you, cleanse you, inform you, hold and support you and allow you the deep healing of rest. Feel the incredible expansiveness and drift of the universe in your cells and in your peaceful body. Allow yourself to sink in.

(Music/sounds to support the transitional state into sleep. Next 15-20minutes)

(Towards ends of the recording, leave with this whispered prompt):

As the music fades you find yourself sinking even deeper into rest. The silence brings you a peace greater than you have known and carries you in sleep for exactly the right amount of time for you.

You breathe and find peace in being.

You are exactly where you need to be.

You are just perfect as you are.

You continue to breathe and release.

As the world too, breathes and unfolds.

# Chapter 24

# Guided Meditation for Self-Esteem Script

There are too many moments in our life when we are our own worst critics. If you are constantly bashing your body, putting yourself down, or feel you generally have low self-esteem, this script is going to be perfect for you! Through meditation, you can boost your confidence and your self-esteem. When you feel good about yourself, your body will be able to relax and just live life the way it's meant to be.

As always, I now invite you to relax. You will want to find your most comfortable position and allow all of the tension to begin melting away from your limbs. As you find your breath, I want to paint a picture for you. Simply do nothing right now but allow for your breath to become natural.

As you breathe, I want you to picture a staircase in your mind. Right now, you are standing at the top of these stairs. As you look down at the bottom, there is a pool of relaxation and peace. When you are looking down, I invite you to take a mental note of how you are feeling right now.

Take a deep breath and picture yourself taking a soft step down. With this step, you are already closer to the relaxation pool you want to be floating in. Each step you take down, feel how much more relaxed your body is becoming. Your arms are relaxing; your legs are relaxing; your jaw is becoming loose as you step closer and closer to the bottom of the stairs.

One step at a time, you are making your way down the stairs. Your arms are feeling heavier, your legs are heavier, the relaxation is pulling you down gently, and it feels comfortable. You are safe in this moment and slipping into the pool of relaxation will be such a relief. Allow for gravity to pull you down gently.

Feel now as your back and your neck are both relaxing, too. Your shoulders being pulled away from being shrugged up into your shoulders, your eyes becoming heavy with relaxation and every part of your body is becoming calm and relaxed. Go ahead and allow for your mind to drift away from you. Everything is feeling wonderful as you approach the bottom of the stairs.

Now, you are taking the final steps to the bottom of the stairs. Go ahead and admire the pool of relaxation as you gently step in. Allow for your mind to drift as you settle into the calmness of the pool and rest your eyes. Your whole body is loose and relaxed; you haven't a care in the world.

I would like you to allow your mind to drift now. As it does, I would like to go over some positive affirmations for your self-esteem. You can listen to them and repeat them if you would like to. While some may apply to you, others may not. Listen to your mind and your heart as we go over the affirmations. Once we are done, you can allow your mind to continue drifting. Simply breathe, relax, and we can begin.

You are capable of doing so many amazing things with your life.

You are a loving person, and you deserve to be happy.

You are strong, but you do not need to be strong all of the time.

You are worth it.

You have the power to control your emotions.

It's okay to accept yourself.

You need to be kind to yourself.

You are absolutely perfect the way you are in this moment.

It's okay to be happy.

It's okay to be proud of yourself.

Now, repeat after me.

I'm capable of doing so many amazing things with my life.

I'm a loving person, and I deserve to be happy.

I'm strong, but I do not need to be strong all of the time.

I'm worth it.

I have the power to control my emotions.

It's okay to accept myself.

I need to be kind to myself.

I'm absolutely perfect the way I am in this moment.

It's okay to be happy.

It's okay to be proud of myself.

Allow for your mind to drift and repeat these affirmations as needed. You can repeat them until you believe them. These are all true for you, and you deserve to build your sense of self-assurance and confidence. At the end of the day, you will always have yourself. It's up to you to become your biggest cheerleader!

You can, and you will make positive changes in your life. When you increase your self-esteem and gain a positive mindset, you will begin to attract positive events and positive people into your life.

Now, I want you to bring awareness back to your mind. Feel now how much happier and relaxed you feel. Notice how calm you are and take a moment to enjoy this new sensation. Any time you are feeling down on yourself, I want you to repeat these affirmations to yourself. You deserve to feel good. Be in charge of your own happiness.

When you are ready to return to your day, take a few more deep breaths. Gently bring your awareness back to your space and return to your day with positivity and gratitude.

# Chapter 25

# Guided Meditation: Overcome Fear

Welcome to session one of overcoming anxiety, fear and discontentment every day for 1 week...

I'm honored to guide you through this relaxing session so that you can let go of all doubts that hold you back from attaining the life that you deserve ....

meditation is a wonderful tool for being able to calm the mind and relax the body so that you can think clearly about all that you want to achieve and strive for ... in a state of deep relaxation you are able to let go of fear, doubt, and suffering when the art of meditation is practiced on a daily basis ...

so let's begin ...

making sure you're in a place where nothing will disturb you from the outside world ... please take a nice deep breath in and out allowing your eyes to close as you exhale ... ensure that you are very relaxed by having your head fully supported and all of your muscles can fully let go as we go along through this session ...

continue taking deep breaths in and out counting to 7 breaths as you go along ...

breathing in .... and breathing out any worries from your day ... 1...

breathing in fresh oxygen .... and breathing out your stress and concerns... 2...

inhaling a new peaceful sense of being ... exhaling any tension ... 3...

inhale serenity .... exhale troubles ... 4...

breathing in that fresh new air ... and breathing out anything that holds you back ... 5...

inhale peace .... exhale stress ... 6...

last one, so make it really full and deep ... and breathing out into a nice state of relaxation ... 7...

good...

let your breath return to a natural flow now... but try to follow closely along with it... notice how your breath is slowing to a nice rhythm and you body is gently expanding and contracting as you breathe automatically...

(pause)

Now draw your attention to the tips of your toes ... notice any sensations in your toes ... the temperature ... the nearby textures ...

(pause)

bring your awareness now to the soles of your feet ... notice how the soles of your feet feel ...

(pause)

allow for a nice relaxing sensation to begin in the soles of your feet … you can imagine that each time you inhale this relaxation expands … breathe in and let your feet become completely relaxed…

(pause)

now allow this relaxation to spread into your ankles …. notice how good your feet feel when you imagine this comforting feeling …

(pause)

allow for relaxation to travel up into your calves, filling your lower legs with a sense of calm… each breath you take, the relaxation intensifies ….

(pause)

breathing … relaxing … notice how your knees are letting go of any tension … just by placing your awareness on them ….

(pause)

this nice feeling travels up into your upper legs … relaxing your quadriceps … hamstrings … your entire thighs let go of any tension … and sink deeply into the surface that supports your legs …

(pause)

notice how each leg is so very relaxed in this very moment …. can you become aware of any differences between the left leg and the right leg?

I don't know if one is more relaxed than the other ... or perhaps one might feel lighter, or heavier ... whatever you notice is perfectly fine ...

(pause)

imagine that this relaxation is spreading into your pelvis and hips ... it is so soothing and so wonderful ... you deserve this deep relaxation ....

(pause)

allow for your abdomen to receive this same love ... letting go of any tension in the gut ... stress that you hold here seems to melt away ... disappearing as each moment passes by ... allow it to go ....

(pause)

your stomach is so very relaxed ... calm. soothed ... in a state of automatic flow... feeling appreciation for this nice sensation in your abdomen ....

(pause)

as you follow along with your breath ... allow for this comforting feeling to travel up into your ribs and chest ... deeply relaxing your heart ... imagine you can focus directly on your heart ... this strong muscle beats kindly for you ... it deserves to relax ... it deserves your love .... send your heart love right now in whatever way feels best for you ...

(pause)

Good...

witness your lungs gently expanding and contracting with the breath ....
allow this sensation to relax you even more ....

(pause)

Now imagine that this beautiful sensation of relaxation is slowly
traveling down each arm... melting away any tension as it moves ever
so slowly...

(pause)

Feel this profound comfort from the neck down... you are almost fully
immersed in deep relaxation...

(pause)

You are ready to allow this wonderful feeling to slowly travel up your
neck now, relaxing any tension that may be present in the jaw... and
cheeks... and mouth... and nose... feel your eyes even relaxing behind
the eyelids... you deserve this...

(pause)

Let your entire forehead feel as if it is melting away all the years of
anxiety or stress.... Let it all go...

(pause)

You are doing so well...

(pause)

Right now, this time is fully for you... time for you to let go and feel a deep state of relaxation... the perfect amount of comfort that is right for you in this very moment... allow it...

(pause)

By now, your entire head is so very relaxed... laying heavy upon a pillow... resting...

(pause)

On the count of three, send a signal to all of your muscles in the body to let go of any last remaining tension... you can do this...

1.... 2.... 3....

Let any stress or pressure release.... Returning to your natural state of balance...

(pause)

You may be feeling a soothing heaviness.... Or a gentle lightness... whatever you are feeling is right for you... experience it... allow it... enjoy it...

(pause)

It is impossible for anxiety to be present in this deep state of relaxation you have cultivated, so really soak up the feeling of being perfectly balanced... aligned with how you truly are meant to feel...

(pause)

Right now,... right here... you are relaxed... you have no where to be and nothing to do... no one needs you and you don't need to do anything... simply rest...

(pause)

This deep state of relaxation allows for any healing to take place on a cellular level, so please tune in to the great power of natural regeneration...

(pause)

All of your body's systems are in perfect working order... your body is working as a unit... all is well... all is sound...

(pause)

Your mind is free to roam through thoughts as they pass on by... your emotions calm and tuned into the perfect state of being...

(pause)

Relax...

(pause)

Now, if you'd like you can imagine something that brings you fear, but since you are in such a wonderful state of calm, you can witness this fear without getting emotionally involved... what is it that commonly makes you afraid? Just see it, as if you are watching a black and white movie...

(pause)

See this fear on a screen in front of you... the movie is called "something that holds me back"

Fear is simply a signal that you are being presented with something you need to overcome in order to be truly free and happy...

(pause)

What is it that stops you from being your best?

(pause)

As the movie plays through, you are shown what life would be like if you stepped through this fear and made it safely to the other side... notice how the movie flushes out into full and vibrant color...

(pause)

What are you doing in this beautiful movie now that you are on the other side of what held you back?

(pause)

See the movie in radiant colors and magnificent scenes that show you living out your dreams... you are successful... you are glowing with good health... you are amazing... hear all the sounds...

(pause)

Now, imagine that you can step directly into this movie and actually FEEL how it is on the other side of fear...

(pause)

Touch something in your surroundings.... Witness the people who are around... see if you can smell any fragrances... what kinds of clothes do you wear when you are free from fear?

(pause)

Very good...

Breathe in very deeply once more, and say to yourself "I am determined to make this my reality"

And begin drawing your awareness to the present moment... feeling confident... calm... and a boost in self-esteem that you can overcome anything...

Wiggle your fingers to become aware of your body... open your eyes to reorient yourself to the room... you did it... welcome back.

# Chapter 26

# 30 Minute Guided Meditation for Sleep, Relaxation, & Stress Relief

[Introduction- Stretch and positioning: 3 minutes]

Prepare your room by turning off any devices that might be a distraction. You may need to put your phone in another room if you are tempted to check it repeatedly. Turn off the TV or any music that is playing. You want to set the stage for a night of rest and relaxation. Dim the lights.

Lie down, on your back and settle into a position that is comfortable for you. If you are not comfortable lying on your back, you might want to put a or rolled blanket under your knees. Make sure that your head and neck are supported as well.

If it is comfortable for you, try moving your head back and forth and turning it side to side to loosen up your neck muscles.

Let it relax back into a comfortable position

Wiggle your shoulders and let them fall back into a relaxed position

Keeping your buttocks on the bed, move your hips a bit and then let them fall back into a relaxed position.

You want your body to be in a neutral and comfortable position so:

Make sure that your chin is not pointing too far up. Tuck in in just a bit to allow the neck to lengthen and the jaw to relax.

Tuck your shoulders underneath you and then let them relax into a natural position

Let your hands rest at your sides, palms up or down, or on your abdomen.

Let your legs relax, your feet and knees may roll out when they are relaxed. Try not to hold them in any specific position, just let them fall naturally.

Pause to allow participants a couple minutes to adopt a comfortable position.

## [Intention Setting And Focus On Breathing: 10 Minutes]

You may find that you will doze during this meditation. That is ok. Don't force yourself to stay awake if you feel that you are sleepy.

Close your eyes lightly. For this time, you aren't going to try to do anything. There is no need to worry about things that happened today or things that might happen tomorrow. Right now, all you need to do is to be here, in your body, on your bed letting your mind do what it needs to do to relax for a good night's sleep.

Thank yourself for taking this time for self-care. You deserve a night of restful sleep and to wake up feeling refreshed and ready for the day. This is one thing that you can do that is just for yourself. No guilt, no worries.

Know that whatever worries you and stops you from sleeping won't be fixed by keeping you awake.

Know that no matter how you slept last night, or the night before, you can sleep well tonight. This is the only night that matters.

Pause a minute for reflection

Breath in and out naturally a few times.

Pause a minute for reflection

Take a few deep breaths and exhale whatever tension you feel. Inhale slowly and really feel where the air is going. It is normal to breath less than we can. Right in this moment, you want to breath as fully as possible.

Take a deep breath and feel the air as it flows through your nostrils, down into your lungs and fully into your abdomen. Breathe in as deeply as you can.

Exhale slowly, pushing the air out, first from your abdomen and then from your lungs.

Think about any areas of tightness you may have had when you took that breath. If it felt stuck anywhere, feel what it would be like to relax that area.

You are going to take a few deep breaths again and think about relaxing into the breath. I will be giving you instructions for relaxation but don't feel that you need to match the pace of your breath with my instructions. Just keep breathing deeply and try to apply the instructions with each breath.

When you exhale, don't push out the air so much that you are pulling in your stomach.

On your next deep inhale, feel the flow through your nostrils, down behind your jaw into your throat. Sometimes people tighten their throat when breathing deeply. Try to tuck your chin, just a bit, to lengthen your neck relax your jaw and think about opening your throat to allow the air to pass freely through and into your lungs.

Exhale slowly, feeling the air flow out of your body.

Pause a minute for reflection

Exhale naturally.

Pause a minute for reflection

On your next deep inhale, feel the airflow from your nostril, down your throat and into your lungs. Feel your abdomen rise as you fill your lungs. Relax your stomach and let it push out. Don't worry, no one is watching. Use your stomach to help your lungs fill more fully. A lot of us aren't used to relaxing our stomachs this way. We don't like to push it out and look fat but know that no one is watching you right now.

Exhale naturally, relax your stomach and try that again. Inhale deeply, feeling the air in your lungs and your abdomen pushing out. Relaxing your shoulders and letting your stomach push out.

Take three more deep breaths at your own pace, feel for any remaining areas of tension. Meet those areas without judgment and try to relax them. Don't worry if they still feel tight. Just take note of them as you move your attention elsewhere.

Let your breath relax and become natural again.

Pause a minute for reflection

## [Body Scan: 10 Minutes]

As your body relaxes, it may begin to feel heavy. Feel how it rests on the bed. You are supported in this meditation by the things around you. They hold you and allow you to do the work you need to do to unclutter your mind.

Like your breath, your body may hold areas of tension that distract you. As we scan the body, we will try to release these areas and achieve a fuller relaxation. When you notice tension, try to relax those muscles. You may find that a small stretch and release of the muscles helps reduce the tension. This doesn't have to be a big movement. It is something that resets the muscle memory into one of relaxation rather than tension.

Bring your attention to the top of your head. Focus on what that feels like. Maybe it's warm or maybe you feel a breeze. If you don't think about it much, it might be hard to feel the top of your head. Imagine it touching the air around you. You might feel something strongly, like heat or a breeze. Whatever you feel, or don't feel, is ok. Just notice whatever it is, without judgment.

Pause a minute for reflection

Move your attention to your cheeks and around your mouth. Notice if you are holding tension in either of these places. Think about what to would feel like to let that tension go. Try bringing your lips into a soft small smile. This smile is mostly internal. It always feels better to smile and helps to relax your whole face. Don't worry if this all feels a little funny, just relax and let it happen or not without judgment.

Pause a minute for reflection

Now bring your attention to your neck and shoulders. These are very common areas for storing stress and tension. If you keep them tight, you may not even be able to imagine what they would feel like relaxed. Try shrugging your shoulders and tucking them back. Move your head back and forth a little bit. If any of these actions hurts, stop. Let your shoulders feel heavy and fall away from your neck. Notice whatever you feel in your neck and shoulders without judgment. However much you relax them is more than they were relaxed before!

Pause a minute for reflection

Focus on your heart area, stomach, and abdomen. Notice if you are holding any tension on those areas. Nerves and worries like to settle there. You can let those go for now. You have already promised yourself that you will get to those things when you are finished with this. You can let the wait for just a few more minutes while you prepare your mind for them. Holding tension in your stomach won't help them to get done. Try to imagine your chest and stomach relaxed and not distracting you from things you want to focus on.

Pause a minute for reflection

Move your attention to your arms. They might feel heavy to you, that is how they are when they are relaxed. Let them rest however is comfortable to you. Notice if you have any tension in your hands and stretch your fingers just a bit to let that go. Let them relax again, resting on your legs or the floor.

Pause a minute for reflection

Bring your attention into your lower back and pelvis. You've been sitting still for a few minutes and may find that you are tight. Feel free to wiggle a bit to get comfortable and release any tension that may be in your lower back. Notice any areas of tension in your pelvis. Let any tension go without letting yourself slump or slouch.

Pause a minute for reflection

Now move your attention to your legs and feet. Sometimes, we are so used to holding ourselves up with our legs that we don't even notice the tension we have in our thighs. Lt the fall naturally while keeping your feet connected to the floor. If you are lying down, let your knees and feet fall naturally to the side. You may want to stretch or wiggle them a bit to feel the relaxation.

Take three deep breaths at your own pace, linger a bit on the exhale but don't force it.

Feel what this state of full relaxation feels like. Maybe you haven't felt this relaxed in a while. Know that you can create this for yourself at any time.

Pause for moment for reflection

## [Conclusion: 7 Minutes]

Shift your focus back to your breath. Let your breathing become natural and notice the inhale and exhale. Try not to force it. If you find yourself breathing slower or faster than normal, notice that and try to let the need to control the breath go. Normally, you don't think much about your breathing so it's common for people to change how they breathe when they start to pay attention to it.

This is a light focus on your breath.

It's just in …. And out….

One breath, in…. And out

When your mind drifts, notice that you have become distracted and, without judging, bring your attention back to this one breath.

Focus on just this breath….

Take each breath one at a time.

Pause for a couple minutes of silence.

As you end this meditation, thank yourself for taking this time to prepare yourself and settle your mind and body for a restful night's sleep. It might not feel like it, but you have taken an important step towards clearing your mind and practicing relaxation. This will help you to let go of whatever thoughts or worries might prevent you for sleeping well.

Know that you can achieve this level of relaxation every night before bed. When you want this, just take a moment to feel your breath and remind yourself that worries, and tension are just distractions that you can put aside while you focus on more important things. Whenever you feel them creeping into your mind, bring your attention back to the breath.

Inhale

Exhale

Take one more deep breath and feel the weight of your body on the bed. This is rest. This is how you replenish.

Let yourself feel this fully and completely

Let yourself rest.

# Chapter 27

# Guided Meditation for Anxiety

Find a comfortable place to sit. Either on a chair or on the ground.

Adjust your posture accordingly and sit upright with your spine straight, neck tall and shoulders relaxed.

When you are ready, gently close your eyes.

Allow yourself to settle in the here and now.

(10 seconds)

Become aware of your surroundings. Notice any sounds around you. They may be loud or subtle. Maybe there is a sound of the clock ticking. Or, the humming noise of your air conditioning. Or, noise from the streets. Maybe you can hear the chirping of the birds outside. Or, it is completely silent. Just notice whatever sounds or silence in your environment.

(20 seconds)

Now, pay attention to your thoughts and notice what thoughts are popping up in your mind

(5 seconds)

What are you thinking about?

Are you thinking of your problems or your plans for the day?

Just become aware of the thoughts in your mind and let them go.

(10 seconds)

Now, bring your attention to your breathing.

Take a deep breath in through your nose and feel it fill your body.

(5 seconds)

Exhale completely and let the air leave your body.

(5 seconds)

Keep breathing deeply.

(30 seconds)

When you notice your mind wandering, just focus on your breathing and bring your attention back to my voice.

(30 seconds)

Feel the sensation in your nose as the air touches it.

(15 seconds)

Become aware of the air as it fills your lungs till they are fully inflated.

(5 seconds)

Then, gently release your breath and feel as your lungs become deflated. Feel the air leave your body through the nose.

(5 Seconds)

Now, return to your normal breathing rhythm. Let your breathing assume its own natural rhythm and just observe each inhale and exhale.

(30 seconds)

Remain alert and aware. If your mind wanders, bring your attention back to your breathing.

(30 seconds)

Now, notice the parts of your body that are in contact with the ground. Fell the support of the surface beneath you.

(10 seconds)

Direct your focus to your toes. Wiggle all your ten toes and feel them relaxing.

(10 seconds)

Make circles with your feet and let your ankles relax.

(10 seconds)

Notice your calf muscles and knees. Tighten the muscles around them and let go.

(10 seconds)

Bring your attention to your thighs, squeeze them together and release allowing them to relax.

(10 seconds)

Take your attention to your buttocks and feel them pressing down the surface beneath you. Relax them and let go of any tension around them.

(10 seconds)

Focus on your pelvic area and relax it.

(10 seconds)

Move your attention to your back. Do you feel any tension?

Tighten the muscles in your back and release them. Feel them relax as the tension around your back dissolves away.

(10 seconds)

Gently, take a deep breath through your nose and feel the air fill your entire body and then exhale completely releasing it.

(10 seconds)

Take a deep breath in and fill your belly completely allowing it to expand as much as possible and then exhale letting it fall and completely relax.

(10 seconds)

Round your shoulders and upper back and squeeze your chest muscles and then release and assume an upright position allowing the chest to open au.

(10 seconds)

Now, bring your attention to the shoulders. Squeeze them up towards your ears and then release them down letting go any tension as you feel them relax.

(10 seconds)

Stretch out your hands in front of you and make tight fists and then release spreading your fingers wide.

(10 seconds)

Rets your hands on your lap.

Drop your chin towards your collar bone and let the back of your neck stretch and release and tension.

(10 seconds)

Lift your chin as up as possible and allow the front of your neck to stretch and release tension.

(10 seconds)

Clench your jaw, close your eyes and tighten your facial muscles. Breath in deeply and hold your breath in for 7,6,5,4,3,2,1 and exhale gently as you allow your jaw and facial muscles to relax and then open your eyes.

(10 seconds)

Sit in the awareness of your entire body. It is relaxed and alert.

(30 seconds)

Bring back your attention to your breathing.

Inhale deeply and silently repeat the mantra 'I am inhaling.'

Exhale slowly as you silently say to yourself, 'I am exhaling.'

Keep breathing and reciting the mantras "I am inhaling", "I am exhaling".

(30 seconds)

When you notice your mind wandering, gently bring you attention back to your breathing and repeat the mantra.

I am inhaling.

I am exhaling

(30 seconds)

Gently direct your awareness to your body.

Feel the surface you are sitting on.

(5 seconds)

Notice the temperature on your skin.

(5 seconds)

Listen to the sounds around you.

(5 seconds)

Listen to your breathing.

(5 seconds)

Notice the sensations in your body.

(5 seconds)

Gently wiggle your fingers and your toes.

When you feel ready, open your eyes.

You are now ready to go on with your plans for the rest of the day.

## Quick Guided Meditation For Anxiety

Sit comfortably in your chair and relax.

Gently close your eyes and begin to become aware of your breath. Bring your attention to your nose and notice the air as it comes in and goes out.

(20 seconds)

Take a deep breath in and release it slowly.

Take three more deep breaths.

(30 seconds)

Allow your body to relax and adapt to your breathing rhythm.

10 seconds

Notice the sounds in and out of the room; These sounds are not distractions but simply an expression of what is happening in your surroundings. Notice them and continue to breathe deeply and let your body continue to relax.

(30 seconds)

Is your mind wandering? It is okay for your mind to move from one thought to another. Slowly, focus your attention back to your breath. Notice how your chest is rising as you breathe in and gently falling as you breath out.

(20 seconds)

Make each inhale deep until your lungs cannot accommodate any more air.

(10 seconds)

And then breathe out completely allowing all the air out.

(10 seconds)

Keep focusing on your breathing, and if you feel your mind wandering gently guide it back to your breathing.

(30 seconds)

Breath in deeply.

Breath out gently.

Release all the expectations that you are holding on for this practice.

(10 seconds)

Your only responsibility at this moment is to consciously breath in and slowly release your breath.

Let go of all the judgments that you hold on this meditation. About whether you are being perfect or not.

(10 seconds)

As you breathe in notice your belly rises and as your breath out slowly notice the belly fall.

(20 seconds)

Allow yourself to relax and be present to this moment.

(30 seconds)

Now, take three deep breaths.

(30 seconds)

When you are ready, gently open your eyes and move your body slowly.

# Chapter 28

# Guided Meditation for Anxiety and Stress

**T**ry to practice this exercise daily, in a place where nobody is going to disturb you.

During this exercise I'm going to ask you

to contract your muscles but this

shouldn't be something uncomfortable or painful.

As I direct you, try to contract

your muscles up to 60 to 70 percent of

your capacity.

Also, keep in mind that is

completely normal if your mind loses

focus or you get distracted.

If any thoughts come to your mind,

simply watch them without any judgment.

Some people are not used to being relaxed

and they may think this is just a waste of time,

but achieving mastery of the art of

relaxation is a very important element

to get rid of anxiety and stress.

If you find it difficult to relax, that is a

very powerful reason to practice this

exercise more often.

As with any other discipline,

the more you practice it,

the better you get at it and the more

you're going to be able to enjoy it.

This is very critical to achieve the results you

want, so let's begin...

Put yourself in a comfortable position.

You might be sitting on a chair or a

couch... a place that gives support to your

back, where you can keep your back

straight.

Or if you want to do it laying on your bed,

it's perfectly fine. Just feel comfortable.

Now I invite you to close your eyes and begin

bringing your attention to your breath.

Notice when you inhale and when

you exhale.

Breathe deeply and slowly through your

Nose.

Try to breathe filling up your belly

with air and then let it go.

Put your focus on filling your belly with

air and exhale letting go of any tension.

If you find it easier, you can put your

hand on top of your belly and feel your

hand going up when you breathe in and going down when you breathe
out.

Notice how the fresh air feels when it

goes through your nose and goes inside

your body.

Notice how your belly moves as you

inhale and exhale.

Every time you breathe out, let go of any

Tension.

With every breath you take, you get more and more relaxed.

Continue to bring your attention to your

breath. Take a deep breath slowly.

Hold the air for a second and slowly breathe out letting go of any tension.

Take another deep breath.

Hold the air and slowly let it go let go any stress

and tension.

Take another deep breath.

Hold the air and breathe out letting go any accumulated tension in your body, in your mind.

Now bring your attention to your

Feet. Notice how they feel.

Are they warm?

Are they cold?

Or heavy?

Do you feel any tingling?

And whenever you're ready, start to

contract and tense the muscles of your

feet.

Feel the tension for a few moments

and then relax the tension.

Relax your feet and your toes.

With every breath,

relax your feet more and more.

Now bring your attention to your legs.

Bring your attention to your ankles, your

Knees, your thighs…

All your legs.

Pay attention to any sensation

that you might be feeling on your legs

and whenever you're ready,

contract and tense the muscles of your

legs.

Sustain the tension, maintain the

contraction.

And now, let it go slowly.

Invite your legs to relax.

Take a deep breath

and allow yourself to experience more

and more relaxation as you breathe.

Now bring your attention

to the muscles of your pelvis and your

back.

Pay attention to any tension that

is present in this area,

identify any tension

and whenever you are ready start to

contract the muscles of your buttocks,

by pressing them tightly.

Arch your back up and away from the floor or chair.

Pay attention to these sensations of

tension as you contract your muscles...

[wait a few seconds]

and then relax those muscles.

Relax any tension.

Breathe out and let go of any tension.

Now bring your attention to your

shoulders and your neck. Notice if you

are experiencing any tension

in this area.

Notice how it feels

and what sensations you may experience

around this area.

Whenever you're ready, contract and tense the muscles of your shoulders and your neck.

Press the back of your head

against the chair or your bed.

Now shrug your shoulders.

Just try to lift your shoulders to

your ears and bring your chin as

close as you can to your chest.

Sustain the tension and pay attention to any sensation that you are experiencing

right now, …

Now relax and let go the tension on

your shoulders and your neck.

With every breath you take, relax your

shoulders and your neck more and more.

Now bring your attention to your hands

and your arms. Notice how they feel.

Are they warm?

Are they cold?

Heavy?

Do you feel any tingling?

Pay attention to those sensations.

Take a deep and a slow breath

and whenever you're ready, start to

contract those muscles.

Lift your arms in front of you.

Contract your hands, clench them,

making a fist and

bend your hands back at the wrist.

Feel the tension in your arms for a few

moments.

Slowly let the tension go

and allow your hands and your arms to

relax. Let them rest.

Take a deep breath

and as you breathe out, let go of any

tension that may have remained in your

arms.

Now bring your attention to your face

and your head. Notice any sensation in

your lips, in your cheeks, in your eyelids,

your nose, in your forehead and your skull.

Continue to breathe slowly and

deeply as you pay attention and try to

identify any sensation in your face and

your head…

And whenever you're ready, begin

to contract and tense those muscles

closing your eyes firmly, lift your eyebrows as much as you can.

Press your lips together tightly and extend your lips pulling them outward.

Tense every muscle in your face.

Feel and experience any sensation of

tension in your face or your head, and

whenever you're ready... relax!

Relax all those muscles.

As you relax those muscles

You may open your mouth slightly and

continue to relax all the other muscles

in your face.

Notice the difference between

the state of tension and

relaxation.

Now bring your attention back to your

Breath. Make sure you're breathing deeply and slowly and allow yourself to relax more and more, letting go of any tension.

Now I'm going to invite you to scan your

whole body and try to find any source of

tension that may have remained.

Start by your feet.

Check on your legs, your back, your pelvis.

Continue scanning your shoulders,

your arms. Check your neck,

your face and your head.

Pay attention to the feeling of relaxation

and let go of any tension

that you may have found now.

Bring your attention back to your breath

and enjoy the feeling of relaxation all

around your body.

Keep enjoying it. Enjoy

all these for as long as you want

And whenever you're ready,

without any rush, start moving

your toes, your fingers and bring back

your attention to the place where you

are.

You can open your eyes and stay in a

state of total peace and relaxation.

As I already mentioned, try to practice this exercise more often. Ideally every day at least once a day to maximize its benefits.

Also, I would like to ask you if you can please leave a comment about how your experience with this exercise has been.

# Chapter 29

# Guided Chakra Meditation for Anxiety and Stress Relief

Find a comfortable position either seated or lying down and gently close your eyes.

(5 seconds)

Become aware of your surroundings. Are there any sounds in your immediate environment?

(5 seconds)

Is it warm or cold? Is the air humid?

(5 seconds)

The air you are breathing is it warm or cold? Does it have a smell, or it is odorless?

(5 seconds)

Now, become aware of the parts of your body that are in contact with the ground. Allow your body to become limp and for the surface beneath you to support you.

(10 seconds)

Notice any sensations on your skin.

(10 seconds)

Notice any sensations on the different parts of your body.

(10 seconds)

Begin to take deep breaths.

(20 seconds)

Let the inhales and exhales allow you relax.

(20 seconds)

Notice as your chest rise and fall with every inhale and exhale.

(10 seconds)

Feel the sensation in your nostrils as you breathe in and out.

(10 seconds)

Become aware of the difference in temperature of the air that you are inhaling and the one that you are exhaling.

(20 seconds)

Now bring your attention to your tailbone, the bottom of your spine where the root chakra is located. Visualize a red circle of energy pulsating on the area around your tailbone. Take some deep breaths and visualize the energy going to your root chakra, easing any tension held on this part of your body

(30 seconds)

This root chakra is responsible for connecting you to the energy of the earth. When your root chakra is balanced, you feel grounded and supported. On the other hand, when your root chakra is overactive, you feel jittery and anxious. It might also manifest physically as digestive problems, lower back pain, hip pain, ovarian issues and prostate issues in men.

To balance your root chakra every day, incorporate grounding activities such as meditating and prayer in your everyday life. Also spend time in nature.

(10 seconds)

Repeat the following mantras to help you get grounded:

"I am here."

(5 seconds)

"I deserve to be here."

(5 seconds)

"The Earth is my support."

(5 seconds)

Take a few deep breaths here as you pay attention to the surface beneath you.

(30 seconds)

Now bring your attention to the area just below the belly button where your sacral chakra is located. Visualize an orange circle of energy pulsating around this area. Take some deep breaths and visualize the energy going to your sacral chakra, easing any tension held on this part of your body

(30 seconds)

This sacral chakra is responsible for your creative and sexual energy. When your sacral chakra is balanced, you feel motivated and relish in the joys of life without needing to overindulge. You are also sexually and creatively expressive. On the other hand, when your sacral chakra is overactive you have addictive and overindulgent tendencies. When it is underactive you experience a lack of passion, decreased sex drive and lack of creativity. Physically, an manifest as depression, obesity, hormonal imbalance and addiction.

To balance your sacral chakra, engage in creative activities often.

Repeat the following mantras,

"I am infinitely creative"

(5 seconds)

"It is ok for me to enjoy life"

(5 seconds)

"I let go the need to overindulge"

Take a few deep breaths as you pay attention to your sacral chakra.

(30 seconds)

Bring your attention the area on the top of your stomach where your ribs meet. This is where your solar plexus chakra is located. Visualize a yellow circle of energy pulsating around this area. Take some deep breaths and visualize the energy going to your solar plexus, easing any tension held on this part of your body

(30 seconds)

This solar plexus chakra is responsible for your sense of confidence and personal power. When your solar plexus chakra is balanced, you feel confident, a sense of wisdom, as sense of personal power and you are decisive. Otherwise, when it is underactive, you may feel timid, indecisive, insecure and needy. When it is overactive you may feel too energized, greedy, angry and have a need to control and micromanage.

Physically, in imbalanced solar plexus chakra manifests as digestive issues or issues on internal organs such as kidneys, liver, appendix and pancreas.

To balance your solar plexus chakra, recite self-esteem and self-confidence affirmations.

Repeat the following affirmation:

"I am enough"

(5 seconds)

"I am worthy"

(5 seconds)

"I am confident"

(5 seconds)

Take a few deep breaths here as you pay attention to the area around your solar plexus.

(30 seconds)

Now, move your attention to center of your chest where your heart chakra is located. Visualize a green circle of energy pulsating around this area. Take some deep breaths and visualize the energy pulsating in your chest area, easing any tension held on this part of your body

(30 seconds)

The heart chakra is responsible for your ability to give and receive love. It is also associated with compassion, kindness, empathy, joy and peace. of confidence and personal power. When your heart chakra is balanced you give and receive love with ease. You are kind and compassionate to others. When it is overactive, you may find it difficult to set healthy boundaries for yourself or you may experience interpersonal relationship issues. When it is underactive, you might find it difficult getting close to other people.

To balance your heart chakra, offer yourself self-love. Treat yourself with compassion and kindness and extend the same to other people. Engage in acts of service that are within your boundaries.

Repeat the following affirmation:

"I accept myself"

(5 seconds)

"I am willing to learn to love myself unconditionally"

(5 seconds)

"I am kind and compassionate to myself and others"

(5 seconds)

Take a few deep breaths here as you pay attention to the area around your heart center.

(30 seconds)

Now, move your attention to your throat where the throat chakra is located. Visualize a purple circle of energy pulsating around this area. Take some deep breaths and visualize the energy pulsating in your throat area, easing any tension held on this part of your body

(30 seconds)

The throat chakra is responsible for expressing your personal truth with clarity, love and kindness. If your throat chakra is overactive or interrupting others. When it is underactive, you may feel shy or opt to remain silent even on issues that are important to you. Physically, an imbalanced throat chakra may manifest as loss of voice, throat pain, cavities, or mouth ulcers

When speaking always think:

"Is it the truth?"

"Is it necessary?"

"Is it kind?"

To balance your throat chakra practice expressing your emotions and truths.

Repeat the following affirmation:

"It is ok for me to speak my truth"

(5 seconds)

"Even when I feel like my truth does not matter, I will say it anyway"

(5 seconds)

"It is becoming easier and easier for me to speak my truth"

(5 seconds)

Take a few deep breaths here as you pay attention to the area around your collarbone and throat area.

(30 seconds)

Now, move your attention to the space between your eyebrows. This is where the third crown chakra is located. Visualize an indigo circle of energy pulsating around this area. Take some deep breaths and visualize the energy pulsating on the area around you're the space between your eyebrows, easing any tension held on this part of your body

(30 seconds)

The crown chakra is responsible for intuition. It is believed to give the brain access to information that is beyond the material world and what your five senses can detect. When it is balanced you feel in tune with both yourself as well as the physical and material world. You will receive intuitive messages with ease.

When it is overactive you may become obsessed with getting psychic information. On the other hand, when it is underactive, you may feel spiritually disconnected. Physically, an imbalanced crown chakra may manifest as headaches, vision problems or sinuses.

To balance your crown chakra, spend time in nature and engage in spiritual activities regularly.

Repeat the following affirmation:

"I am tuned in to my intuition"

(5 seconds)

"I am in alignment with the universe"

(5 seconds)

"I am divinely guided"

(5 seconds)

Take a few deep breaths here as you pay attention to the area between your eyebrows.

(30 seconds)

Now, move your attention to the top of your head where your crown chakra is located. Visualize a white circle of energy pulsating around this area. Take some deep breaths and visualize the energy pulsating on the area on the top your head, easing any tension held on this part of your body.

(30 seconds)

The crown chakra is responsible for pure conscious energy. It is the center of enlightenment and spiritual connection with your higher self. When it is balanced you feel in tune with your higher self and divine consciousness. When it is underactive, you may feel spiritually disconnected. Physically, an imbalanced crown chakra may manifest as headaches.

To balance your crown chakra, engage in spiritual activities regularly and balance the other chakras.

Repeat the following affirmation:

"I am spiritual being experiencing humanness"

(5 seconds)

"I am connected to my highest self"

(5 seconds)

Take a few deep breaths here as you pay attention to the area around the crown of your head.

(30 seconds)

Once more visualize the various energy circles pulsating on all your chakras. A red circle of energy on your tailbone, orange circle of energy two inches below your belly button, a yellow circle of energy on your solar plexus, a green circle of energy on your chest, a purple circle of energy on your throat, an indigo circle of energy between your eyebrows and a white circle of energy on the crown of your head. See all the circles of energy vibrating simultaneously.

(30 seconds)

Now, bring your attention your body. Notice how your body feels and any sensations. Notice how calm, grounded and peaceful you feel and rest in this awareness.

(60 seconds)

Begin to deepen your breath.

(10 seconds)

Gently move your head from side to side.

(10 seconds)

Come to stillness and when you are ready gently open your eyes.

# Chapter 30

# Guided Meditation for Happiness

I n this exercise, I will guide you through a simple meditation that includes breathing exercises to help you relax and focus on your breathing. This exercise includes different strategies that you can use to increase your happiness quotient. I will help you hold onto all positive thoughts and let go of all the negativity within and around you.

This meditation you to this mediation that will help you cultivate happiness.

Before I begin, find yourself something comfortable to wear and avoid any tight-fitting clothes.

You can either lie down or sit comfortably. You can sit in a chair or sit on the ground with your legs crossed. Let your hands rest one over the other in a standard meditation pose.

If you feel uncomfortable at any time, you can stop the recording.

Now, you need to close your eyes and listen to the recording.

During this time, you can release yourself from the stress and tensions of the day and from all your responsibilities, for a while at least.

Let your mind be free to explore, to smile and experience happiness.

Concentrate on your breathing and nothing else.

Feel your breaths becoming deep and long.

Take a couple of moments, breathe in and breathe out, allow yourself to let go of the world outside

Start to visualize a path in your mind. The path can be anything that you want it to be, but at the end of it, you need to be able to see a door. This door opens up the path to your inner world. Now, open the door and you can see a ray of bright light. The light is warm, welcoming, and helps you to relax.

You can see the bright inner world of yours and you need to step into this beautiful world.

Relax into all the warmth and harmony existing within.

You are the only one that knows this place and you are the only one with the key to open up this world.

Take a deep breath and shut the door to the outer world.

Give yourself the permission to enter this place and fully immerse yourself into this world of inner peace. It is a world where you feel safe and you can experience happiness here.

Give yourself this time to work on your happiness so that it spreads joy within your body and eventually radiates from you.

It is okay even if your mind wanders. It is perfectly alright even if you realize that your thoughts have gone off tangent.

You are in charge of your thoughts and if you feel like your thoughts are wandering, you can bring awareness back. Listen to the sound of my voice and concentrate on my voice.

Now, take a deep breath.

Start with your feet; feel your toes relax and then feel your feet relax.

Feel your legs relax slowly.

Feel the muscles in your thigh loosen and then the muscles in your abdomen relax.

Gently will them to relax.

Shift your focus towards your chest. Will the muscles around your ribcage to relax, then move onto your back?

You can now feel the muscles in your shoulders relax and all the tension starts to fade away.

Now, allow the muscles in your neck to relax and move towards your head.

Take a deep breath and allow your entire body to relax.

Your breath fills up your lungs with air.

Start to exhale slowly until there is no air in your lungs.

Take a deep breath to fill your lungs with air. Allow your lungs to expand and once they do, breathe out.

Breathe in through your nose for a count of four.

One, two, three and four.

Hold your breath.

Exhale through your mouth for a count of eight.

One, two, three, four, five, six, seven and eight.

Breathe in again. One, two, three and four.

Breathe out. One, two, three, four, five, six, seven, and eight.

Visualize the path that you took to enter your inner world.

Walk on the same path and the same bright light that you saw now surrounds you.

Walk on the path that leads you through an alpine forest.

There are white pine trees that line the path.

The morning sun is shining brightly and is casting soft golden rays of warm sunlight all around you.

Continue to walk on this path and you will find a rock outcrop overlooking a landscape of mountains.

There are hundreds of peaks all around you; some seem closer than the others.

Let your gaze take in the expanse of mountains in front of you and you will feel a feeling of peace wash over you.

Appreciate the beauty of nature that's all around you. Revel in this gift and be thankful for it.

Enjoy the view and give yourself a moment to smile. Smile at the beauty that's present in front of you.

The golden rays of sunlight are illuminating the landscape. The colors are gently mixing with each other all around you and it looks like a beautiful painting.

Smile and become aware of all the flora and fauna around you.

Imagine the sounds of birds chirping happily and smile.

Now, you will notice a large tree near you. The tree is quite old, and its trunk looks large.

Now, visualize this tree in detail. The bark of the tree looks like that of a sweet birch; its leaves smell sweet.

A gentle wind is blowing, and it blows a couple of leaves away from the tree. One such leaf lands in your hand and you smile as the leaf leaves a slight sweet-smelling minty scent.

Smile at this marvel of nature and take a deep breath.

There is something else besides the wonderful aroma. The leaves start to gently rustle and it sounds like a stringed dulcimer.

Light and airy sounds surround you.

Everything sounds melodious and they complement the wonderful landscape around you.

You are now surrounded by the warm golden light and the wonderful sounds.

Listen to the music of nature; you can feel your heart fill up with joy. There is so much beauty around you and it makes you feel happy.

Look around; there is a bush with emerald leaves next to the tree. The leaves have triangular points and the bush is filled with small berries like raspberries. Go ahead, pick a few berries and eat them.

Enjoy the flavors of these berries and savor how wonderful they feel in your mouth.

Start to slowly chew and swallow these delicious berries.

You can feel warmth and energy radiate from your core as these berries slide down your throat and into your stomach.

You can feel the energy rise within you.

This energy spreads from your stomach to your head, arms and legs. This energy is now pulsing through your body.

All your senses feel ecstatic. You feel a sense of calm and appreciation wash over you as you enjoy this wonderful bounty.

Look at the bush, the old tree, and the landscape around you.

The sun is higher in the sky and the landscape looks more beautiful than ever.

There are more wonderful scents all around you.

Allow yourself to enjoy the richness of nature and let your body soak it all up. This powerful energy continues to radiate through your body and it is casting a light halo all around you.

You can see a golden aura emanating from your body.

A pure energy makes you smile.

Bask in this wonderful energy. Let it wash over every muscle, bone, and cell of your being. Let your body be infused with nature's wonderful energy.

Stay in this place for a couple of moments and smile some more.

Now that your body is infused with this wonderful energy, it is time for you to return to the outer world.

Your inner world has given you the tools that you need to return to your day feeling energized, refreshed, and happy.

The beautiful landscape looks more golden than ever because of your aura. You feel strong and happy.

Smile more widely and you can feel this energy shine brighter. Let the sense of gratitude and appreciation wash all over you.

Whenever you feel low or dull, you can return to this place.

It is time for you to turn and go, but the sound of nature makes you linger for a while longer.

Take a deep breath and bid adieu to this wonderful place, for now.

Slowly, start to walk back up the path through which you entered. Allow yourself to soak up all the energy that this place emits. Let this energy make you feel alive.

You feel good about yourself and you are looking forward to going back to your world.

As you walk, you will notice the door to the outer world. Slowly open the door, take a deep breath, and step inside.

You are now back in the real world and you are full of happiness and positivity.

Now, breathe in slowly and deeply.

Take a deep breath through your nose and hold it for a count of four.

One, two, three and four.

Now, breathe out through your mouth and hold it to the count of eight.

One, two, three, four, five, six, seven and eight.

Take another deep breath through your nose and exhale through your mouth.

Start to slowly open your eyes and you can feel the energy of the inner world shine brightly in your body.

Take a deep breath, smile and return to your day.

You can follow this exercise whenever you want a burst of happiness. It will help you to appreciate all that is good in your life and let go of your worries.

# Chapter 31

# Meditation to Fall Asleep Instantly

T his final meditation in this set is one that is going to help you fall asleep instantly. It is a quicker and shorter meditation that will take you through the visualization exercise.

This process makes it easier for your mindset to go from one where you might be thinking of specific things in your life to a place where you can get into a more dreamlike trance. You will be able to easily fall asleep and get that deep rest you need in order to conquer the day tomorrow. Again, ensure that you are in a comfortable place where you will be able to fall asleep for several hours at a time. This is best at night but if you plan on taking a rather long nap you could do this as well. Keep an open mind and focus on your breathing.

## Meditation For A Deep And Quick Sleep

Sleep is incredibly important, but sometimes falling asleep can be difficult if we are not in the right mindset.

For this activity, we are going to take you through a visualization that will help ensure that you can get a deep sleep. It's important before falling asleep to relax your mind so that you can travel gently throughout your brain.

Start off by noticing your breath. Breathe in through your nose and out through your mouth. This is going to help calm you down so that you are able to breathe easier.

Begin by breathing in for five and out for five as we count down from twenty. Once we reach one, your mind will be completely clear. Each time a thought passes in, you will think of nothing. You will have nothing in your sight, and you will only think with your mind.

Make sure that you are in a comfortable place where you can sink into the space around you. Let your body become heavy as it falls into the bed. Keep your eyes closed and see nothing in front of you but darkness.

Each time a thought comes in, keep pushing it away. Breathe in through your nose and out through your mouth.

Remember to breathe in for five and out for five. Keep an empty mind and be ready to travel through a journey that will take you to a restful place.

You see nothing in front of you, it is completely dark, and you feel your body lifting gently up like a feather. You are light against the bed, and nothing is keeping you down. Continue to feel your body rise higher and higher. You are floating in space. There's black nothingness around you. You are gently drifting around.

You can see a few stars dotting the sky so far away, but for the most part, you see nothing. You feel yourself slowly moving through space. Your body is light and free, and nothing is keeping you strapped down. You're not afraid in this moment.

You are simply feeling easy and free. Breathe in and out, in and out.

You start to drift more towards a few planets, throughout your journey in space. You can really see now that you are up in the highest parts of the galaxy. You see out of the corner of your eye that you can actually catch a glimpse of Earth. You start gently floating towards it, having to put no effort in at all as your body is like a space rock floating through the stars.

Nothing is holding you down.

Nothing is violently pushing you either. Everything that you feel is a gentle and free emotion. You get closer and closer to Earth now and can see all the clouds that surround you. You start to move down, and you gently enter into the cloud area. Normally gravity would pull you down so fast, but right now you're just simply a gentle body drifting through the air. You get closer and closer to the land. You can see some birds here and there and a few cars and lights on the ground beneath you.

You pass all of this. Gently floating over a sleepy town.

Look down and let your mind explore what is it that you see down there. What is it that is in front of your eyes? What do you notice about this world around you as you continue to go closer and closer to home?

You are gently drifting throughout the sky. You can see trees beneath you. Now, if you reached your hand down, you'd even be able to gently feel a few leaves on the tops of the tallest trees. You don't do this now because you're just concerned with continuing to float through the sky. That's all that you really care about in this moment.

You're getting closer and closer and closer to home now, almost ready to fall asleep. You start to see that there is a lake.

You gently float down to the surface of the lake, and you land right in a boat. Your body is a little bit heavier now. You feel it relax into the bottom of the boat. Nothing around you is concerning you right now. You feel no stress or tension in any part of your body. You are simply floating through this space now.

The boat starts to gently drift on the lake. It is dark out now and you look up and see all the stars in the sky. All of this reminds you of the place that you were just a few moments ago. You start to drift closer and closer to sleep.

Do you feel as the tension leaves your body? You are peaceful throughout. You are not holding on to anything that causes you stress or anxiety. You are at ease in this moment. Everything feels good and you have no fear. You drift around in the water now for a little bit longer. You can see everything so clearly in this night sky. Just because it is dark does not mean that it's hard to see. The moon casts a beautiful glow over everything around you. You can feel the moon charging your skin. As you drift closer and closer to sleep, you feel almost nothing in your body now. You continue to focus on your breathing. You are safe, and you are at peace. You are calm, and you are relaxed. You feel incredible in this moment.

The boat starts to lift from the water. You feel as it gets higher above the water. You are even heavier now. Now you are completely glued to this comfortable surface as the boat starts to fly through the sky. You can look down and see that the city beneath you has drifted to sleep. You're getting closer and closer to home now. You can actually see your home beneath you. The boat gently takes you to your front door, and you float right in. No need to walk or climb stairs. You simply float in and straight to your bed.

You fall delicately into your bed with your head resting nicely on a pillow.

Here you are, in this moment, so peaceful and so relaxed. You are completely at ease. There's nothing that stresses you out or causes any anxiety or tension now. You are simply a body that is trying to fall asleep.

As we count down from 20, you will drift off to sleep. You will be in a very relaxed state where nothing stresses you out. You're not concerned with things that happened in the past, and you aren't going to stay up in fear of what might happen tomorrow, you are asleep. You are relaxed.

Breathe in and out. Breathe in and out.

# Conclusion

These meditations are going to be an important part of a healthy sleep routine. In order to really alleviate your mind from any anxious thoughts or other things that keep you awake at night; you will want to ensure that you are calming down and becoming more relaxed before you go to bed. These meditations will be your key to becoming a happier and healthier person because of the consistent amount of rest that you'll be able to get.

The more that you practice these meditations, the easier it will be for you to get the restful sleep you deserve. You can also check out other meditations and series of books to find something with a more specific purpose, such as weight loss or positive thinking.

If you are going through a stressful time, remind yourself to gain control of your breath and that these feelings will pass. Through meditation, you have now been gifted the skill sets to help you get through just about anything whether you are dealing with anxiety, panic, or a combination of both!

If you are ever going through a rough patch, I hope you think of these meditations and take a few moments for yourself. Even if you only have several minutes, a simple breathing meditation can help put everything into perspective with you. Remember that the more you practice, the stronger your peace of mind will become. I hope that you have enjoyed learning meditation, now go forth and lead your very best life.

The key to a happy life is a happy mind and these meditations will do just that.

Meditation can bridge the gap between you and many worldly wants as well: your sleep gets better, you are able to regulate your weight, your relationships become more satisfactory and you have the ability to reduce physical pains that occasionally come and go.

Although its practice is still being blindsided by many factors, the practice is bound to receive the recognition it deserves eventually. With the internet of things, the spread of the practice is almost reaching a rampant state with the topic of meditation resting on the lips of both professionals and paupers. Even in the event that most of these people are just talking about it without putting any practice, the fact that it has gained such a massive amount of popularity is nothing but astounding. This is a positive thing though, as the positives of meditation outweigh the negatives.

For those who are a bit skeptical about engaging in it because of various reasons, I hope this serves as a beacon of light to dispel any misbeliefs and doubts one might carry about the practice. The main purpose of meditation is to reach within and access oneself. We all spend so much time on a daily basis trying to find people and things. It all falls in place easier if you discover the most important thing to find is yourself.

So, thank you once again for your kind attention. If you have found this to be useful or helpful, in any way, please tell your friends and family, or anyone whom you believe to be interested in this topic. It will surely help them find the balance they seek in life. In addition, they are surely going to benefit in the long run.

Hopefully, you now have a better understanding of how meditation can benefit you. From reading this guide, you will have gained a deeper understanding of how your mind works and how meditation alters your brain to work at its optimum. From producing the hormones and chemicals, we need to live without stress, anxiety, or depression. To be happy and balanced in our thoughts and actions.

The true test, of course, is to try it out for yourself. By this I mean really try it. Give yourself a window of time each day that you safeguard for meditation. Although it is far easier for a beginner to do this somewhere quiet and without disturbance, it will eventually be possible for you to practice meditation almost anywhere.

Make it part of your daily life, like eating, drinking, or brushing your teeth – you do brush your teeth, right? If you can make meditation habitual, then you will reap the benefits for the rest of your life.

Don't be shy about it either, spread the word, tell your friends just how awesome it is and help change someone else's life too.

People suffer in different ways, and one of the most common ways to experience pain is through anxiety. Understanding the best ways to deal with anxiety is crucial because it will enable you to deal with these issues that we face daily.

I believe that the steps outlined can help you to deal with anxiety and at the same time master how you can be in control of your life and do the things that enable you to excel and take your life to the right direction.

Start practicing these guided meditations from today, and you will see how your life will change and the positive advantages you will start experiencing once you start doing these guided meditations. Comprehending anxiety is the first step in managing it. Knowing its impulsive nature, we can get a good sense of what triggers and how our worries work - and this is where to look.

Anxiety is a state of cognition linked to an inability to control emotions. But research shows that constant feedback stimulates the brain's brain pathways, and thus enhances our ability to control emotions.

Ideally, we learn about ourselves through stressful thoughts and narratives. We learn to see, sit down and let go. In doing so, we learn two important things: ideas define us, and opinions are not real. With this new perspective, we can gradually shift our relationship to anxiety, by distinguishing between what is impossible and what is real.

Another benefit of this skill is the study of physical awareness, which teaches us to draw attention to our bodily sensations in the present moment. This technique involves examining the brain, about an inch, which makes us better aware of what we experienced physically. When exploring these emotions, you will sit with your senses in the same way as you sit with your thoughts. This new way to go can give you a safe and accessible place to go whenever stress arises

If you have been disciplined enough to follow the meditation exercises, you must have started seeing some real benefits. Although, if you follow the instructions given, you can master everything and even start doing the exercises without having to look at the instructions.

Whenever you find that you are stuck somewhere and you do not know how to go with a meditation, you can always refer to this manuscript and find what you need to do to move with the exercises smoothly.

The importance of focusing on other areas of your life is that you will maintain your goals for a long time. Therefore, I have covered these tips in this manuscript because you should not go back to where you started. The best way to achieve this goal is to ensure that all areas of your life are functioning well. When these aspects are good, you are now able to have the strength that you need to maintain the current weight that you have achieved. The concept is that you need to remain in this state for the rest of your life since this makes you enjoy your life to the fullest.

It is fair to say that this information is useful to you and many others who have considered using it in their program. As you have discovered already, meditation is a crucial tool that you can use in your daily life. Apart from that, it has helped you to achieve the goals that you desire it can also help you in other areas of your life. This means that you can keep on practicing these meditation tips as long as you find them helpful and contributing positively to the growth and development of all angles of your life. For many years, those who have discovered the many benefits that come with meditation have been doing it for various reasons. There are some who do meditation for spiritual purposes, while others do it when they are faced with a lot of stress. Although many people have found help with meditation and many have solved their problem, this does not mean that everyone can gain the same results others have gained. It largely depends on the effort that you put as an individual. Working hard will help you to achieve this, and therefore, you find that maintaining focus has been emphasized a lot in this manuscript.

What can you do if you find that you have done everything that is required for your meditation exercises, but still, you do not see any results? Truly, there are people who say that meditation is not their thing and they have tried it severally, yet it has not worked. If this is the experience you have had with the meditation exercises that we have covered in this manuscript, then you do not have to curse yourself. This may not be your problem since different people can get varying results with the mediation program they plan to use. There are other ways that are also useful, and you can use them to attain the goals you want.

This has been "Guided Meditation For Mindfulness And Relaxation: How And To Change And Calm Your Mind. Stress Free With Self Healing. Understanding And Practicing Buddhism. Yoga And Zen Made Plain For Beginners"

Written By : Peace of Soul & Brain Foundation.

This has been "Self Guide Meditation For Beginners: The Collection To Learn Mindfulness And Relaxation Meditation. Stop Anxiety And Fall Asleep With Hypnosis For Deep Sleep. Self Healing Guide To Declutter Your Mind" Written By : Peace of Soul & Brain Foundation.

10% of the sale of this book is destined for "Fundación Letras Itinerantes", dedicated to promoting reading in Mayan communities, preserving the language and providing quality education in Quintana Roo, Mexico.